COUNTRY COTTAGE
Conservation

A GUIDE TO MAINTENANCE AND REPAIR

COUNTRY COTTAGE
Conservation

A GUIDE TO MAINTENANCE AND REPAIR

Bevis Claxton

THE CROWOOD PRESS

First published in 2010 by
The Crowood Press Ltd
Ramsbury, Marlborough
Wiltshire SN8 2HR

www.crowood.com

British Library Cataloguing-in-Publication Data
A catalogue record for this book is available from the British Library.

ISBN 978 1 84797 179 1

Disclaimer
The author and the publisher do not accept liability of any kind for the use of material contained in this book or any reliance placed upon it, nor any responsibility for any error or omission. The author and publisher have no control over how the information contained in this book may be used and can accept no liability for any loss, damage, injury or adverse outcome however caused. Third parties and websites are referred to in good faith but with no responsibility for their advice, behaviour or the content of their publications. Laws and regulations are subject to variations across the United Kingdom and to changes with time. Conservation experience, living conditions and the adjustments necessary to cope with climate change may develop and alter over time. The information contained in this book is necessarily generic and cannot relate to each individual building or circumstance and should not be seen as a substitute for specific professional and technical advice.

Drawings and photographs all copyright Bevis Claxton/Old House Info Ltd

Frontispiece: A country cottage shows how to build to last using sustainable local materials; it also records human capabilities, and recalls human experience, from before the machine age.

Typeset by Jean Cussons Typesetting, Diss, Norfolk

Printed and bound in Malaysia by Times Offset (M) Sdn Bhd

Contents

Dedication

To my parents who, as children, experienced real rural life in several country cottages – and have stayed well clear of them ever since.

Acknowledgements

The photographs in this book include a few of the author's own projects, but mainly the images are as noticed around the country and assembled to illustrate the contents in a wider context. Information has been gathered in a similar way, much directly experienced and much learnt from sources too widespread and too numerous to acknowledge individually. Thanks are due to all those who have contributed in some way whether by passing on information and experience at some point in the past, or by keeping their cottages looking fine enough now to photograph. Two of the author's drawings first appeared in different form in *Old House Care and Repair* by Janet Collings (Donhead, 2002), and a couple more in *Maintaining and Repairing Old Houses: A Guide to Conservation, Sustainability and Economy* by Bevis Claxton (Crowood, 2008). Some of the information presented here has also appeared in different forms in articles and on the website www.oldhouse.info.

Introduction

WHAT THIS BOOK IS ABOUT

The information

This book sets out practical information that can help owners to keep their cottages viable and attractive. It aims to help bridge the information gap – between recognizing the need for action and deciding on what action to take – by providing some understanding of the special nature of cottages and how repairs and redecorations may affect them for good or ill. This information can be of help to owners whether they propose to carry out work themselves or engage others to do it for them. Cottages were designed cleverly to keep themselves intact despite dampness and movement. This technical performance is due to the way in which they were designed to use natural, sustainable materials, and it was also linked to the way in which people lived in their cottages. The visual appeal of cottages follows naturally from the authentic materials and their technical design. This book explains how some of this original look and function might be restored and preserved for the future.

Identifying the problems faced now

This book also looks at the condition in which most cottages have arrived in the twenty-first century. In addition to the problems of time and wear, cottages have not been served particularly well by many of the industrialized products and building methods of the twentieth century that have been, mainly innocently, applied to them. Most country cottages have been through several rounds of refurbishment since rural workers began to leave them a century ago. Books published since the 1950s have often tended to address bringing cottages up to contemporary standards of comfort, 'doing them up', frequently involving extreme rebuilding in the twentieth-century manner.

But the problems faced by a new owner today are much more likely to be about whether those twentieth-century repairs are mismatched with the original construction, and failing in some way, and whether recent refurbishments have also robbed the cottage of the character that once made it so attractive. What can be left of a cottage in many cases is not so much cottage, more a poor imitation of a modern house.

HOW THIS BOOK IS ORGANIZED

The chapters are organized within five sections, each identified by coloured pages:

The first section, 'OLD AND WISE – A cottage is not a modern house', introduces some essential information about taking on a cottage today and where help can be found in assessing a property for purchase or repair. It also explains in a straightforward way the big differences between a cottage and a modern house in terms of how damp and movement is managed. The persistent and continuing misunderstanding of these important qualities by owners, builders and professionals has arguably been responsible for the advancement of decay in countless cottages during much of the last century – so it's worth knowing before considering new work on any cottage.

The second section, 'THE WAY WE WERE – Cottages as they were built', examines some of the more common constructions used in cottage building, including some principal variations of materials used for roofs, walls, doors and windows as found in different regions of Britain. This section also looks at how those traditional constructions emerged from the necessity to make use of what the countryside was able to provide, and the limitations imposed by lack of transport and machinery at the time. These intrinsically sustainable methods and materials should, nowadays, also be of use, informing modern environmentally conscious design in new housing.

The fourth section, 'IN THE YEAR 2525 – Preparing for the future', imagines the cottage in the future. Cottages can offer practical lessons to the twenty-first century on how to build durable, sustainable and beautiful low-impact dwellings from what was once immediately available, all without using up fossil fuels or industrial quantities of energy. Cottages were highly sustainable when their occupants had no choice but to live sustainably themselves. But now we have become used to living unsustainably, and because most people in Britain are likely to continue to feel that they deserve more than nineteenth-century levels of comfort, this section looks at how we can try to match our own unsustainable needs with a cottage's sustainable heritage – including insulating cottages appropriately.

Section three is 'THE PRESENT – And what the twentieth century did'. For the best part of a hundred years now, most cottages have not been used or repaired in the ways that were originally intended. In many cases cottages were cast off as slums and then perhaps taken on by wealthier people to use as holiday homes; some have survived as permanent homes, most have been 'modernized'. Like many a collectable antique item or classic vehicle, they have passed through a period of being underestimated before they emerged as desirable survivors. This section looks at appropriate maintenance and repairs, and also what might be done to redress past works that may have been inappropriate.

Finally section five, 'STYLE COUNSEL – Keeping the look alive', offers some ideas on presentation, inside and out. This is not intended to impose any particular 'period lifestyle' but rather to highlight how easy it is to over-dress a cottage and to lose the simplicity that is, after all, the essence of a cottage's attraction. This section also examines a few of the practical problems often faced, including getting a fireplace to work properly, extending a cottage sensitively, and incorporating kitchens and bathrooms.

ABOUT TO BUY A COTTAGE?

Cottages are often less convenient to live in and more expensive to buy than the equivalent modern house, so there is something that puts them into a similar category to antiques and classic cars. The owners of those items happily accept some limitations in performance in return for the interest they give and the attention they attract. Those owners also tend to take great care to use only authentic materials in their repair. The same is reasonable for a cottage – but the message that one day a cottage could be worth less if it has been poorly 'modernized' has to fight to be heard above the clamour of sales pitches for home improvement products. Owning a cottage can present an opportunity to engage with a different sector of the economy, one that is involved with natural materials and ancient crafts.

THEN, WHAT IS A COTTAGE?

This book assumes that a country cottage was built for rural workers any time up to the modern period, when modern industrialized building materials took over. This 'modern period' was a result of the nineteenth-century's industrial revolution, but there were still country cottages being put up with basically mediaeval technology for some time after, perhaps as late as the 1930s. Estate agents sometimes like to extend the term 'cottage' to urban terraces and 'artisans' dwellings', and indeed some of those built in the late nineteenth century and early twentieth will owe much more to the traditional construction that this book is concerned with, than to the newer conventional 'modern house' methods.

It took some time for industrialized materials to displace old habits. Those late Victorian, Edwardian and later urban 'cottages' are, however, likely to exhibit 'hybrid' constructions – blends of ancient and modern. In a similar way many 'genuine' country cottages will have become hybrids in that they have been extensively altered in the modern period. But even in those cases an understanding of traditional building ideas is still very useful in making decisions on future repairs.

Country cottages may be grouped in a hamlet...

... or equally in a village or country town and then, when do they become houses?

Perhaps the typical country cottage stands alone in the countryside. Its accommodation may often have been tied to a particular job of work ...

... or cottages may have served other needs such as almshouses; sometimes a larger house was subdivided into cottages, or the other way round, and back again.

The nineteenth century produced the 'cottage orné', an elaborate and probably quite expensively embellished version motivated either by a desire to improve the lot of tenants or to make a country estate look more jolly. By the end of the cottage era, cottages were more often designed by draughtsmen than by the 'builder's eye', and their technology and function were often assimilated into the council house.

RESPECT FOR THE PAST

Gone ...

Too much has been done to most cottages to 'turn back the clock' and recreate an authentic restoration of their past, either in technical function or in visual appearance. A full restoration would anyway be more appropriate to a museum because it would have to reflect the life of people living perhaps six to a bedroom with one main wood fire that had to be tended all day, every day. Some of those folk lived in the shadow of perpetual fear of eviction, disease, star-

vation and infant mortality – the echoes of that way of life are still remembered by some. Needless to say there were no bathrooms, no indoor WCs, no electricity, no central heating and often no piped water. Cottagers were poor, way beyond the scope of modern British definitions, and cottage life itself was nearly drawing to an end before most were allowed any political voice or offered any significant state safety net.

... But not forgotten

We may have a romantic vision of cheery ploughmen

A rare sight now, cottages no longer inhabited but still in their original form. It was the availability of many so-called 'slum' dwellings in similar circumstances that fuelled the country cottage boom of the mid-twentieth century, helped by government grants. Conservation knowledge was rarely applied then, and many such cottages went on to become, literally, modernized.

Nowadays untouched cottages are considerably rarer, and the more likely situation is a cottage that was modernized years ago but which would now, once again, be considered in need of attention. This book hopes to help bring cottages together with a more sympathetic kind of attention this time round.

and rosy-cheeked milkmaids, some of whom may actually have been lucky enough to have enjoyed an uncomplicated life under the paternalistic care of others. But cottage dwellers were, in practice, slaves to their condition, and their labour in the countryside provided essential services, such as putting food on the tables of the nation. The simple, frugal and obedient way of life they were required to adopt has inspired some onlookers to label their condition as noble and romantic; others considered them exploited.

So if we do examine ways in which to 'restore the past', then perhaps it should be with respect for the memory of past occupants, their fragile lives and their building skills. In looking after cottages we can do this by preserving the old materials and artefacts that survive, and resisting the temptation to apply a sugary varnish to the events they record. The smallest evidence of the real past can be beautiful, human and touching enough.

THE FUTURE

Gone …

There is a common thread between the emptying of rural labour from cottages and the refilling of those same cottages by commuters or holidaymakers, and that common thread is mechanized transport. As the steam traction engines and diesel tractors came to the countryside, so the manual labour and horse-power began to be shown out.

Then steam trains, petrol-powered cars and buses allowed people to work in the towns and live or play in the countryside. Ironically some of the new 'townie' incomers will have been descended from the agricultural workers who previously had to leave the countryside, and this perhaps accounts for the nostalgia that surrounds cottages.

… But coming back?

But it is becoming possible that, in the near future, fossil-fuel depletion could turn back the clock. Even if we do not see a reduction in the use of powered vehicles, we are increasingly likely to have to create our new homes almost entirely sustainably, as our forbears did, and that means with much less reliance on imported and highly processed materials.

This book examines some of the lessons from inherently sustainable traditional building materials and techniques that were used for centuries before our dependence upon fossil fuels. These ancient ideas are already being dusted off in preparation for being re-adopted for sustainable building in the future, and these old traditions of sustainable building have even more to offer than most people perhaps yet suspect. The future may not consist of the exciting silver things on stilts that we were promised in the 1960s but, instead, revived versions of the cottages that the 1960s saw being demolished.

Using proven and reliable resources

The sustainable and naturally abundant materials that have been used to build cottages were understood for a thousand years, the traditions handed down through practical apprenticeship. The modern age almost wiped out that knowledge. Many are now pioneering an alternative sustainable construction using 'waste' materials such as used tyres and straw bales, which is admirable. But those materials are arguably only available as by-products of an industrialized system of living, farming and transport that may well have to change soon. The traditional materials used in cottages were well understood, better than our conventional modern materials, and better also than the new 'recycled' materials. There was simply more time to get to know them over a millennium. There is no need to wonder how well traditional construction may perform over time – every surviving cottage is evidence of what can be achieved using what the natural world delivered, without waste. All we have to do to ensure a continued supply of natural materials is to look after the natural world.

Preserving interest: preserving value

Apart from what cottages can teach us to help cope with the future, they are also records of the past. This may be a novel idea to those who are more used to new houses and who have wanted to make them their own and alter them to take account of new fashions. But the reason that a cottage may well cost more than a new house is that it is, in effect, an antique – and a unique one at that. Alter or modernize an antique and its value generally diminishes.

Old country cottages may now have found a new type of owner, but will there be a new generation of cottages built in the countryside for farming use again, using some of the same sustainable materials?

So this book addresses the ideas of repairing and retaining original fabric rather than just renewing something when it needs attention. A related idea is that of 'reversibility', which here means that, in order not to devalue the antique nature of the cottage, any necessary changes should be made, if at all possible, so that they can be completely undone in the future without leaving a permanent scar on the cottage.

ABOVE: The corrugated iron porch may be practical rather than elegant but it is a reflection of the reality of cottage life until recently; the smartened version of the porch next door has not been over-elaborated, and seems commendably restrained.

ABOVE LEFT: A small example of the frailty of the past: the burn mark made by a candle or taper where it was routinely attached to a post hundreds of years ago; a coat of varnish would obscure it, or a coat of paint, and it might be lost forever.

OLD AND WISE
A cottage is not a modern house

Cottages were the simplest of dwellings, which might originally have been built straight on to trampled earth and using scraps of wood, mud, straw, twigs, blood, hair and dung. Despite the primitive farmyard flavour of that list, all the ingredients would have been assembled and used to best advantage in accordance with a thousand years of word-of-mouth research and development. Although it lacked our modern calculations, certificates and official approvals, a cottage had to be every bit as technically integrated a product as the most modern building is today. But much of that building skill and understanding was wiped out by the social upheaval and technological change following an industrial revolution and two world wars.

When the twentieth century devised new building materials, the well tried ways of building with what nature provided began to be forgotten. Newer substitutes sometimes offered apparently enhanced performance, sometimes needing less time or less skill to use. This new building technology obviously works well on its own and has provided clean and efficient homes for around a century. But modern building technology functions in some *very* different ways to traditional sustainable rural building technology, and mixing the two technologies in the same building can cause one or both to fail. Acceptance of this came, through bitter experience, late last century – yet some find that experience hard to accept, and will still try to force the two technologies together.

The simple materials that our ancestors spent so long refining and understanding were also, in our modern terms, highly sustainable and largely natural materials. In a world that pre-dated the internal combustion engine and electricity, low energy living was a necessity and not a lifestyle choice. They had to be good at it to survive. Recycling (and avoidance of waste in the first place) was also necessarily second nature. Their buildings have been proved capable of very long life – much longer than modern homes dare to claim. Cottages were once designed to be heated, not by imported fossil fuels but by what nature provided locally – wood; and wood we now recognize as a 'carbon-neutral' fuel in our world that is threatened by climate change.

So a cottage has real answers to our present building crisis: highly sustainable, long life, natural materials, minimal transport, renewable energy and carbon-neutral heating. Yet despite these clear virtues, old housing has long been under threat of being swept away to be replaced by something flimsier made from components that come from factories hundreds of miles away. Cottages can teach us so much about how we might adapt to live responsibly with our planet in the future. If only we would stop trying to force them to conform to last century's outdated and unsustainable ways. But that is for Section Four, first …

The chapters in this first section introduce some differences between cottages and modern homes that can affect the way they are lived in and looked after, and which it would be useful for any prospective cottage owner to understand before crossing the threshold:

Chapter 1: Thinking of Living the Dream? – *Some perspectives on the idyll*
Chapter 2: The Professionals – *The right help when needed*
Chapter 3: Don't Bring Me Down – *Traditional management of movement in cottages*
Chapter 4: The Air that I Breathe – *Traditional management of damp in cottages*

CHAPTER ONE

Thinking of Living the Dream?
Some perspectives on the idyll

THE EMOTIONAL SIDE

Many of us are attracted to a country cottage in much the same way that people are attracted to chocolate: it is an in-built yearning that was implanted in us very early in our lives. So it is probably no accident that chocolate boxes have had a long history of being adorned with pictures of cottages. But chocolate is a craving that is quite cheap to satisfy, while cottages are more expensive.

If already gripped by a desire to live in a cottage it can be difficult to step back and analyse what makes the idea attractive, but as there is a lot of money and happiness at stake, it's worth making the effort. The appeal of a cottage is often visual, so we can try an experiment with that side of things first. Take a good look at a real cottage: for this to be as scientific as possible, find a cottage that is close to its original appearance. (A village or holiday cottage owned and maintained by one of the National Trust charities, one of the national conservation organizations, or perhaps a large country estate might be good places to look – the majority of cottages found in country lanes and in print are, like many of the examples photographed in this book, already well in the grip of the twentieth century.)

Now take a good look at the cottage pictured. No two examples in the country will be the same because the British Isles have a rich variety of landscapes and geology, from which cottage building materials came. But despite regional differences there is every chance that a good example from anywhere in the country will display many of these characteristics:

- The walls and roof may appear irregular, or downright 'wonky'.

Much of the character of a cottage is linked to evidence of its original purpose and condition, so the less this is overlaid with suburban neatness, the more of a cottage it will appear.

Cross-dressing: the use of modern materials for repair and decoration can now give cottages an industrial age veneer. At the same time, new houses are deliberately being built to try to look pre-industrial.

The reflections from the window in the red wall (above) show the contrast between older, slightly 'crinkly' glass, bottom left pane, and more perfect later glass. The straw-coloured wall (below) shows that an informal 'imperfect' quality also gives character to walls. Much cottage character is due to subtle visual imperfections and irregularities; iron those out and some charm evaporates.

- The doors and windows may be familiar-looking, but not standard designs.
- There may be evidence of charmingly crude, but effective, hand-made repairs.
- Surfaces, even when soundly decorated, may appear uneven or blemished.
- There may be features left over from the past that make no current sense.

Now picture an image of this cottage on a computer screen about to be manipulated by some software – by which the outlines are first straightened, the doors and windows are replaced with modern standard patterns, the old repairs are swept away, the surfaces are made much more uniform in colour and texture, and all the old superfluous features are done away with. The result the computer screen shows might be cleaner looking and more rational, but would it still look like a cottage?

The real life version of the imaginary computer exercise described above is almost precisely what so many cottage owners have actually done to their homes, and at great financial cost. Not at all because they are mad or vandals, and no one would doubt that they love their homes, but because they have been drawn into the modern-home way of looking at things that promotes straight, clean, tidy and new. Nothing wrong with those things in the right places, they just don't seem very 'cottage'. Maybe they did not know that there are other ways of going about repairs and redecorations that can preserve character.

Or maybe they would have been happier with a new house instead. A lot of people are put off real cottages by some of the 'down sides' sometimes associated with them:

- No off-street parking, or difficult access.
- Curious boundary arrangements, including 'flying freeholds' and remote gardens.
- Poor acoustic insulation between attached properties.
- Necessity to negotiate some routine repairs and redecorations with neighbours who are under the same roof.
- Inability to totally exclude unwelcome wildlife, such as rats, mice, birds, insects and spiders, from old walls, floors and roofs.
- Poor thermal insulation that does not sit happily with current heating methods, and which might be awkward to improve without destroying the character or fabric of the cottage – and therefore necessitates lower indoor temperatures.

These 'deficiencies' are not so much due to age or deterioration, but more to do with the modern expectations we have learnt from modern houses and the modern levels of comfort that we demand. In other words they are not so much a result of a cottage being old and worn out, it is because we are new, we have become more fastidious, and we are trying to make cottages do different tricks to the ones they are good at.

But there is one last possible drawback with cottages that demonstrates how hearts can rule heads:

- A cottage has frequently tended to cost more than a modern house offering similar accommodation.

Just old-fashioned

There is a lot of debate about whether new buildings should be styled according to traditional values or be entirely free from past constraints. Fair enough when it comes to the style of a new large public building, but when people have decided that they want an old country cottage there seems little question that what is wanted *is* the past, and in spadefuls.

Horse sense

If the modern owners of an old cottage also had a horse, they wouldn't dream of feeding it diesel instead of hay; nevertheless, many will happily force feed their cottage on modern building and decoration materials that are potentially just as ridiculously inappropriate. A mis-fuelled horse may fall over and die quite quickly, but a mis-decorated house can continue to stand and even look reasonably sound – yet within its walls, softening and decay could be taking hold.

This should, even for the non-romantic, be a persuasive argument for keeping their investment looking more like a cottage and less like a modern house.

THE TECHNICAL SIDE

The cottages that people might now dream of living in would have been built in the days when horses were still everyday transport: a very different age. Nowadays, a small modern house might even try to look a little like an old cottage, if a little smoother and straighter. It might have similar-looking bricks, timber, paint and render. But if this modern small house is built in the conventional modern way, there the similarity ends – because modern houses, and many of their materials (including the bricks, timber, paint and render), can perform entirely differently to olden traditional construction in several very important ways. And so a cottage needs to be looked after in a different way to a modern house – simple enough.

The problem is that people have been seduced into applying modern maintenance methods to their cottages, and unwittingly they have created problems involving dampness and decay. So they have had to go on and spend more money rectifying those problems. The time has now come when a lot more is understood about how old buildings worked, and how cleverly they coped with ageing. Cottages can't be bludgeoned into being new buildings, and it can often be better for them, their owners and their bank balances, if they all decide to work in the same way – the way the original builders intended. Those men and women had, after all, been building on a thousand years of 'trial and error' experience in their locality. Our modern building regulations have been around for only a twentieth of that time, during which they have had to be revised as problems have come to light – and more will no doubt have to be readdressed. Cottages were built on a more mature set of 'rules' that are worth trying to understand.

So it is not simply judgements about visual quality that make conservation architects, planners and historians unhappy when they see some modern materials and modern building practices applied to old buildings: there may be sound practical reasons why some of these innovations could be unsatisfactory or why they might cause serious problems in the future. The modern cottage dweller needs to be aware of them.

Cottages breathe, or at least they should

House building in the pre-industrial world (the changeover happened some time between the late nineteenth century up until several decades into the twentieth) had to rely on what is called 'breathable' construction rather than the modern practice of near-total water-tightness. This was simply because there were very, very, few traditional building materials that were reliably totally watertight in long-term use. So buildings were assembled to shed what rainwater they could, while other sources of damp, such as ground dampness and internal condensation, were dealt with by the constant and unavoidable ventilation that fed open fires and ranges. Walls and floors would have been in a constant cycle of wetting and drying, and they relied on the drying power of the sun and wind externally, and a permanent fire and its draughts internally.

Like an old-fashioned woollen overcoat, an old cottage might have kept its contents dry in a shower by a combination of deflecting most, and soaking up some, rainwater, but all the time letting out the wearer's perspiration. With luck it stopped raining before the cottage walls, or our overcoat, were saturated and began actually to admit water. Once the rain did stop, then like the coat, the walls would dry out in the sun and wind, and in that way mould and rot were less able to take hold.

But cottage owners need to understand that applying a coat of modern waterproof paint or render to an old cottage will have similar results to trading in the woollen overcoat for a bin liner: pretty good for the first fifteen minutes, pretty dire after an hour or two when the inside is running with sweat. In terms of a cottage this sweat translates into condensation and dampness that becomes trapped inside the building materials, and that can cause decay.

The modern-built house can take advantage of modern waterproof construction and finishes that should have been assembled within an integrated design, soundly joined together to banish all damp and wet. The insides of things, we hope, never get wet in modern construction. But in a cottage they do, and it is too late and too costly to rebuild them so that they don't (and if we did they would no longer be cottages). The cottage with just a few modern finishes applied here and there would still be taking in water in some places, yet unable to get it to dry out completely through the waterproof bits. Imagine what condition parts of your body would be in if wrapped permanently in plastic. Exactly. (*See also* Chapter 4: The Air that I Breathe.)

Cottages may flex, like they always have

Cottages were by definition not top-of-the-range housing. In the rockier areas of the country they might have been lucky enough to have had really firm walls of stone founded on good solid rock. But cottages were often built in rock-free areas out of less firm materials such as sticks and mud, and they were put straight on to the soil, or as near to it as made little difference. Mobile subsoils, such as clay, could affect the walls then, and still will now, so seasonal movement has always been likely. A cottage of timber construction is particularly prone to seasonal movement, as the timber itself responds to atmospheric and seasonal humidity, regardless of any soil movement.

Regular minor movement translates into minor cracks and niggly defects such as binding doors and windows, or draughts. But without destroying everything that is there and rebuilding the cottage from the ground up as a new house instead, and with modern materials, this slight to-and-fro movement is unlikely ever to be arrested. Not recommended! To the original cottagers the movement was of little consequence because, happily, old-fashioned building and decorating materials and styles happened to be quite tolerant of movement (modern ones can be less forgiving). There is no reason why we should not go with the flow and use those same movement-tolerant materials today. They are usually very simple, and can even be cheap, it just needs some patience to find someone who knows their mud, clay, lime, or whatever.

Modern building and decorating materials, on the other hand, have been designed with modern houses in mind. Modern houses are designed with deep, rigid foundations so as not to flex and settle, and applying to them the modern renders and coatings formulated for a stable background such as a new house is as simple and effective as icing a good solid fruit cake; any fragile coatings are unlikely to be tested by movement. But applying some of the more brittle modern materials and coatings to an old cottage that is bound to move is just not going to be as successful. Instead of being like icing a good solid fruit cake, it is probably going to be more like icing a sleeping dog: promising at first perhaps. (Don't try this at home, *see also* Chapter 3: Don't Bring Me Down – 'Why new houses don't like to move, but old cottages don't mind', page 38).

Even the draughts caused by movement (perhaps as it had affected the fit of doors and windows) were useful to a degree in a traditionally run cottage: there was most likely a permanent fire in the hearth, which provided heat, light and served all cooking, and this fire actively needed draughts to feed it with oxygen to burn. What was also useful was that those same draughts picked up much of the dampness that the cottage's simple building materials had not been able to banish. Nowadays, without a permanent open fire but with expensive central heating, those useful draughts are often sealed up, and this might worsen a damp problem already made bad by incarcerating the cottage in modern waterproof paints. So all in all it would be better to keep modern materials and old cottages entirely separate. Except that in most cases it is too late (for some compromises *see also* Chapter 11: Get It Right Next Time).

The ability of cottage construction to cope with slight movement has contributed to their visual interest. But while some cottages have changed shape slightly over time, a great deal of cottage construction was never capable of being straight, plumb or level in the first place. So cottages are not necessarily crooked or uneven because they are old and worn out – many were built that way. And that is why we love them.

New-fangled cracks

When an old house or cottage is being redecorated there are often cracks seen being filled that run from the corners of the windows and doors. This can be a symptom of cement render having been used at some time in the recent past: being relatively brittle, cement can crack in big squares as if it were thin, hard icing on a cake that has been bent. Traditional lime render, on the other hand, can accommodate little shifts in the building – more like marzipan.

WHAT ARE YOU LOOKING AT?

It has been a long time since cottages were routinely repaired and redecorated using the very same materials with which they were built. It has been so long that even chocolate boxes, calendars and jigsaw puzzles now routinely feature cottages painted in 'plastic' paint in eye-watering 1970s colours, and with 1980s designs of windows and doors. Most of what is actually visible to our eyes could often be a late twentieth-century veneer entirely dependent on our oil-fired economy, with only the bare outline of the original hand-crafted cottage left.

Even inside, cottages have been stripped of original surfaces and their previously spartan interiors adorned with fitted carpets, fitted kitchens and fitted bathrooms. These upgrades are inevitable as many cottages originally had no floor other than bare earth, and certainly no bathroom or WC. In so many cases all that survives is a selection of carefully chosen 'beams' and a planked door or two, but even these are most likely pickled behind several coats of thick, gooey, suffocating modern varnish.

There is obviously a practical balance that has to be struck between twenty-first-century living and pre-twentieth-century aesthetics. But if, as this book hopes to show, there are common-sense technical reasons to re-employ some pre-nineteenth-century finishes, then cottages could also benefit by looking much more authentic as a result. Nor should we forget that, in period properties, 'authentic', which equals historical worth, must sooner or later come to dictate financial worth. It has happened with other antique items, and who wants to be left with something that might have been more valuable if only it hadn't been spoilt?

Pick on something else

Cottages are small and unsophisticated and therefore easily bullied by those who feel the need to gut an old building and fill its skin with reproduction antiquity or minimalist modernity. A cottage is more likely to be happy in its original skin if its insides are all of compatible construction technology.

ON THE THRESHOLD OF A DREAM
I didn't know it would be like this

Getting to know what an old cottage might be like to

Four in a row; cottage styles from several centuries happily side by side.

Make it easy on yourself

Once a cottage is chosen, it can be a very good idea to take time to get to know it, rather than immediately embarking on a regime of change. Having gone through the process of carefully choosing a cottage, then it should be mainly right for the occupants already – and if not, then perhaps the wrong cottage has been chosen? Cottages are individual, so try not to import prejudices from outside about decorations, alterations and fittings as soon as the keys are handed over. Even if it means living with the previous owner's brown shag pile carpet and a classic avocado green bathroom suite for a few months, that time should be what informs how the place is going to work and what are its best features. If the cottage is not given a chance to show its best features, then those things could be inadvertently swept away. Unnoticed treasures, tricks of light, views – all gone forever. The same applies to the garden – and that ideally needs a full run of all the seasons to tell you everything it can offer. (*See also* Chapter 2: The Professionals – 'Timetables for work to older properties', page 34.)

live in is very useful if you don't already have that experience. A spell in a holiday cottage, perhaps run by one of Britain's National Trust charities or one of the national heritage 'quangos', can be a useful introduction. Those people who are inclined to fret over creaking floorboards or doors that are not quite straight may take time adjusting to the reality of cottages; some places can appear a bit rough and ready, they can harbour a rich variety of wildlife and insects, and they will always, always, need some routine care and attention. In some ways a cottage is like a pet that needs constant attention – and it is never established quite who owns whom. But cottages have lasted much longer than pets or their owners, and will be around to influence future generations – today's owner is merely one in a long time-line of custodians.

The idea of custodianship

Taking on a cottage in poor condition and returning it to health and beauty might leave some owners feeling that they have put in more effort than they are likely to see returned. But the repayment is partly in the satisfaction of passing on something of value to the future: there are few other projects that most people have the opportunity to initiate almost

---

Roots

Owners can become involved in the history of their own cottage, and this can improve the experience of living there and help explain some of the things they may find while exploring the building. Historical local census returns can show the occupation of former occupants, local archives may have maps and records such as old farm and estate plans. General reading on the artefacts and customs of the period could also shed light on things found on the cottage, some related to the occupation of the householder, others of more general life. (*See also* Chapter 6: Sticks and Stones – 'Timber Frame – Further interest', page 85.) This book tries to give a feel for the diversity of British cottage construction, but there is not space to catalogue every type – the variations are many, and almost every county has its own style, if not its own materials. It is worth finding out more.

---

genuine antique fabric has actually survived from the past. Of course there will be the need to make repairs, maybe carry out some updating to plumbing and electrics, and possibly some selective adaptations: these are examined in the later chapters of this book (Sections Three and Four). Even though humans are intelligent enough to adapt to buildings, frequently people will embark on a costly programme of building alteration before they have allowed themselves time to work out how to use what is there more ingeniously and more economically.

Understanding old methods, and buyers' surveys

This book aims to smooth the path towards a happy relationship between cottage and occupant, in part by explaining some of the common-sense logic of old buildings – logic learnt over a thousand years of building that has come to be forgotten and disregarded, sometimes with expensive and damaging consequences.

When setting out to buy a building, prospective owners are normally advised to get a full professional technical survey, not just a valuation, from a properly qualified surveyor. In the case of a cottage, its age will normally justify seeking a surveyor who is in addition experienced and accredited in conservation (the RICS www.rics.org organizes such accreditation for surveyors, the AABC www.aabc-register.co.uk for architects). This is because the modern building industry has moved on tremendously fast in the last hundred years and has forgotten most of the old-fashioned construction wisdom that was once everyday knowledge. If anyone is thinking of spending a substantial sum of money on something, then it makes sense to have it examined by someone who knows better than most how it was put together.

The next chapter introduces some of the professional and building skills that a cottage owner may need to engage, as well as looking at some of the implications of grants and taxes. Chapters 8: This Old House and 9: Reasons to be Careful look at a selection of common maintenance and hazard problems that could also be relevant for anyone who is looking at a cottage for the first time with a view to making it their home.

single-handedly which would improve the environment. The payback is not from the owner having imposed their will on a small building, but in having passed it on to the next generation with its genuine features intact and better equipped to survive. While there are always going to be surprise pitfalls, with proper information and appropriate help, preserving a cottage and returning it to a more sustainable balance can be satisfying, and a rewarding and lasting achievement. And it can make the country look a little bit better.

Selection

The necessity for sustainability has brought to the fore the idea that we should preserve the 'embodied' energy and materials that were used long ago to create old buildings. So it makes environmental, not just financial, sense when buying a cottage to try to choose one that is suitable just the way it is. Avoiding alterations avoids wasting what is already provided, avoids the unnecessary use of energy and resources, avoids expense, and avoids further eroding whatever

CHAPTER TWO

The Professionals
The right help when needed

PEOPLE

Unfortunately, cottages are unlikely to come complete with original plans and specifications or even an instruction book, and the owner would be lucky to have records of past alterations, even quite recent ones. So where does the owner turn to find help?

Horses for courses

A slightly crooked appearance is often considered to be part of a cottage's charm, and it would be sad, or mad, to straighten it just for neatness. But who is to know when quirky crookedness is about to turn into dangerous off-balance? Who also can judge what grim decay might be lurking beneath the surface of an old cottage, even if (as can easily be the case with some modern materials that are wrongly used on an old building) the surface looks absolutely perfect?

Obvious

Everyone accepts that horses have horseshoes, and cars need rubber tyres. Likewise cottages can need to have distinctly different maintenance to modern houses. What is so difficult about that? But what often happens is that cottages are repaired and decorated with materials intended for modern houses. That is like nailing car tyres to a horse: neither will work properly afterwards. Sadly, there is still a widespread and misguided belief that modern maintenance is the best for old buildings.

Everybody may feel entitled to be a pundit on the subject of building, but as long as it remains an almost everyday occurrence to find potentially harmful things still being done to cottages and other old buildings, then experts need to be chosen with care. Regrettably, even ordinary respectable builders and professionals can still be found stripping off the original materials that are part of a cottage's survival mechanism and replacing them with modern materials that fight it. They do this because they do not understand the way the old materials worked, and they also expect that the new materials and methods will work on an old building in the same predictable way that they are used to on a new building.

It's building, but not as we know it

Superficial similarities between old and new construction have misled many owners, architects, surveyors, builders and decorators into assuming that not only can old buildings take all modern repair methods, but they can even benefit from them. It is now clear that this is not always the case. Old cottages are not modern houses and they were often intended to cope with damp and with movement in very different ways to modern construction. Modern finishes that seal cottages up and stop them 'breathing' can set off rot, while modern repairs that are too rigid can fail when old cottage fabric flexes naturally, as it must.

The experience gathered by builders and craftspeople over the centuries, the result of painstaking trial and error, was largely wiped away by the adoption of modern building methods during the twentieth century. Fortunately, traditional skills and

We still build with brick now, so what can be simpler than finding a bricklayer for repairs? But it can be surprising how much the search needs to be narrowed when looking for one who is comfortable using traditional lime mortar.

design techniques are being re-established for conservation projects, and each link in the chain of the building team can now be made up from people with appropriate skills and experience. But they are not everywhere yet, so where to find them?

Where to look for expert help

Before selecting professionals and builders the cottage owner might usefully contact their local authority's conservation officer to seek some local knowledge. The local authority might even be able to provide records of past planning and Building Regulations applications relevant to a particular property. A useful source of general information is the charity The Society for the Protection of Ancient Buildings (www.spab.org.uk), whose members also

have access to courses and facilities, and there is also general information on www.oldhouse.info.

Whether looking for a builder or an architect, there is a distinct difference between someone who has 'done work to' old houses and someone who understands how old houses function. That difference is sometimes between those who try to beat old buildings into submission by extreme modernization, and those who cleverly work with them. Not surprisingly, adapting to what is already in place can cost less than an extreme makeover, but it can require the confidence of experience on the part of the adviser – plus, on the part of the client, a willingness to be open to the cottage's needs as well as their own. An additional advantage in getting the right help is that someone who knows how old buildings work is less likely to be frightened into carrying out excessive work where it is not necessary.

Before looking at some of the specialists available, there are some general points that can apply to all building work. In addition to looking for the best combination of competence, experience, evidence of satisfied customers and price, anyone engaged to work on your home is going to have to be around you for some time and be trusted with designing or building the things that may surround you well into the future. Selecting someone 'on the same wavelength' can mean that communication is that much easier, and they may be able to anticipate a lot of your requirements for you.

The cost of it all

People like to get a visible return for their money, and paying fees for intangible things such as advice and design goes against the grain for many Britons. So when, for example, owners are faced with a tiresome problem such as damp, rather than paying a conservation architect, say, a three-figure sum to at least diagnose the problem and propose a course of action, many home owners elect to skip that step and go straight to a contractor to do whatever it is they want to do to tackle the perceived problem at a cost of a, say, four-figure sum.

But impartial advice from such people as conservation architects and surveyors, who are not tied to any one product or solution, can analyse and specify solutions, which can range in cost from next to nothing (yes) and which should then work upwards only if necessary and appropriate to the problem and to the budget. And if the eventual solution still costs a four-figure sum, surely it is better that it was selected from an array of options offered through experience in order to target the problem. Buying a repair to an old property is not like buying a television set, it is more like buying a medical operation – risky if performed without experienced diagnosis, and reckless if it treats something that is not a problem.

Client – the head of the team

A project starts with the client, and for a minor DIY repair the client may be the entire team as well. Clients can help themselves by trying to understand some of the principles of the care of old building fabric. That may help them understand some of the possibilities as well as helping them to select appropriately qualified help from designers and professional advisers to analyse the problem, and tradespeople who have relevant skills and experience. If a client is engaging others to work for them, they can help keep costs down by giving a clear brief in good time, and by making properly informed decisions and trying to avoid changes. To enable the whole team to meet their own obligations further down the line, payments to them on time are necessary (to pay staff, to be able to buy materials, to eat).

Some projects might not warrant a full-time professional, but whatever the extent of their input, professional advice can be worth having even for quite small projects: the professional ethos should be about providing impartial advice and experience to suit the client's circumstances, rather than maximizing the amount of work. Faced with a building problem, impartiality and experience are more likely to deliver a solution that is right for the building and for the client – rather than going to someone who simply sells a 'one-size-fits-all' solution.

Clients will, reasonably enough, not want to be a cash-cow for anyone they engage so, whether seeking professional advisers or builders, they will need to call on their own instincts as well as taking up references to ensure the team is right. If they select wisely and treat them fairly, they might be surprised at the care and loyalty that a good team of advisers and tradespeople returns.

There are bureaucratic reasons for having professional guidance. For example, architects and surveyors can handle things such as Listed Building or National Park and Conservation Area consents (sometimes needed even for repairs), Building Regulations and Party Wall Awards, and they may even be able to alert a client to procedures that could result in more favourable tax rates (subject to rules applying at the time) for certain works to listed buildings and some other categories of work.

One important thing that the client can do to save their own money is to make decisions based on as full an understanding as possible and try to stick to them, as changes can be expensive, disruptive and time-wasting. Sadly, changes can be forced on a project for various reasons even if no one wants them, so be

Professional guidance, whether fully in charge or in the background, can contribute significantly to that hoped-for sunny outcome.

prepared for costs and time-scales to creep upwards once a project is started. Because every building project is a 'one-off', even professional advice cannot foresee every pitfall that lies ahead, but it can often eliminate the many routine traps that will be lying in wait for the inexperienced homeowner who is 'going it alone', while it can also help to plan a programme of work realistically according to permissions schedules and weather, for example.

Architects and surveyors

Architects tend to be thought of as designers of new work, especially for those seeking a blend of appearance and performance, while building surveyors have been linked with maintenance and the practical issues of building. In conservation the boundaries are perhaps a little more blurred than that, as both professions tend to look at remedial works to old buildings, and the differences are sometimes more to do with an individual's skills and training than which set of letters they have after their name.

Architects, who ought to be able to bring their profession's aesthetic skills to seeking a visually sensitive as well as a practical solution, can be registered as accredited in building conservation by a board of their conservation 'peers' issuing AABC status (Architect Accredited in Building Conservation) following examination of submitted evidence of experience over a number of years. The surveyors' institution, the RICS, also has a register of members it has accredited in building conservation following similar assessment. These are different and more rigorous examinations of competence relevant to the care of old buildings than where a professional simply ticks a box to claim such expertise, or puts an advertisement in a local paper. As there are fundamental physical differences in performance in old buildings, the client needs to be sure what degree of understanding they are paying for.

A professional adviser as 'lead consultant' can take the strain of selecting builders, obtaining prices and administering contracts. More importantly, the client is buying some thinking time and experience, which saves having to 're-invent the wheel' tracking down a solution when the principles of an answer may already be well established. Therefore if considering buying an old cottage it is advisable that a survey is carried out by a properly conservation-accredited professional who understands how old buildings work.

Structural engineers

Structural engineers are frequently called upon either to arrest things that look as though they are about to fall over, or alternatively to become involved with the structural design of alterations. Like all other members of the building team, it is very important that the engineer is already familiar with the strengths as well as the limitations of traditional buildings, otherwise there might be a tendency for repairs and interventions to be heavy handed and unsympathetic to the long-term performance of the building. As with architects and surveyors there are now conservation-accredited engineers, and their professional institutes (ICE and IStructE) have a register, CARE. Also, like surveyors and architects, the boundaries of responsibilities and knowledge between professions have become less clear cut recently, and some engineers have specialities in a variety of conservation repairs.

Other professionals

Legislation over the last decade or so has introduced the need, in certain works, for a special consultant to deal with health and safety issues (the 'CDM' regulations – Construction, Design and Management regulations). Another relatively recent introduction of legislation, brought to the countryside from some towns, is that works to, or near to, boundaries with neighbouring owners, not just to 'party walls' themselves, need a Party Wall Agreement, for which one, or more, separate specialist surveyors might possibly be needed (information may be obtained from the local authority, or from www.planningportal.gov.uk). A lead consultant – an architect, surveyor or engineer – should be able to advise on appointing these additional skills where they are necessary. If there are no professionals appointed yet, it could be worth the building's owner having a word with the local authority's Building Control Department to try to find out what obligations, and perhaps hazards, there are in any particular project.

Some larger projects might have a quantity surveyor (QS) as part of the professional team to look after the finances; this usually applies to larger or more complex projects than a small cottage might usually generate (the lead consultant should have a feel for whether a QS is justified). Building services – the plumbing, heating, electrics and some 'eco' features – can be handled by an 'M&E' ('mechanical and electrical') engineer if they are likely to need special design (*see also* Chapter 10: Heat, Light and Water). These extra professionals would benefit a project based around a period property by being properly attuned to working *with* and adapting old buildings (as opposed to 'modernizing' or 'refurbishing' them).

Building contractors

Professional builders range from one-person outfits to large firms usually styled 'building contractors'. For work to old houses it can be inadvisable to go straight to a builder who normally carries out conventional modern work without, at the very least, the advice of a conservation-accredited professional.

A century ago every country builder would have been well versed in traditional 'period' construction techniques, but not so now. There are specialist builders who have excellent experience and track records in this area of work, and who may be expected to know more about the detailed practicalities than the conservation professionals. But many builders would still be uncomfortable making design or conservation repair decisions for the client; they may feel they have enough on their plate without taking on the responsibilities of a professional adviser or negotiating with statutory authorities.

For smaller projects there need be nothing intrinsically wrong in using a 'one-man-band' general builder provided they either have a broad range of genuine conservation skills and understanding themselves or, again, are being closely guided by a professional conservation-accredited consultant. But, as with the building professions, it is experience in working *with* old buildings that helps preserve a cottage rather than experience in dominating and modernizing old buildings, which tends to turn them into hybrid modern buildings. The difference can be difficult for the lay person to distinguish at first sight, which is why background reading and membership of conservation organizations can be of use to understand some of the technical issues.

Sourcing traditional crafts

Once commonplace, certain crafts and skills are now extremely hard to find. Thatchers, however, might be easier to locate because they have established trade bodies and because their work has never been totally displaced by twentieth-century roofing methods. And green oak woodworking, to take a less well known craft, all but died out but is thriving again if you know which forest to look in (a council conservation officer could help).

All traditional crafts are inherently 'low technology', however, while some skills can be learnt by more or less anyone for a particular task, others require a lifetime of endeavour. For example, mixing and applying a traditional 'daub' for walling needs skill, but it may be a reasonably accessible skill to many that is also fun to learn for a small one-off project. On the other hand a craft such as blacksmithing involves equipment, training and a degree

of nerve that would put it beyond most people's grasp for a one-off use.

Again, the Society for the Protection of Ancient Buildings (SPAB) is a useful source of information, as well as the local authority's conservation officer. A conservation-accredited professional adviser ought to know how to locate and select appropriate specialist skills. The SPAB (www.spab.org.uk) and other organizations (for example, the Scottish Lime Centre www.scotlime.org and Essex County Council www.cressingtemple.org.uk) run hands-on courses on traditional building crafts.

When selecting specialist trades be aware that, years ago, every skill was learnt through apprenticeship, and before the age of the van, a craftsperson was limited to working in a small area, so they had to work responsibly and well to gain a good reputation and keep working. Apprenticeships have all but disappeared (for now), and there is now little regulation on who may claim to be a craftsperson in many of these traditional trades, so references should always be thoroughly followed up.

SOURCING TRADITIONAL MATERIALS

Some conservation materials, such as lime, are once again available from regular builders' merchants (*see also* Chapter 6: Sticks and Stones – 'Drawing: Quick Guide to Lime', page 68). Generally, a competent craftsperson will know exactly where to get what they need. Some conservation materials come lovingly packaged and priced at a premium for the retail market, playing on associations with the idea of wholesome naturalness. These are aimed at the hobbyist, as real builders are not going to be seen undoing brown paper parcels tied up with organic ribbon. Cottages were originally built from the free

OPPOSITE: Flint and thatch experts might once have been found in the pub across the road every evening, but now that these materials are no longer mainstream in new building work, cottage owners may need to look further afield for appropriate skills.

mud and clay, sticks and trees and general farming 'left-overs' found in the countryside; however, it could be illegal, not to say dangerous, to try to follow this course of procurement today. Apart from that, there is usually a degree of time-consuming processing involved with any 'natural' building material, so there is often no option but to pay someone who has specially cultivated or otherwise nurtured the necessary materials.

Again, conservation officers and the SPAB are good starting points to find out more. The internet may help, subject to the usual 'buyer beware' advice. Without an experienced craftsperson or adviser it can be easy to buy embarrassing amounts of the wrong product, so at the very least do some detailed research if aiming to be your own craftsperson, and arrange for some hands-on training from organizations such as mentioned above.

TENDERS, PRICES AND CONTRACTS

Where architects or surveyors have prepared written specifications, or drawings, it has been usual for building contractors to be selected on the basis of a competitive tender. Remember that builders' prices may be quoted net of VAT as is common between businesses. For smaller jobs without a professionally administered tender, it can be useful to know that there is an accepted distinction between the words 'estimate' and 'quote', the former being vaguer and more likely to change, as its name suggests. A builder can only reasonably be expected to give a firm quotation if they have reasonably good information about what will be involved. The larger the job, the less likely it is that all contingencies have been imagined – especially if the project is being organized without the benefit of appropriate professional experience.

Because building work inevitably contains 'unknowns' – and because it can be complex and also potentially contentious – it is essential that works are thoroughly described, and that a written contract exists to specify how, for example, any alterations to the scope of the works will be treated. There are 'standard forms' of contract based upon long experience in the industry of what is seen to be reasonable in various circumstances. A professional adviser such as

Traditional materials such as limewash are now much easier to find; they are not particularly complicated to use, but they operate differently to modern materials and so need to be properly understood for safe and effective use.

an architect would normally insist on a client having one of those written contracts with their builder. Entering into a building project without any form of written contract is inadvisable and reckless.

There are also standard contract forms for house-holders to engage contractors for small works, though these would not be as comprehensive as the versions that professionals use. Clients owe it to themselves and the builder to be clear about their instructions, and in turn to have understood the implications of what they are asking the builder to do. It can be difficult to visualize and administer a building operation if one has never experienced it before, which is where an architect or surveyor earns their fee.

Timetables for work to older properties

Traditional materials can be very beneficial to the preservation of an old cottage, not just in looks but also in terms of controlling decay and limiting the effects of movement. A number of modern materials, on the other hand, look wrong and can even harm the way the rest of the traditional fabric copes with damp and movement. But we should not forget that

modern materials became popular in modern build-ings because, for example, they might dry more quickly, or because they could be used all year round, or simply because less skill was required to use them at all. So to get the full benefit from using traditional materials the work often needs to be programmed to allow for any limitations – such as the very common one of frost sensitivity, which usually means a start in the spring and finish before autumn. Therefore any planning and other permissions, obtaining prices and so on, needs to be dealt with before the previous winter is over.

Time and spending over-runs are legendary in building work. If everyone cooperates, and unfore-seen circumstances can be cleverly managed as they occur, then the programme and budget can remain intact. But sometimes compromises are necessary to keep things on track, and completion dates need to start realistic and even then be elastic.

The end result

Selecting the right professionals and builders for the job should ensure that the project correctly interprets the client's requirements and meets their budget. A building project is something that can unavoidably change as it progresses, so professional involvement should ideally be there until the end to manage the change. People are, quite understandably, wary of the cost of hiring professionals for the full term – but those fees, which might be less than the builder's profit margin or even the VAT on the work, can be the difference between success and failure in a project that inevitably affects the value of the house.

SOME RED TAPE

Listed building and planning controls

Many cottages are listed buildings, or may be within conservation areas. The planning process in the UK is designed to help preserve the quality and interest of listed buildings (identified as of historic or architec-tural interest in various grades) and conservation areas. These designations are not conceived as an obstacle to the continuing use of any one building, and ought to be beneficial to the continuing value of a property if that value relies upon its period

Opportunities

Where listed building controls apply, or if the cottage is in a conservation area or similarly protected area such as a national park, official consents are likely to be required for any changes. These can cover ordinary repairs as well as alterations, also seemingly minor work such as redecorating, and apparently non-controversial work such as removing blatantly modern additions. Listed building status applies to everything, inside, outside and about the building's site, even outbuildings; it is not limited to just what the listing summary mentions.

People can sometimes feel threatened by the idea that there are enforceable planning controls governing their home and the local environment, but if you look at these measures as a help and not a hindrance, they can take on a new light. Cottages appeal to a different market than do new homes, and if they are to retain that special appeal then it is worth preserving their character rather than obliterating it. Statutory listing need not be seen as an obstacle to 'doing what I want in my own home', but instead as the opportunity to benefit from first-stop advice from the council on 'preserving the value of my investment'. Planning control can involve some give and take: it might mean that no one who lives around a particular village green is 'free' to have plastic-framed double glazing – but it might also mean that the village green does not become a supermarket car park.

buying any house it is essential to check that all planning and other statutory requirements have been kept in order, but if buying a listed property those checks need to be especially thorough. Listed building status applies not just to the outside, as some people wrongly believe, but to everything, whether original, old or recent, and it applies just about everywhere inside the building, outside the building and over the whole site – in some situations extending beyond the present extent of the site to take in the perceived original 'curtilage' (sometimes being equivalent to the 'natural' or former boundaries). Even the colour of the paint or an innocuous repair might be critical and require local authority consultation.

Grants

Improvement
Local and national government organizations have grant programmes from time to time to assist the suitable preservation of certain old properties. Grants are not particularly common and are usually subject to meeting specified requirements, so their availability and relevance should not be automatically assumed. But always ask – the local authority is a good starting place. With public money, expect strict administrative procedures and the requirement to use accredited professionals: it is not unknown for the effort necessary to comply with grant conditions to eat up the additional value of a grant.

Insulation and energy
Due to the need for fuel economy there are grants appearing that support insulation or installation of energy-saving or energy-generating devices. The same cautions as above apply, and in addition cottage owners should be aware that as their properties are relatively small, the proper application of insulation could have serious effects on appearance as well as on the preservation of other aspects of performance (*see* Chapter 15: Hot Love). Grant conditions may be too generalized to take that into account.

Also because a cottage is by definition a small building, features such as solar collectors and wind turbines can be obtrusive so are probably best located away from the cottage if there is a suitable garden,

character being judged to remain intact. So it makes sense to work with that process rather than treat it as an imposition. Local authorities often have conservation officers who can be an excellent first contact for seeking appropriate help and skills, as well as offering advice on the planning process itself.

Being enshrined in law, there are some stringent penalties for contravention of listed building legislation, and this could even, in certain circumstances, have the effect of making new owners liable to correct the misdeeds and omissions of former owners. If

Conservation areas try to help preserve an area's unique character; these designated areas might, variously, aim to improve the look of a neglected area that has potential, or help an area that is already perceived as attractive cope with its popularity. Logically, if people are attracted to visit conservation areas, then these visitors should also welcome the idea of adopting the same ideals into their own home area.

otherwise it could quickly begin to resemble a space station. If the grant itself has not been thought through thoroughly, and if the customer does not take the trouble to examine the actual benefits compared with any non-grant options, then there is the potential for customers to be pressurized into spending a lot of money that may not benefit the environment or reach a 'pay-back' point within any reasonable time frame. (*See also* Chapter 14: Future Past.)

Insurance

General

If a cottage suffers a fire or other disaster then it needs repair appropriate to its fabric. An owner of a vintage car whose original wire wheels were stolen would expect insurers to replace them like for like. If a wall of a listed timber-frame house is knocked down in an accident there is quite likely to be a planning requirement that it has to be rebuilt as it was, not in concrete blocks. Insurers should want to know about what they are insuring – and they might also be interested to know that properly applied traditional repairs are not automatically more expensive than the modern

repairs that might otherwise be carried out. However, some highly artistic or craft-based work could be expensive to replace, and to enable this to be done well, and indeed to provide a record of every cottage in the event of rebuilding becoming necessary after some disaster, a thorough photographic record would be useful, stored well away from the property in question.

During building work

A professionally administered building contract or other formal contract usually specifies whether builder, owner or both provide insurance of the works. Insurers would normally want to know of events such as building work since it could affect their assessment of risk, and might affect their view of cover. It is also worth clarifying whether insurances held are for the appropriate contingencies, as there are now many different types of insurance required, sometimes statutorily, to cover quite different risks: thus the insurance that might cover a visitor falling into a hole may not be the same, or even be held by the same person, as the insurance to cover the theft of building materials.

CHAPTER THREE

Don't Bring Me Down
Traditional management of movement in cottages

MOVEMENT IN COTTAGES

When they were first built it is likely that even the most crooked-looking of our old buildings were reasonably straight, plumb and true. What can have happened since is that the structure has become slowly distorted over time for various reasons. This kind of gentle historical movement may sometimes need checking, but it need not always be a cause for concern, and actually can provide a welcome visual contrast to bland and straight modern housing. Otherwise why would people have driven miles on Sunday afternoons for the last half a century to look at villages full of crooked old cottages?

Why new houses don't like to move, but old cottages don't mind

We have the technology
For a little over a century now houses have been built

Movement that could look alarming in a modern building might be accommodated in an old one by the movement-tolerant materials with which it was first built – and some continuing adaptations.

with rigid concrete foundations. These, if properly designed, should ensure the new house is adequately and uniformly supported. Particularly weak ground conditions have more recently been overcome by techniques such as piling or 'floating' rigid rafts of concrete, work that would have been considered luxuriously extravagant even for important bridges and lighthouses in the days when our cottages were built, even if the technology had been available. Because modern foundations are so firm it is usually perfectly reasonable to build on to them with rigid modern materials, even brittle ones such as huge sheets of glass, confident that the foundations should not move and stress them into cracking.

They didn't have our technology,
so they used their own
Cottages had to make the best of the ground as found – and often the ground has given way very slightly. The building materials used in olden times were capable of accommodating such slight movement: this is either by fortunate accident, or as a result of centuries of trial and error. Lime mortar seems, almost magically, to re-set itself – usually without cracking the bricks – when an old brickwork

wall moves due to slowly shifting ground. These old walls were not built crooked but have slowly settled that way.

By contrast, a modern wall relies on firm foundations to eliminate that movement: it has to, because hard cement mortar cannot cope with movement, not from the ground, and not even from the slight movement that comes with thermal expansion – which is why modern brickwork of any length is deliberately divided into bays separated by expansion joints (vertical breaks in the wall filled with a rubbery compound). So, while cement is all very well in its place on modern buildings, it should be obvious that it is not a good idea to introduce cement mortar into old brickwork on an old house, old garden wall or cottage: it would be out of its league.

Extensions
On a larger scale, adding a modern-built extension to an old cottage is bound to highlight some structural incompatibilities, as they will each behave differently according to their construction and the way they cope with movement. The design would need to allow for this movement to happen without damage or inconvenience as far as possible. The more substantial foundations that are normally indicated

No need for modern movement joints or even pillars here: the traditional East Anglian 'crinkle-crankle' wall proves that lime can absorb all the movement without fracturing the bricks and so allow a different structural solution.

for an extension by modern regulations can some-times be counter-productive to the health of the original cottage: a conservation professional would need to propose and justify any alternative that was to be put forward for official consideration. (*See also* Chapter 17: Come Outside – 'A Bit on the Side', page 194.)

Seasonal movement …

Timber is sensitive to changes in temperature and humidity so will be expected to move back and forth with the seasons. For example, a door in a timber-framed house may itself change size and shape very slightly during the year, while the timber frame surrounding it may also be having its ups and downs. To avoid frustration the full seasonal pattern needs to be understood before contemplating any trimming or patching, and a flexible and 'reversible' solution is probably worth investigating. These kinds of problem might also have been made worse by the doors and windows being suffocated inside modern paints or varnishes that unhelpfully inhibit the passage of water vapour out of the timber.

… and seasoning

In today's high-volume house building, modern timber-framed houses are built on rigid foundations and they also use seasoned timber. This means that any damaging effects caused by shifting ground conditions should be largely eliminated by modern foundations, and similarly the changes caused by the timber distorting over time should be considerably reduced by the use of more stable timber.

This is not, however, the case with the old timber-framed cottages. Even if the earth does not move under them, the unseasoned 'green' oak from which they were mainly first assembled would very slowly be seasoning itself as its internal moisture dries out, causing twisting, shrinking and tightening. This can produce some very dramatic results, but because timber-frame construction can often be very well tied together, the resulting framework could act like a giant basket that can hold itself together in tension despite looking precariously unbalanced. This same quality means that timber-framed build-ings can also be better at coping with failed foundations.

What you see is not necessarily what you have got

Although it is comforting to think that a wobbly-looking timber-framed house is happily defying gravity, it is sometimes doing so more by luck than design. Anyone who has worked on old timber-framed houses will know that it is not unusual to find that important-looking structural timbers have been quite carelessly cut away to allow in, at a later point in time, doors, stairs and windows – particularly dormer windows. If those really were important structural members, where is the stress being taken now? Is it safe to remove anything more? That skinny, innocent-looking post at the back of the downstairs WC might be doing a lot more than just holding the toilet-roll!

Historical remedies

Buttresses

Although there appears to have been much more tolerance of slight structural movement in the past amongst our cottage-dwelling ancestors, there is plenty of evidence that sometimes enough was enough. A common sign of this is the buttress: if cleverly designed it can always be leaning slightly on the wall it is trying to hold back. However, as a buttress is almost certainly going to be founded on the same suspect ground as the wall it is supposed to be propping up, it might simply end up adding its weight to the problem, and pull the wall over, rather than being the rock-solid support it was intended to be.

Tie bars and spreader plates

Another long-practised remedy to outward-leaning walls is the tie-bar, a long iron rod that the local blacksmith would have made up, and which was poked right through the house or perhaps bolted to a substantial floor or roof timber. Where the bar emerged on the outside wall of masonry buildings it would need to be fixed to a device to spread the pressure and stop it being pulled back through the wall. Hence the 'S'- or 'X'-shaped blacksmith-made wrought-iron devices seen on the walls of some old houses, or later circular pre-fabricated cast-iron plates.

Buttresses have been known to lend a helping hand in the past but are not always reliably designed and are used less now. Spreader plates for tie bars indicate that there are old repairs in place.

Obviously it would normally be extremely unwise to remove or cut tie-bars, but equally it cannot always be assumed that they are still up to the job they were made for. After a couple of hundred years buried in a wall a wrought-iron bar might have rusted, or the timber around any internal fixing bolts shrunk back, due to central heating perhaps. A conservation-accredited engineer's assessment could be useful if any irregularities are suspected.

Modern remedies

The earth moves

When the earth literally does move under a cottage, a solution that frequently comes to mind is 'underpinning'. This is often taken to mean scooping out the weak, failed subsoil and replacing it with a good dose of concrete. This sounds fine in theory, and may work on modern buildings where the original foundations themselves would have been of rigid concrete, but with an old cottage the original foundations would probably have been rather hit and miss

all round and unlikely ever to have been thick concrete, so they were never rigid in the first place.

Replacing a small section with really rigid concrete is going to be an uncomfortable thing for the cottage – rather like putting a brick under a soft spot in a mattress on a bed. If the wall sitting on the new concrete underpinning is now held so firmly that it no longer moves at all, then the rest of the cottage's walls that always used to shuffle about more or less together, could start to crack away from the under-pinned section as most of the rest of the cottage continues its age-old seasonal or ground-based movement. So by being too rigid (too good, even), the 'solution' could create cracks that look just as serious as the cracks due to the instability that brought about the underpinning in the first place.

Think again, think better

Situations like this are demonstrating to owners, insurers and repairers of all old buildings that it is simply no use assuming that techniques developed for modern building repairs are automatically going

41

Don't leave me this way

Even if not faced with any serious structural problem, cottage owners can make life easier for themselves and their homes by trying to avoid introducing too rigid modern materials that could interfere with their home's natural defences against the effects of movement. For example, by avoiding cement-based renders and mortars and considering more mobile lime-based ones in appropriate circumstances, an old house owner would not only be looking to recreate some of the original defences against the effects of movement, but with matching traditional decoration on top, could also stand to benefit from increased 'breathability' – plus a more authentic period appearance as a bonus. But proper advice and craftsmanship are essential, because although traditional materials are good for doing traditional things, they will not be able to stretch to some of the structural feats that modern houses take for granted.

to work on old buildings. Structural engineers, like their architect and surveyor colleagues, have a register of professionals attuned to old buildings, who should be able to take a reasoned view on repairs to cottages and old buildings. The engineers' register is called CARE, and more information can be found on the web sites of their institutes, the ICE and IStructE.

Internal struggles

Lime render and lath and plaster
Indoors, too, cracks can be either superficial or serious. The finish to a wall might be cracking because the render itself has been replaced with something too rigid for the softer wall it is applied to – often gypsum plasters or cement renders have been smeared over the original lime render – or the cracks might go deeper than the finish layers and signal something more troublesome. Old ceilings of lath and plaster (older plaster is often a lime and sand mix rather than plaster of Paris or a gypsum plaster product) are relations of the lime-rendered walls that

tend to accommodate movement, so dips and bulges may not necessarily be a problem provided that everything is dipping and bulging together and all elements are still firmly attached to each other and to the structure of the cottage.

Lath and plaster repairs
Where the lime plaster has separated from the timber laths, or the laths from the ceiling joists, then the ceiling most definitely needs repair. A feature of lath and plaster that is not often exploited by ordinary builders and decorators is that it can be satisfactorily patched and re-made provided the timber framework is sound or can be properly reattached. Not having asked the right people is not a sound reason to strip out a repairable lath and plaster ceiling and replace it with plasterboard. Plasterboard, being relatively rigid in one plane, may anyway also crack along its joints as the house continues to move. Lath and plaster is worth keeping and repairing because it can, subjectively at least, offer a useful degree of sound insulation.

A common twentieth-century repair to lath and plaster was not to repair it at all but to cover it with plasterboard: this is inadvisable, because if the lath and plaster is really failing then it will add its weight to the plasterboard, and the nail fixings that hold up the plasterboard sheets are then being asked to do much more work that they were designed for. Another repair was to pin expanded metal mesh over the old ceiling and put a skim coat of plaster over that. Depending on the security of the fixings, that may have been a somewhat better option, but if the original lath and plaster was repairable traditionally, then the mesh and plaster was a waste of money and an extra load on the floor. (*See also* Chapter 6: Sticks and Stones – 'Lime mix on timber laths', page 90, and 'Lath and plaster ceilings', page 95.)

The effects of central heating
Introducing central heating into a cottage for the first time will risk the timberwork and joinery drying, shrinking and distorting further than it has managed of its own accord over several centuries or with regular seasonal movement. So once the heating is in, it should be applied gradually at first, similarly at the beginning of each winter thereafter. Attention should

An appropriate response

Applying a modern structural or even decorative repair solution that is too rigid or too complex can fight against the more easy-going nature of a cottage. Without comprehensively rebuilding it from the ground up using different materials (that is, as a modern fake), it is unlikely to be practicable to eliminate the affinity for movement from most cottages. Traditional buildings usually not only tolerate their own movement, they originally came equipped to cope with some of the movement inflicted from outside. Unfortunately, much of what helped them to cope has been stripped off in twentieth-century redecorations. Traditional finishes and materials tend to be softer, more mobile and more forgiving of movement than modern versions developed for rigid modern houses.

The technology and understanding that was used to build cottages out of simple materials developed over a long period. To function properly all parts need to be compatible. Twentieth-century industry presumed it knew better than a thousand years of building experience, and while twentieth-century buildings are usually successful, it is not always successful to mix ancient and modern methods – particularly when movement is concerned. A cottage is not exactly frisky, but it is unlikely to behave quite as obediently as those who work with modern buildings and materials would like to expect.

be paid to humidity levels, since having central heating also implies that the draughts that once delivered moist fresh air will have been blocked up, and will no longer be able to redress any over-drying of the air. Furthermore, many cottages will have become slightly over-damp in their post-open fire days, so the transition to central heating's over-dry tendency needs to be handled very carefully.

Few would expect a fifty-year-old car to be compatible with components designed for the latest models, so why expect centuries-old cottages to be at their best with products developed for modern buildings?

CHAPTER FOUR

The Air that I Breathe
Traditional management of damp in cottages

WATER VAPOUR

Water and air are part of the cycle of life and in a healthy cottage, just as in nature, these two elements have to be balanced. Traditional buildings were designed and built with this in mind, but unfortunately some more recent decoration and repair materials have upset that balance at times and are preventing the beneficial 'breathing' that once ventilated the building's fabric and kept it sound.

Dress for the country

Damp is probably the most feared defect in old property. It is associated with rot and decay, with musty smells, peeling wallpaper and mouldy carpets. When cottages were first converted to suit more suburban tastes, owners tried to force their homes to wear suburban décor that was designed for city homes. Modern cottage owners may now be better at dressing themselves for the country, but many still have to make the same allowances for their cottages. If a cottage was built to allow the gentle and continual release of low levels of damp from its walls and floors, then what is likely to happen if those surfaces are swathed in highly water vapour-resistant vinyl wall coverings or foam-backed carpets?

The twentieth century's solutions to peeling wallpaper and mildewy carpets included covering the

OPPOSITE: Water evaporating back into the atmosphere from the countryside after a soaking in a summer rainstorm: this same process also needs to be permitted in traditionally built cottages.

walls and floors with various waterproof paints, renders and sealers, then standing back satisfied, thinking the problem was solved because the damp was now hidden out of sight. But the sealed-in damp could continue to feed decay within the walls and floors, attacking timbers and mortar and leading to expensive repairs. At best the damp could push at the back of these new painted-on coatings, causing bubbles and blisters.

Now, conservationists are keen to reintroduce the simple idea of 'breathability' to old buildings, so that damp is dried out through more permeable décor and finishes, rather than just being bottled up. Their message is not supported, however, by the sort of big advertising budgets that promote decorating fashions and remedies for damp that are, presumably, formulated for newer buildings: these have proved inappropriate on many old buildings, but are all that most householders may have heard about.

Damp: a three-part problem

The damp problem can be separated into three parts. First, undeniably, old cottages tend to be rooted more closely to the soil, and in many cases were built literally on to the ground and constructed from relatively porous materials that seem to absorb dampness.

Secondly, many people who live in cottages nowadays want, perhaps not surprisingly, to live in them as if they were just like modern houses, with fitted carpets, tiled showers, central heating, and wallpaper or emulsion paint on the walls. By blocking the exit of water vapour these modern features can fight against the mechanisms that a cottage has traditionally used to free itself from harmful damp.

45

Thirdly, most of the routine repair, maintenance and decoration materials and processes that are now applied to cottages, indeed all buildings, were probably designed primarily with the market of new buildings in mind. It means they are all likely to work in a different way to the original, traditional construction of most cottages.

Examining each of these parts of the damp problem should help the cottager understand how excess damp was once managed in old houses, how that came to be disrupted in the last century, and how it might be rediscovered now that we have learnt some bitter lessons through hindsight.

Part one: were cottages damp when they were new?

Imagine being back in the nineteenth century and entering a farm labourer's cottage that had been boarded up for a year or two. It would probably smell musty, and the chalky paint on the walls might feel damp or even slimy to the touch. Weeds might be growing up between the floorboards, while spiders, beetles, woodlice and mice would be scurrying across the floor.

Now imagine a family moving in. We are still in the nineteenth century, remember, so they would immediately have started a log fire and kept it burning all day, every day, for all their cooking, even in summer. The fire would pull draughts in through open doors and windows in the summer, through smaller gaps and cracks in the winter, and all the time these draughts would be drawing dampness out of walls and floors. The chalky paint would dry and revert to a slightly powdery surface, and would be quickly and cheaply cheered up by a new coat of the same mix, perhaps in a fresh colour if the family could run to the cost of adding some simple pigments. The weeds would be plucked out from between the floorboards, while cats would help keep wildlife down in return for a place by the fire.

The house might still feel a bit earthy and agricultural by our standards, but it would be relatively dry and warm in the main downstairs room. Bedrooms might rely on that heat rising rather than having their own separate fires, so they would probably not be a place to spend much time in unless well wrapped up in bed. There would be no baths or showers to create condensation, and even the continual steam from a kettle or stewpot over the fire would escape directly up into the chimney and not hang around to moisten walls and windows.

Without the damp-proof courses, waterproofed concrete floors and foundations of modern-day housing there would always have been a suspicion of damp about the walls and any solid earth or brick floors in that cottage, while the whitewashed exterior walls would seem to soak up rain like blotting paper. But it does not rain for ever, and outside walls can dry out in the wind or sun, also drawing out damp that has found its way into the depth of the wall. So a cycle of wetting and drying – that conservationists like to call 'breathing' – was set up in the old cottage, and with luck the walls usually dried out before the damp got bad enough to cause serious problems of decay.

Part two: a modern lifestyle in an old cottage

At some point by the early twentieth century the lifestyle described above came finally to an end. Gradually changes would have been made: floorboards covered with foam-backed carpet or sheet flooring, screeds and plastic tiles laid over brick floors, walls papered with wipe-clean vinyl papers, a downstairs room converted into a kitchen, another into a bathroom, perhaps chimneys became disused and were sealed up when electric fires and central heating took over.

At first things may not have gone well: the carpet might have gone black and mouldy around the edge because it was trapping damp that used to get out into the room, to be whisked up the chimney. The wallpaper might have peeled off for much the same reason, and new-fangled cookers and baths would belch steam that condensed on to the walls and windows, causing black mould and making the new emulsion paint peel away from powdery old distemper underneath. Any new central heating would dry the air inside the room, but it would not be able to draw damp from the floor and wall surfaces so well if they were now sealed up behind waterproof oil or plastic paints or covered in plastic flooring or wall coverings. And there would be nowhere for damp to be whisked away to, if chimneys and draughts were all sealed up and the open fires that drove the circulation of air were all put out.

Cottages, and all old buildings, were simply expected to play host to a modern lifestyle and work properly despite being treated, well, badly. No one seemed to think that modern fashions and modern materials were incompatible with old properties and were suffocating them. If the new emulsion paints did not obediently stick to the old distemper, then special primers were devised to tame the distemper – and few then considered that distemper was actually a much better, more useful surface, which could let harmful damp out: it was simply victimized as old-fashioned, dusty and boring.

If a cottage could not adapt to all that was expected of it, it was then required to undergo extreme 'refurbishment' to try to make it change its ways. When that failed, thousands of old homes were unimaginatively condemned to demolition as 'slums'. Little over half a century ago a cottage could be found cheaply almost anywhere in Britain. But today's survivors, even one that has been savaged by ugly 'restoration', would each probably cost more to buy than a decently equipped 'average' modern house.

Part three: attempts to improve things make them worse

While cottages were first struggling to keep up with the demands of their twentieth-century occupants, new houses were being built alongside that showed how it could be done. These new houses may not have been pretty enough to make people drive out to see them on a Sunday afternoon, but they had waterproofed concrete floors and foundations, firm walls that would take modern renders and paints without cracking and splitting them, plus, as technology progressed, all sorts of clever innovations such as vapour barriers to stop condensation getting into the walls, insulation to keep the heat in, wall cavities as a bar against damp, and even extractor fans to remove condensation. All these could keep damp at bay if they worked together – at least that was the theory – but even with new houses there has had to be some significant rethinking over the years. People naturally thought 'Why not apply these things to our very old houses, too?' A lot of people did, and there are now few cottages and old houses that have not imported some of these ideas, sometimes with disastrous results.

Limewash can be used to permit a suspected damp-related problem to dry out – as an alternative to a modern 'plastic' paint that would trap the damp, and blister and bubble. It may look unsightly until things settle down, and that may take a long time, but eventually the worst affected area can quite easily be overcoated with further coats of limewash, usually without the tedious stripping back necessary with damaged 'plastic' paint. The important thing is that damp is allowed to exit the building via the limewash, rather than being trapped inside and disguised by a film of plastic. Though this picture helps to make the point more noticeably, in this case the staining seems very much more unsightly than simple dampness might produce, and might perhaps be due to another cause, such as long-term tar build-up behind a fireplace.

What was not properly understood when applying these new ideas to cottages was that in a new house all these useful innovations were designed in from the ground up, and they could be carefully coordinated to work together. Each damp-proof (or water vapour-resisting) part relied on all the others being in place, and being properly joined to them as necessary. Applying just a few of these measures to a cottage could leave big gaps in the defences, and it was not practicable to apply the full set of measures without virtually dismantling the whole cottage. The result of half-applied modern damp-proofing measures in an old cottage was that some parts were now waterproof, but some still let water vapour through (remember that before, all the parts were able to let water vapour through). Result: water vapour becomes trapped inside walls, floors, timber, decorations, everything. When it cools it has to condense out (turn to water) right where it is, rather than being able to escape the building. That water is also trapped, so it stays and it dampens and dissolves materials, feeds the fungi that cause rot, and soften wood, encouraging wood-boring insects.

It seemed a good idea at the time

So where are we now? Cottages were not perfect in the first place, but at least they had a system for dealing with damp. Unfortunately, changes in the way people used their houses upset that system. Twentieth-century people were not prepared to find out how their cottages worked before living in them. Worse, the innocent misapplication of new products and materials to old houses has sometimes created disastrous problems of rot, damp and decay. Much of that mistaken work is now quite difficult to undo: for example, a timber-framed house that is covered in cement render, or simply painted in plastic masonry paint, is potentially at increased risk of timber decay due to trapped dampness.

It is not yet universally understood by the general building industry, let alone the average owner, how such well intentioned and apparently ordinary work can actually harm old property. So it keeps

---

Crystal confusion

Long-term damp, especially when trapped by waterproof finishes, can have caused soluble salts to have been deposited near the surface of walls. Some of these can attract damp from the air, as does table salt, and this gives a false impression of dampness still coming from the wall. The salts can remain within the render and the wall behind long after any damp problem has gone, and with 'breathable' finishes, they can be brushed off from time to time without causing much damage. But they should not be washed, as that can redissolve them into the wall.

Bottle it up, or let it go?

Many cottage owners have in the past elected to have, or been forced to have, a damp-proof course installed. There have been various types, including injected chemical ones, which try to make old porous fabric impervious, physical ones, which cut in a waterproof barrier to the wall, electrical ones, which are applied to the wall via a conductor to try to dissuade water at an atomic level, and various porous inserts, which are drilled in and aim to do the job of a complete breathing wall in small spots.

Sometimes these various methods achieve what they set out to do, sometimes they don't. Even if they work, some of them are working counter to the way a cottage is likely to have been designed (though some later cottages may have been built with the physical barrier type as a slate damp-proof course), as explained earlier in this chapter. At worst a 'remedial' damp-proof course may be 'bottling up' damp that used to get out somehow – so where is that damp going now? What is it up to?

If remedial damp-proof courses don't work, it is probably because they are simply very difficult to retro-fit precisely into something as unknown and unpredictable as an old cottage wall. If a damp-proof course were installed with the condition that nearby vapour-permeable renders were replaced with waterproof ones, that would have introduced further alien material into the cottage. Some of the other conditions of guarantees may have included the sorts of common-sense damp-management measures that might have solved the damp without resorting to a damp-proof course at all: ensuring soil levels were not 'wicking' damp in, ensuring rainwater goods were not leaking, and so on. If a cottage has had a damp-proof course installed without considering the side effects on how the whole cottage deals with damp, then it may be time for some conservation-oriented advice.

happening. For example, a quick redecoration of an old limewashed cellar using masonry paint might appear to smarten the place up: beads of damp might no longer appear on the walls of the cellar. But if that damp now gets trapped in the bricks and mortar instead and makes them soft, or has to climb as high as the timbers of the living-room floor to escape, then the 'solution' has risked creating a worse problem for the future.

Another example that can still be witnessed virtually every day in the country is where owners are persuaded that old lime mortar on exterior brickwork has failed simply because it is soft. But it was never meant to be harder than the bricks: that is how it coped benignly with damp and movement (*see also* Chapters 3: Don't Bring Me Down, and 6: Sticks and Stones). If old lime mortar really has degenerated to the point where replacement is necessary, then the first option ought to be to look at a like-for-like replacement with lime mortar again. But often cement mortar is sold as a replacement to householders, most likely because the general building industry has forgotten about lime, and builders are unfamiliar with lime mortar. What can then happen is that the new, hard cement traps water in the brickwork, and the old, soft, damp bricks freeze in winter, which eventually causes them to crumble to dust.

Owners should remember that old and new do not necessarily go together before letting anyone near their home with trowels or paintbrushes.

What to do with a mixed-up cottage: a hybrid

Unfortunately, most cottages have by now been generously, lovingly but most usually mistakenly sealed up with paints or renders that inhibit their ability to 'breathe'. Many were forced by, arguably misguided, mortgage lenders to have damp-proof courses installed regardless of whether the walls were already handling damp adequately or not. Many cottages are also now inhabited by people who keep them hotter and less well ventilated than was ever likely when they were first built. Some of these things can be accelerating decay due to damp becoming trapped, where once it could pass freely and escape (*see also* Chapters 8: This Old House, and 11: Get It Right Next Time). Some cottages may appear to have settled down to coexist with their modifications fairly amicably, sometimes this might actually be the case, but sometimes unpleasant things are happening unseen under the surface.

Every property will be different, and sometimes it can pay to invest in an impartial assessment from someone who understands old buildings, rather than face expensive repairs later. Remedies such as stripping paint or render that is suffocating walls might be recommended in specific circumstances, but not everyone can do this and there may be other, less onerous ways to try to manage the risks. For the majority of cottages it makes sense generally to take simple steps to help traditional fabric make the best of whatever 'breathing' is available, and to limit damp ingress generally. For example, by allowing some through-ventilation in warm, dry weather; by keeping gutters and down pipes in good order; by keeping existing paint (even the 'wrong' kind) sound; by preventing the build-up of soil against external walls; by examining roof spaces and cellars to see that timbers are appropriately ventilated, and to check on leaks. It could save a lot of money in the long run.

Chapter 2 The Professionals makes the case for getting advice from those who know the original 'anatomy' of a cottage before committing it to any surgery. Above all this applies to the management of damp, since a damp remedy that seals in or 'bottles up' damp is no remedy at all. That simply risks a new and perhaps even more serious problem for the future.

The answer

There is no guaranteed 'magic bullet' for damp, but there is experience and there is a vast range of simple, cottage-friendly measures that start small and can be tried one at a time. One of these is the French drain (*see* the drawing opposite). However, much of the rest of this book is concerned with the issues of 'breathability' in an old cottage, and understanding and applying those principles can be a significant step towards retuning a cottage to its natural ability to manage dampness. But the modern cottager needs to come to terms with using their building in accordance with its capabilities, which might mean forgoing some modern state-of-the-art decoration and instead using something more, well, cottagey.

Persistent wetting, here apparently connected with water dripping from hanging baskets, can quickly translate into a building problem that at first sight looks like 'rising damp'.

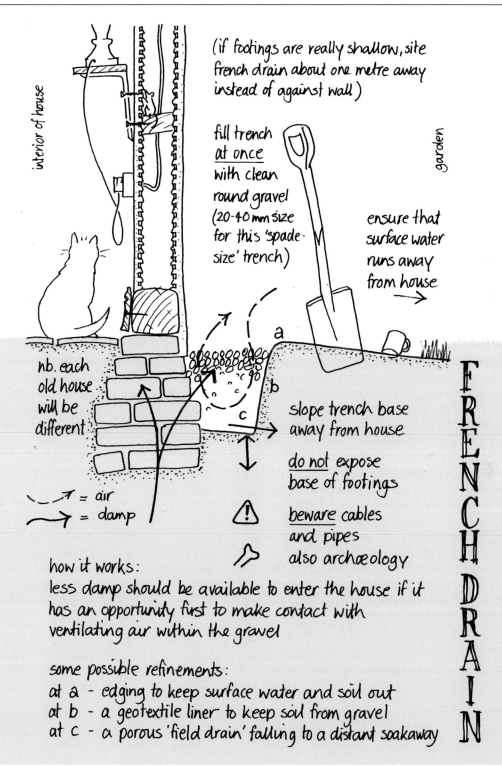

(if footings are really shallow, site french drain about one metre away instead of against wall)

interior of house

garden

fill trench at once with clean round gravel (20-40 mm size for this 'spade-size' trench)

ensure that surface water runs away from house →

nb. each old house will be different

a

b

c

slope trench base away from house

do not expose base of footings

beware cables and pipes

also archæology

⌣↗ = air

→ = damp

FRENCH DRAIN

how it works:
less damp should be available to enter the house if it has an opportunity first to make contact with ventilating air within the gravel

some possible refinements:
at a - edging to keep surface water and soil out
at b - a geotextile liner to keep soil from gravel
at c - a porous 'field drain' falling to a distant soakaway

THE WAY WE WERE
Cottages as they were built

A cottage is an old building, built by people now long forgotten. They used materials and techniques that had slowly been refined over a thousand years, before our minds and capabilities were expanded by the Industrial Revolution and the modern age.

During those past centuries, builders of cottages would mostly have remained living and working close to their buildings. They noticed any defects in design and materials, and if they didn't, the people who lived in the building probably helpfully pointed them out at the village inn or during archery practice. As a result the thousand years or so in which the same simple materials were used resulted in a thorough understanding of their possibilities and limitations. This, by and large, was what cottages were based on until the twentieth century.

That age-old experience and thoroughly understood use of materials still lies at the heart of just about every old cottage, but has mostly been distorted by the products and methods inspired by the Industrial Revolution and applied ever since by a couple of recent generations who have forgotten the lessons of the previous thousand years. The newer methods have been tested over only a fraction of the time of the old methods, and already it is obvious that the two systems can sometimes be seriously incompatible.

Even with a building that has become a hybrid of traditional and modern construction, it is worth understanding what was in place before the modern age because the old methods and materials still exert a strong effect on the building, and it could be useful to use the knowledge, even the materials themselves, in repairs. And, as the fuels of our industrial age are said to be running out, we might soon have to re-learn what was second nature to our forbears and adapt some of those pre-industrial methods and materials for ourselves as mainstream building. Pre-industrial techniques as applied to the homes of the poor were indisputably sustainable: there was no other way for them.

The chapters in this second section explore some of the main traditional materials and methods to be found in a British cottage, looking at their maintenance and repair using traditional techniques where possible:

CHAPTER FIVE

A Hard Rain
Traditional roofing

HERE COMES THE RAIN AGAIN

A badly leaking roof is one of the most unfortunate failures in any building, since keeping the rain off is a basic requirement of shelter. The very earliest roofers would no doubt recognize thatch as still used today on cottages, and although a century of recent industrial development has produced some new roofing solutions, it has not completely swept away the traditional clay tiles or stone slates that were first introduced here before the Middle Ages, and which are still being produced.

Thatch

Britain is a fertile country with a wide variety of natural vegetation that was adaptable to thatching. Turf and heather roofs can still be seen, especially in the north and west of the country and its outlying islands. Long ago, once farming had been established, it made sense to recycle the long stems of cereal crops for roofing (it was also in demand for human and animal bedding, not to mention more labour-intensive applications such as corn dollies and straw hats).

Thatching went through a lean period last century after hybrid cereal crops were developed with less useful short stems, which, even then, were broken up by mechanical harvesters, making them doubly useless for roofing. As a result many straw-thatched cottages turned to tiles or corrugated iron for roofing material, or were re-thatched in reed, another traditional thatching material usually confined to wetland corners of the country and with a slightly different look to the more common straw thatch. The Norfolk Broads, one of the traditional reed-thatch areas, continues to harvest reeds just for thatching. Now, 'old-fashioned' thatching straw is specially grown (some thatching materials come from abroad), and local planning authorities may insist on properties reverting to straw when they are re-thatched. This might be a temporary situation, however, as expected pressures on farming land could make the production of food the first preference for cereal crops, rather than a 'luxury' roofing product, which is, ironically, what thatch has become in the eyes of some.

A conservation plea: if re-thatching, particularly if forced to change from one material to another, bear in mind that in thatching traditions such as long-straw the lower layers might never be replaced. This means that they could be five hundred years old or more, perhaps even blackened with soot from the days before chimneys and upper floors were inserted in houses. This is valuable historical evidence, and steps should be taken to preserve it intact and in place. Speak to the local conservation officer for local advice. (*See also* 'Repairs and re-roofing', page 60.)

One of the predicted effects of climate change is wetter winters, nevertheless there are certainly thatching traditions on the west coast of Britain that have proven resistance to high and persistent rainfall. Even the traditions from the drier east will have developed through many centuries of climate change already – if only with the experience of some bad years. An ability to dry out between soakings is crucial to thatch and the roof beneath, so anything that might be introduced into the roof construction or thatch that hinders this may be unwise, and proposed alterations to proven roofing and thatching traditions need to be properly evaluated and understood.

Clay tiles

Plain, by royal decree
Ordinary 'plain tiles' were standardized in size by royal decrees back in the Middle Ages, with gradually increasing degrees of public obedience. The lawmakers may not have had sustainability on their minds, but this was good environmental legislation since it reduced waste and has made repair and replacement that much simpler for hundreds of years since, so well done them. These simple, flattish rectangular tiles can be nailed to the timber

Norfolk remains well known for its reedbeds that still produce thatching reed, much as they have for centuries. But the long-stemmed cereal straw for 'long straw' thatch, once much more common in England, and for 'combed wheat reed' thatch, is no longer a by-product of regular farming methods, although it is still available, specially grown.

Similar solutions to coastal winds from two different parts of north-western Britain.

Long straw being laid in shaggy layers (left) before trimming and binding at its edges to keep it in place (right).

Norfolk reed bundles placed at a roof's hip, before being finally shaped (below left). Water reed has quite a sharp profile (below right), and its weight helps keep it in place without visible binding. The ridge on a water reed roof has to be made from a bendier material than reed, such as sedge. The West Country's combed wheat reed tradition uses a similar thatching technique to water reed technique, but with straw instead of reed (below bottom); the 'reed' word here describes the stem, not the plant.

roofing battens but are often simply hung instead, on a nail passed through a pre-formed hole in the tile. Before mechanization made nails cheap, a peg of oak was used – so these tiles are also known as 'peg tiles'. More recent plain tiles also have a built-in 'nib' in the clay so they can be self-hanging.

Hand made, machine made and 'hand made'
Mechanization has been applied to tile-making, and new materials, such as cement, have been used to make tiles for modern buildings. Where formed and cured identically, these tend to look too uniform on a cottage, so it is worth considering the many modern 'hand-made' clay tiles when repairing or re-roofing.

Traditional peg tiles, seen from inside with new 'hand-made' tiles hanging on oak pegs (left), and some very old tiles outside (right) on another roof, where they have been turned around and probably also upside down (the peg holes are now at the bottom). Also, instead of being hung on pegs, these turned tiles are now set in mortar, which hides their worn ends and perhaps gets another hundred years of life out of them – until the mortar washes away, when things can become unsettled.

Some machine-made clay plain tiles (left), from about the Victorian period onwards, are flatter and more regular than mediaeval tiles; modern 'hand-made' tiles can vary from somewhere between the two right up to a reasonably faithful mediaeval copy.

Listed buildings, or those in conservation areas and national parks, for example, are very likely to be required to use their traditional local roof covering when they are re-roofed, and the local planning authority should be able to advise in detail.

When patching it might be desirable to match using a weathered-looking tile whose colour is achieved by mineral coatings fired to the tiles. But if completely re-roofing, then a bright natural clay tile roof, provided it is in a colour appropriate to the locality, should weather to blend with other old roofs better than an artificially coloured tile.

Other profiles

There are many other successful variations of clay tile; perhaps the most ingenious is the pantile, which, because the tiles interlock with each other, makes for less overlapping and therefore uses fewer layers; this produced lighter-weight roofs requiring fewer tiling battens, but which still effectively shed water at lower angles than plain tiles. In the Middle Ages pantiles were traded into the southern and eastern UK ports, sometimes as ballast in ships returning across the Channel from the 'Low Countries', which had a thriving clayware industry. As a result areas such as Midlothian, Avon, Yorkshire and Norfolk can claim a tradition of pantiles that pre-dates local manufacture.

Traditional pantiles (above), and some less universal traditional local variants (below). Pantiles, and many other tile profiles, were also copied in glass to allow light in.

Stone and slate

Slate is stone

Slate, geologically, is a 'metamorphic' rock that started life millions of years ago as fine clay and has been pressed, geologically pummelled and super-heated into a rock that can be split into thin sheets. This is the thin, grey family of slate varying from black, through purple to green and grey, that can be seen everywhere, but which would probably have been quarried in Wales, Scotland, Cornwall or Cumbria. Each area has a distinct dominant colour and texture: Wales grey-purple and very smooth and thin, Scotland grey-black, Cornwall light grey, and Cumbria grey-green. Most people associate one of these with the word 'slate'.

Having exported vast quantities of its slate over the last hundred years, the UK now tends to import new slates: these can sometimes look very different to

Cornish (left) and Scottish (below) slate roofs in their respective homelands.

Welsh slates (left) and Westmoreland (right), here hung on a wall; Welsh slate can be fashioned in larger and thinner sizes than other British slates and can be found extensively outside Wales on nineteenth-century cottages, courtesy of the railways.

native slate and may be difficult to match for thickness, finish or long-term stability of colour when repairing an old roof that is next to one still having the native original slate.

Stones that are slates

There are also stone slates (also called stone tiles) that are not made from slate but are worked from those limestones or sandstones that happen to be cleavable into manageable slabs. Stone slates tend to be chunkier than 'ordinary' grey slate because the bedding planes along which limestone and sandstone might be split are coarser and less regular. Stone slates, and even some of the thinner grey slates, may have originally come from small local quarries, and while there is a growing demand for these to be reopened, it is not always possible economically, nor is it always welcomed locally: if the present residents of old quarry cottages do not owe their livelihoods to stone, the sights and sounds of quarrying might be unpopular enough for objections to be pursued and listened to. New matching slates of various varieties can sometimes be sourced, with persistence, but if selecting second-hand be careful that another old building has not been sacrificed to supply them.

Various parts of Britain have limestone or sandstone of a quality that will bear cleaving into reasonably thin slabs; each area will have its own traditions of shaping, sizing and of eaves and ridge treatments, depending on the qualities of the stone. In many traditions the largest slabs are used at the bottom, as here, so there are fewer joints to leak, while smaller sizes are fine for the top and are not wasted. Colours range from near white through beige and brown to dark grey, depending on the rock. Matching for repairs could mean following the geological seam until a working quarry is found.

Lead and zinc

Good evening, vicar

Lead is regularly stolen from church roofs according to the ups and downs in world metal prices, and house owners should also take extra care of their lead. Cottages may not have been as richly endowed as was the church, but they may have porch, dormer and bay windows roofed in lead, as well as lead valleys and hidden gutters. Some of these might have been replaced over the years with less substantial materials, perhaps because the leadwork was originally poorly designed or was seen as too expensive to replace like for like when it failed.

A lead roof is not absolutely watertight, insofar as it could not be turned upside down and used as a boat, because it still relies on gravity to shed water over laps and across unsealed joints. Lead also needs to be allowed to expand and contract with temperature or it may wrinkle or tear – which is why there have to be those overlaps and unsealed joints.

New lead for old

Owners wishing to replace or reinstate lead should consider taking advantage of current codes of practice for designing and laying lead, which should help avoid any repeat of failure in performance or of the material itself. If an old roof does not seem to accommodate modern best practice for lead, then a conservation professional may need to design a solution, taking advantage of lessons from repairing other old buildings.

And the rest

When lead failed or was stolen it was often replaced with apparently more versatile modern materials such as bituminous roofing felt, but these materials have not proved to last as well as lead. Lead is usually repairable, but if beyond repair the metal is usually readily recyclable. Zinc was used, particularly from the late nineteenth century, as a cheap or lightweight alternative or replacement substitute for lead. It did not catch on in Britain as much as in some other European countries, and tends to have been worked to imitate the look of lead, rather than show itself to be the sharper, thinner material that it is in its own right.

Timber shingles are a traditional roofing material that would have been applicable to cottages; now quite rare as an original survival, they are nevertheless still available. They could be suitable for lightweight applications now, such as 'light touch' first floor extensions.

LETTING IN WATER
Repairs and re-roofing

Serious or not?

Roof leaks are often irritatingly difficult to pin down. Sometimes there can be several leaks operating at once, so careful investigation pays off, and to avoid disappointment, consider letting a few rainstorms go by after roof repairs have been completed and before reinstating internal decorations – just in case. A leak may stem from a dramatic cause such as a slipped tile or slate, but equally it can be from a tiny crack in a flashing or other detail. A different and often simple-to-fix problem might be that water trying to leave the roof via the normal channels, valleys and gutters is being blocked by leaves or debris and as a result is flowing into the house. A related problem is where snow and ice fill valley gutters, damming them and causing a flood 'upstream' through the roof tiles.

Roof problems can be very depressing, but at least they tend to be honest enough to show themselves and, with luck, it is usually obvious when they have been solved, making them a little more straightforward to deal with than some other problems that can lurk unseen in a cottage.

Re-roofing

Complete re-roofing is a difficult call to make: sometimes poor-looking roofs can happily plod on for another five, ten or twenty years with only a relatively small percentage of the covering having to be re-laid; sometimes a completely sound-looking roof can be torn off in the next storm. Some causes of indisputable terminal failure are that the timber battens (that support the tiles or slates) have generally rotted or their nails corroded, the tiles or slates have generally crumbled, or the nails holding these have corroded. In some parts of the country it was the practice to recycle broken tiles by mortaring them to the battens, which makes for extra unpleasantness when that mortar eventually washes away; it can also make trying to work on such a roof an unnerving experience.

Unfortunately, cottages, being at the bottom of the wealth pile, could have experienced a lot of such make-do-and-mend roofing repairs. Care is needed, and needless to say it is normally extremely inadvisable to try to prise tiles out of a mortared-in roof; temporary repairs might have to involve gingerly applied small lead patches, or even – bearing in mind that the tiles are reused already – a local application of a modern fibre-reinforced liquid repair compound (*see also* 'Quick fixes', 'Sticking point', below), provided it does not disfigure the roof.

Re-roofing is not cheap, partly because of scaffolding costs. However, having paid for the scaffolding it would make sense to look at chimney stacks and other high-level features at the same time. But seek the advice of a conservation-accredited architect or building surveyor regarding specifications for an old cottage and a design to last and to fit in visually, rather than leaving it all to the roofers to decide. (*See also* Chapter 17, 'Birds, squirrels and bats', page 198.)

Thatch

Thatch can be repaired within reason, and long straw in particular is laid in such a way that patches can be knitted in relatively easily. All types of thatch will probably need, and benefit from, re-ridging during their lifetime. Repairs and re-thatching, like virtually all cottage repairs, should be by tradespeople who understand old buildings thoroughly. Initial enquiries through the local conservation officer should help the cottage owner get to know how to find a reputable firm or individual.

Insulation

A thatched roof will probably offer good insulation in many cases, but should a tiled or slated roof need complete re-laying, then there is likely to be an opportunity to address the insulation of awkward roof slopes and ceilings. Such insulation would need careful design to maintain proper ventilation and to avoid future problems of condensation – it has to be done much more thoughtfully than just cramming in thick quilts of insulation (*see also* Chapter 15: Hot Love – (Drawing) 'Insulating Sloping Ceilings', page 163).

Quick fixes

First aid

Buckets, trays and polythene sheets may help in emergencies; try to get them as close under the leak as possible to avoid drenching ceilings and walls, since lath and plaster may not recover well from persistent wetting, and make sure they do not overflow. Safe access to carry out temporary repairs is rarely available to the home owner, and this is best left to professional builders and roofers who should be aware of the limitations of the roof itself and the dangers to people and property below. Missing or broken tiles can sometimes be replaced quite efficiently by working a new one into the gap. Missing slates (thin grey ones) can usually be replaced with the help of a 'tingle' – a simple metal strap nailed to the roof and hooked around the bottom of the replacement slate once it is pushed into place. Scaffolding is not always necessary for difficult-to-access spot roof repairs if it is appropriate instead to use a lifting mechanical platform or 'cherry picker'.

Sticking point

Owners need to be wary of seductively simple-sounding remedial treatments that are applied to the top or underside of tiles and slates with a view to sticking them on or re-waterproofing the roof. They may do that for a period, but if they restrict ventilation through the tiles or slates, or if they seal up the

This cottage (left) has got a job with a bank, which might account for its neat rainwater gutters; however, the run-off from thatch usually comes not just from the top surface but from the outer layers too, which needs collecting in a wide trough (right) – that is, if collection is considered necessary at all.

timbers and battens inside, then there is a risk of timber decay. On top of that, once such fabrics or foams are stuck on to the tiles or slates it becomes very difficult to reuse the latter when re-roofing, potentially ruling out a useful cost saving.

Underlay

By the 1950s houses were being built with a second line of defence under the tiles or slates: a black water-proof 'roofing felt' underlay. Some old houses have also acquired this during past re-roofing. But it has been established that this can cut down ventilation to the point where roof timbers can be at risk from damp arising from condensation. As a result, extra ventilation has been insisted upon for roofs in new houses by more recent regulations, and now 'breath-able' underlays are available.

'Breathable' is a relative term (with as yet little in the way of a universally applicable unit of measure-ment for old building use), and not all underlays are breathable or, if they claim breathability, then they do not necessarily all possess this quality to the same useful degree; therefore seek professional advice to help select what is right when re-roofing a tradition-ally built cottage. (*See also* Chapter 14: Future Past –

'The breathability of insulation', page 156.) Breath-able underlays have been around long enough to have revealed that some are light enough to be prone to flapping in the wind, so they need careful placing to reduce or eliminate this. They have not been around long enough to establish whether they might be affected by exposure to sunlight, as was old-fashioned roofing felt, which disintegrated. So it is a good idea to protect them at the exposed edges by designing in an appropriate material to shield them, one that is ultra-violet resistant.

Liquid repair

Degraded and failed flat roofs of built-up felt or asphalt, and cracked lead valleys or parapet gutters, may take some planning and expense to repair or replace. To try to stop leaks in the meantime, cracks can be bridged with various degrees of success using materials from bituminous sealants to proprietary paint-on fibre-reinforced acrylic compounds. How-ever, there is a balance in what is sensible temporarily because applying these over large areas, particularly to lead, might actually prohibit a traditional repair later. Liquid-applied temporary repairs might, for example, satisfactorily keep serviceable a valley gutter

Cast iron is long lasting if properly painted all round; to assist access for this, the pipes can be remounted to stand a little further clear of the wall.

of failed bituminous felt until a repair or complete replacement is possible, but they are unlikely to solve any underlying problem that may have caused the failure in the first place.

RAINWATER GOODS

Pre-nineteenth century cottages were almost certainly originally built without any gutters or downpipes, since it was only during that century that cast iron made such things relatively affordable. And in any event thatch, in which the rain will infiltrate beneath the topmost reeds or straws before issuing at the eaves, is very difficult to contrive an effective gutter for. Broad timber troughs can work, but it seems that traditionally it was rarely worth the trouble unless it was necessary to save the water.

Cast iron

For many years a British Standard enabled the manufacture of a graceful and inter-connectable system of plain 'half-round' gutters and round downpipes that are likely still to be found on many British cottages. Cast iron is very durable, and its solidity keeps down noise in hoppers and pipes. It is also potentially quite resistant to corrosion, but is susceptible to rust, especially where water can be trapped by poorly adhering paint. It is worth the extra effort to ensure that all surfaces are properly and thoroughly primed and painted (*see also* Chapter 12: Paint It … Back – 'Conventional modern paints – For ironwork', page 139), as decoration intervals and the life of the iron can be significantly extended.

Old installations may be rather brutally fixed to walls with spikes, and these may need attention; gutter brackets likewise, and it should not be assumed that these, or the gutters, can take the weight of ladders.

More recent products

Plastic and, before that, asbestos cement are probably the more common alternatives to be found on cottages. There are obviously potential health concerns with asbestos in case it breaks and the fibres are inhaled (*see also* Chapter 9: Reasons to be Careful – 'Asbestos', page 115). Plastic is very versatile, but a faded grey installation on a cottage can unfortunately 'break the spell' by its association with modern housing – although there are some very convincing cast-iron lookalikes in plastic and aluminium rain-water goods. While cast iron can be the preferred medium for reasons of historical association, its firm-ness and also because of its suitability to the existing layout on most old cottages, there can equally be situations where the lightness of plastic and not having to repaint it can be very compelling. Ladders do pose a danger with flexible plastic and brittle old asbestos cement guttering – and if the latter breaks there is more than just a danger of falling.

ROOFSPACES AND FIRE

Thatched and other roofs

It is worth considering equipping roofspaces in any cottage with heat detectors and smoke detectors. This would be essential in thatched cottages, where being able to sense the temperature of critical loca-tions, next to chimneys for example, would be crucial in order to warn of approaching danger, rather than waiting for an actual fire to be detected. These devices should each be capable of sounding a remote alarm in the house below, and should preferably be linked to a central household alarm. Such detection may already be a requirement under a thatched cottage owner's insurance, or may have been advised following inspection by the local fire service.

Chimneys should be inspected for defects such as missing bricks where they pass within roofspaces and elsewhere, and if in use for open fires, should be tested for smoke tightness. Thatch is not a fixed thickness, and the traditions of some thatching will build up the roof thickness with each successive re-thatch – so the chimney may need to be raised exter-nally to compensate. With increased thickness comes more insulation of course, but there would then be a deeper mass of thatch adjacent to the hot chimney, which is where the temperature sensor would be useful – just in case.

Most classes of heating appliance are now required to be accompanied by a suitable chimney liner, but thatched property owners need to consult their insurers, the local building inspector and the fire brigade for their views on the advisability, or not, of particular appliances. Wood-burning and some other stoves are strongly discouraged by some authorities since the heat from flue gases can be transmitted through flue walls into the depth of the thatch at temperatures sufficient to cause ignition.

A spark arrestor – a special metal mesh to en-close the pot – is sometimes used to guard against direct ignition of thatch from embers floating out of the chimney, but these devices need to be kept clean or they might become a hazard in themselves. (*See also* Chapter 6: Sticks and Stones – 'Chimney pots, cowls and terminals', page 70; and Chapter 16: Bits and Pieces – 'Some fireplace practicalities', page 179.)

Terraced and attached properties and fire

Now all newly built attached dwellings are physically separated from their neighbours throughout their full height. In the past it was not considered necessary (or more likely, in the past it was considered unneces-sarily expensive). For security and to guard against the spread of fire, owners of attached cottages should have their roofspaces inspected for adequate fire sepa-ration. It may not be feasible to add a solid masonry fire-resisting wall in all cases because of the weight this would impose – perhaps there is nothing substantial to bear it upon. In these cases a rock-based mineral wool screen (specially made reinforced versions of the insulation material) can be profession-ally designed to do the job with minimum weight. (*See also* Chapter 15: Hot Love – 'Conventional modern insulation products', page 161.)

OPPOSITE: Britain has a wide variety of building stone of various hardness and durability; some can even be split thin enough to use on roofs.

CHAPTER SIX

Sticks and Stones
Traditional walls, partitions, chimneys, floors, ceilings and stairs

BRICK AND STONE MASONRY

The most durable of traditional wall materials, brick and stone masonry can look good for centuries. However, misguided application of modern cement and paints, or even cleaning, can upset the careful original balance and hasten decay.

The development of masonry
The very earliest use of masonry in house construction was probably similar to the drystone wall construction still seen today: roughly hewn chunks of stone nestled together to form a stable heap that could accommodate a door and support a roof. Over time a simple mortar was developed by burning chalk

Stone and brick can have varied in prominence in the same area over time, and clay bricks and roof tiles can have varied in availability and colour in the same locality even before the coming of the machine age.

or limestone to create lime, which, when re-mixed with water and bound with sand, would help the stones adhere (*see also* the drawing, 'Quick Guide to Lime', page 68). This enabled thinner, more economical walls to be built. Stones vary in hardness and durability across the country, and Britain has a great variety to choose from. Nevertheless, it takes a great deal of physical work to fashion stones into usable blocks, especially without power tools, so brick developed alongside stone; this also enabled many stoneless areas to have the advantages of masonry walls.

Brick was arguably the first modular building component, the proportions of each unit geared to the size of the human hand and to ratios of the brick's longest side so as to enable versatility in use and jointing applications. As a result, brick sizes have been able to resist recent attempts to make them conform to metric (whole centimetre) dimensions, though sizes have been adjusted historically in response to tax liability. The humble brick has, for a simple lump of clay, been quite an agile fugitive from bureaucracy.

A balanced construction

One very important feature established with the earliest lime mortars was that they were softer than the accompanying bricks or stones, which meant that any excess wetting or movement of the wall resulted in the gradual decay or attrition of the mortar, rather than of the stones. But the mortar could be replaced easily enough, which is why mortar is often called the 'sacrificial element' of a wall: the lime mortar in a wall might need its surface replacing, known as 'repointing', around every century or two, or maybe even longer.

In fact lime mortar's relative pliability in long-term use is what has enabled very old walls to bend and bow without cracking the bricks or stones. Its vapour permeability allows excess dampness to dry out from within a masonry wall, protecting the masonry from frost damage. Not only that, but lime mortar is considered to have a moisture transmission rate reasonably compatible with building timbers such as oak: this means that timbers buried in the wall – to create lintels and beams, for example – are less likely to become saturated and decay while hidden away.

Upsetting the balance

Unfortunately, once modern cement had been invented, lime mortars were increasingly dismissed as 'weak' and seen as less durable. This may have been

To test that a mortar is properly balanced with the brickwork, assemble some soft bricks in lime mortar and leave in an exposed field for up to two hundred years. If the mortar wears away first then the mix is good – it shows that the mortar is the 'sacrificial element' in the brickwork, and the mortar alone could have been replaced at some point and saved the wall. Modern brickwork that uses the hard cement mortar of today has not been around quite long enough for confidence in the results of equivalent trials, but it is reasonable to suppose that if the bricks had eroded first, then the filigree of mortar left around them would not be standing for long, as the bricks alone could not be replaced.

This is the result of just repointing this old brickwork with cement as a repair (not even laying the whole wall with cement for its whole life): of course the wall may have been suffering before that was done, but evidently the cement has not prevented the bricks wearing away further, and it is likely that it actually hastened that decay by trapping water in the bricks. The bricks have now become the 'sacrificial element'. This is why it is not a good idea to introduce cement into a cottage, however much modern buildings may adore it. Old bricks tended to be softer and more porous than the consistency we now expect from modern bricks.

true in terms of the engineering uses for which the Victorians invented what we generically call 'ordinary Portland cement', but it has proved, with hindsight, a significant mistake to change from lime mortar when repairing the walls of most old buildings. This is because cement can be harder than the stones or bricks, making them the 'sacrificial' elements instead.

So the question needs to be asked: which is easier to replace every hundred or so years without demolishing the wall, the mortar, or the bricks and stones? Sadly many cottages were subjected to the twentieth-century's starry-eyed love affair with cement (yes, it can be brilliant for lighthouses, tunnels, bridges, foundations and giant skyscrapers … but is it really necessary for tiny cottages?), and they have faced the risk of permanent damage as a result.

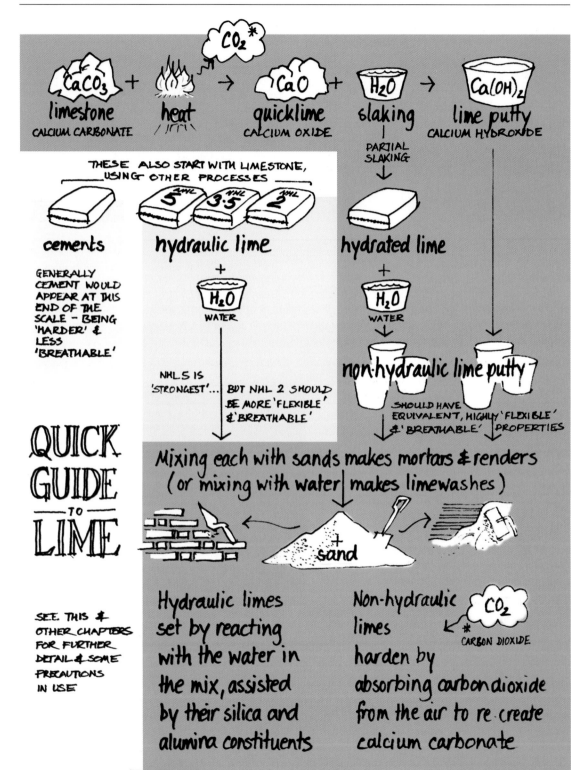

$CaCO_3$ limestone CALCIUM CARBONATE + heat $\rightarrow$ CO_2* CaO quicklime CALCIUM OXIDE + H_2O slaking $\rightarrow$ $Ca(OH)_2$ lime putty CALCIUM HYDROXIDE

THESE ALSO START WITH LIMESTONE, USING OTHER PROCESSES

cements

GENERALLY CEMENT WOULD APPEAR AT THIS END OF THE SCALE — BEING 'HARDER' & LESS 'BREATHABLE'

hydraulic lime

NHL 5 · 3·5 · 2

+ H_2O WATER

NHL 5 IS 'STRONGEST'... BUT NHL 2 SHOULD BE MORE 'FLEXIBLE' & 'BREATHABLE'

PARTIAL SLAKING

hydrated lime

+ H_2O WATER

non-hydraulic lime putty

SHOULD HAVE EQUIVALENT, HIGHLY 'FLEXIBLE' & 'BREATHABLE' PROPERTIES

Mixing each with sands makes mortars & renders (or mixing with water makes limewashes)

QUICK GUIDE — TO — LIME

SEE THIS & OTHER CHAPTERS FOR FURTHER DETAIL & SOME PRECAUTIONS IN USE

+ sand

Hydraulic limes set by reacting with the water in the mix, assisted by their silica and alumina constituents

Non-hydraulic limes harden by absorbing carbon dioxide from the air to re-create calcium carbonate

CO_2 * CARBON DIOXIDE

© 'HARDNESS' SEE TEXT 'BREATHABILITY'

If anyone is lucky enough to have a cement-free old wall, then they should be aware that there is even now a lingering, strongly held, and really quite wrong-headed belief across the building industry that cement is superior in all situations involving old masonry. Do not let your cottage become a victim of this ignorance. Each property will be different and will require a bespoke mix, so it would benefit from proper individual assessment. Enlightened owners might wish to start at their local conservation officer for support and also take note of the published advice from organizations such as English Heritage, Historic Scotland and Cadw.

CHIMNEYS

Masonry was used for constructing chimneys because it offers superior fire resistance, even where brick or stone was considered too costly, or unnecessary, for the construction of the rest of the cottage. Other materials were used but these have not survived in abundance (and probably most of the wooden ones, which oddly did seem to exist, burned down). The long-term durability of masonry in a flue is compromised by it being regularly at different temperatures inside and out, and also because it is subject to internal chemical attack. Traditionally this contingency was acknowledged, and flues were lined (right up to the early twentieth century) with a 'parge' made from cow dung, among other things. This not only smoothed the interior of the flue to allow gases a quick exit, but we must presume that it effectively insulated the masonry, also making for a more efficient flue, as well as filling accidental holes.

It is tempting to scoff at our forbears for building with faeces, but the material was evidently viable, sustainable and freely available. Put a modern scientist on an island with a chimney to line but no money and no factories, just a few cows and goats, and see what answer they come up with. Chimney parging does not last for ever, and because the supply of small children willing to climb chimneys with a bucket of cow manure has dried up, we must in many cases wait for robotic devices and a new attitude to animal droppings before this useful treatment can be resumed.

Twentieth-century efforts to fill the gap with cement or concrete linings of one sort or another were ingenious, but cement and concrete do not always sit successfully with the tendency for old cottages to move and with their need to 'breathe', and there have also been concerns over the weight and inflexibility of such interventions. As a concrete lining was quite a popular repair applied to old chimneys, it is wise to have the existence of such a lining confirmed and its condition checked by video. Video can also be used to examine most chimneys for defects, and other simple tests for smoke fastness are also useful. (*See also* Chapter 5: A Hard Rain – 'Roofspaces and Fire', page 64; and Chapter 16: Bits and Pieces – 'Light My Fire', page 179).

Chimneys may have been built with, or may have acquired later, beam ends or other timbers poking into them. This can easily have happened during alterations last century when the chimney was thought to have finally gone out of use for ever. Along with those timbers may be plumbing or extract pipes and electric wiring deliberately using the chimney as a conduit, or perhaps accidentally appearing out of the back of another wall. Needless to say, these things have to be dealt with, re-routed and any holes properly repaired if the chimney is now going to be used for its original purpose.

Repair considerations

The same considerations apply to ancient chimney masonry as to walls (*see also* 'Upsetting the balance', page 66, and 'Repointing', page 74), but unfortunately the most benign of lime mortars can be too vulnerable to be perched on an exposed chimney. Though it was considered acceptable in the days when a fearless builder could be called upon to shin up a ladder every few years to re-point and to re-flaunch the very top, that process is now inhibited by the expense and scaffolding of our gentler age.

It has to be admitted that in the recent past even hardened conservationists have resorted to cement additives for chimney repairs, and these have surely cracked and trapped damp, but they haven't actually worn away. Fortunately, now there is hope, as the understanding of lime has been more thoroughly rediscovered: 'hydraulic' limes (*see also* Drawing – 'Quick Guide to Lime', opposite) have become widely available again, and these can offer a more tenacious alternative in these situations than ordinary 'non-hydraulic' lime. The 'weaker' grades of hydraulic limes are considered to possess a useful degree of the breathability and mobility advantages that 'regular' non-hydraulic lime provides, but without the harsh absence of them that can come with a pure cement mix. As ever, this product needs careful specifying based on conditions of use and exposure, but the traditional experience in its use is being reassembled, and it is also now making inroads into modern 'sustainable' construction.

Chimney pots, cowls and terminals

Pots were probably a little too expensive and therefore a luxury for cottages for much of their lives. The alternative stone or slate cowls or wide open flues would have been less of a problem when a good fire was burning almost constantly and incoming rain or snow quickly evaporated. Since the abandoning of open fires, many cottages have had flues blocked, and a terracotta cowl or plug or metal cap may have been fitted. If reopening the chimney, then as well as checking on the condition of the flue and having it swept, also make sure that the pot is suitable for a fire and is not just a ventilator designed to keep rain and birds out of an unused flue. Flues turned over to appliances that have superseded open fires must now have appropriate linings and terminals, not only to ensure efficient working of the appliance, but also to protect from blockages and to protect the occupants from leaks and backing-up of combustion gases. (*See also* Chapter 16, Bits and Pieces – 'Light My Fire', page 179.)

Thatched cottages may have a wire grid around the chimney top to try to catch sparks. These can be a mixed blessing if they are not regularly cleaned of the soot and tar that can cause them to catch light themselves. (*See also* Chapter 5: A Hard Rain – 'Roofspaces and Fire', page 64.)

Stays

Tall chimneys may be found restrained with a slender rod fastened at one end to a strap around the stack, while the other passes into the roof to be attached to the structure of the cottage. The traditional versions of these stays are not usually stiff enough to actually hold a leaning stack, but were intended to prevent a

One version of a vented cap (top) that must be removed before lighting a fire. There are other more open designs in metal that are intended to permit a fire to be used while also keeping birds and rain out. Also a spark arrestor to protect thatch (below); these mesh screens must be kept clean otherwise any soot and tar build-up might catch fire – something to remember if cottages suddenly revert to full-time open fires after decades of just having them at Christmas.

swaying rhythm being set up in high wind that could eventually lead to collapse. They ought to be checked for rust and security of connections, as well as water-proofing where they pass through the roof. A conservation engineer would be appropriate to advise on any structural concerns.

THE CARE AND MAINTENANCE OF TRADITIONAL MASONRY

A wall in brick or stone can provide an excellent low-maintenance structure and finish, one that can last hundreds of years without painting or repointing if properly built and looked after. However, fashion, or mistakes, may have intervened.

Paints

Many old masonry walls have acquired a painted finish during their lifetime. Perhaps they were first painted with a watered-down lime product called limewash (*see also* the drawing 'Quick Guide to Lime', page 68), the basis of traditional external whitewash and traditional colourwashes. Over the years new paints came along and were applied over the top, but – you've guessed it – many of those modern paints can just seal up damp in the walls and have proved, again with hindsight, a sad, sad mistake. This is not just technically, but also visually, as modern paint is so ruthlessly uniform that it can drain the character from cottages at the same time as it dams up the damp inside them.

Cottages might not necessarily have had access to the most expensive materials to start with, but if the workmanship was sound then ordinary masonry in lime mortar has the potential to last well over a century, maybe two, without needing attention.

71

Three examples of adding new brickwork to an old wall; each has avoided complete demolition and replacement, and that much at least is good for conservation and for the planet. (Top) shows a very old and heavily eroded wall, which appears to have been newly repointed in lime mortar and repaired with bricks that match how the originals would be expected to have looked new, and are probably also of a similar composition and hardness; (centre) seems not to have found such a good match of brick and unfortunately seems to have opted for cement mortar; while (bottom) shows some fairly neat modern workmanship in uncompromisingly modern materials crashed into some fairly neat period workmanship and materials, with a prominent division that seems to imply that space and time is somehow fractured where they come together: 1860 one side, 1960 the other? Each of these three repairs is honest and probably none would be likely to weather unnoticeably 'as one' within the lifetimes of those commissioning and carrying out the work, but the first example seems to have made the effort to match the materials' technology so that the whole wall can work happily as one without any fighting breaking out, and that should be what repairs try to do. One lesson that owners of brick walls should take from this is that each of the above would be seen by different people as a reasonable response to the basic instruction 'Repair that wall with red bricks, please'.

If their masonry walls have a painted surface, cottages need a gently varied finish to disguise other imperfections and to read as 'natural'. So once again, if in possession of a building that is still limewashed, seek information from those institutions mentioned above before considering redecoration (*see* 'Upsetting the balance', page 66). Limewash is still available and is quite easy to understand and use with appropriate precautions – and it can look much more appropriate on a cottage (*see* Further Information, page 202).

Damp

Even if individual bricks and stones are properly mortared with lime, they may still be subject to some

If a cottage owner is committed to preservation rather than replacement, then when faced with a serious problem, it is worth exploring new options. Here the mortar holding the rubble fill within the front wall had become loosened. Rather than rebuild, the wall was propped and 'corseted' (left) and new mortar poured in. This spared the disruption and expense of totally dismantling and rebuilding the front of the cottage, and in this case it meant the finished job, seen soon afterwards (right) shows only those signs of surgery that should soon heal; even the roses around the door were spared.

retained dampness: poor detailing, inadequate maintenance or the long-term raising of adjacent ground surfaces can channel too much damp into the wall and force it to stay there. The first line of defence would usually be to ensure that the damp is deflected away, and that the wall itself has ample ventilation and is not sealed up inside or out (by, for example, cement renders, emulsion paints, sealers and soil). The application of 'remedial' waterproof renders, or sealing compounds, paints and other non-breathable barriers as a 'solution' to damp, makes about as much sense as rubber gloves to cope with a leaking pen: the problem is still there and will be a nuisance in other ways.

Proper advice is necessary to seek out the cause of the problem so that it can be dealt with – and it's often quite an inexpensive and easy matter to introduce basic ventilation or to remove the worst sources of excess dampness, though time needs to be allowed for thorough drying and the establishment of a stable 'status quo'. This is life in the country – take time! (*See also* Chapter 4: The Air that I Breathe, for more on damp.)

Repairs

Age will still bring about some crumbling of bricks or stones in even the best managed of masonry walls. If the bricks and stones are still in their original lime mortar they can sometimes be taken out individually and turned round to repair a local disfigurement. This can be useful if the original brickworks or quarry has long gone and a match is otherwise impossible. Of course doing this on a large scale is inadvisable, and one does need to understand the engineering of masonry to attempt it at all, as certain bricks and stones are crucial to the structural integrity of the whole wall.

Cracks can have a number of causes, from simple thermal or ground movement to local overloading by, or failure of, the various beams and lintels that bear upon the walls. These will benefit from analysis by a conservation-accredited structural engineer. Once the cause is established and has been dealt with (*see also* Chapter 3: Don't Bring Me Down) any fractured bricks or stones can, according to function and appearance, be filled or replaced. The beauty of lime

a   new bricks
flush-pointed

cross section

b   weathered bricks
recess-pointed

when re-pointing after bricks
have been well-weathered
style b keeps the proportion of
         bricks to mortar close
         to the original (a)
style c   changes the original
         appearance – the mortar
         becomes too dominant

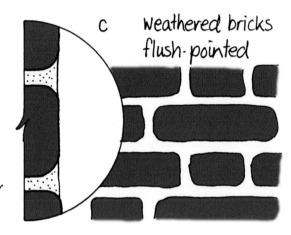

c   weathered bricks
flush-pointed

mortar as originally used in old buildings is that it would bear the brunt of any movement and limit the likelihood of cracks fracturing bricks and stones; therefore repairs to an old lime-mortared wall should employ the same mix, which would normally be appropriate for any filling of cracks in masonry items (in which case it can be coloured to match – *see also* below '"Plastic" repairs to masonry', page 76).

Repointing

Hard or soft option

As mentioned earlier, lime-mortared masonry will probably need repointing after upwards of a century or two, though this might sometimes be less, some-times more. This does not amount to demolishing the wall and rebuilding it: usually it is only necessary to replace the outer inch or so of the mortar joint, and only if the mortar has actually decayed. Softness alone is not indicative of the need to repoint, since lime mortar actually has to be relatively soft to do its job of protecting the bricks or stones. Unfortunately, much sound old lime mortar is condemned because it is not as hard as the cement mortar that people have become used to in modern brickwork – and with olden-day construction, hard mortar is not so good.

Hand tools

Rules of thumb are dangerous in building because

they can quickly usurp common sense. However, bearing that in mind, and also the need for proper on-site advice, it is said that one should remove a depth of failed mortar that is equivalent to two to three times the height of the joint: if a normal traditional joint height is up to 1/2in (about 10 to 12mm), this means roughly 1in at least (25mm+).

It is quite important with soft or uneven old bricks and stones that only hand tools are used to rake out the old mortar. A powered disc cutter can be a big mistake as it can so easily gouge out the edges of the masonry and overrun into the faces of bricks and stones. There are special machines with fine-bladed grinding surfaces to remove mortar from fine historic masonry, but in the ordinary, perhaps uneven jointing to be found in many cottages, it may be reasonable to assume that when a naturally soft mortar really does warrant replacement, it is not going to be a struggle to remove it manually.

How far?

If it proves to be really hard work chipping out sufficient old lime mortar with a fine old chisel, then it probably has not failed. It may be convenient to tackle a whole wall at one time for other non-technical reasons, but arguably those areas that do not succumb to gentle removal techniques do not need urgent attention. Specific on-site conservation advice is necessary, as the condition of lime mortar in an old wall is not likely to be uniform over the whole surface, so it can be a completely unnecessary expense and intervention to replace the lot. Simply removing what has failed and replacing that with a matching mix might be good for a few more decades.

The aim in repairing an old cottage is surely to keep it looking old, so a completely and obviously repointed wall may be a little too brash. There is skill in matching mortar mixes, and perhaps colouring them with matching local sands so that after a year or two the new work can blend in almost unnoticeably with what remains of the old. A sample panel would help convince clients of the tradesperson's abilities here (*see below*).

The materials

Even in these enlightened days when there is a growing awareness of conservation issues, such as the importance of lime mortars to ancient brickwork, there are still legions of 'gung-ho' builders eager to cram cement into your old joints. And even if you think you've found someone who has agreed to use only lime mortar on your precious old lime-mortared wall (maybe they've even put it in writing and sworn an oath), there is still a chance that if pressed they'll give a knowing wink to a passer-by and confide that they've 'slipped a little cement in … just enough to help it go off'. Others swear by some stuff called 'white cement', which was popular with architects around 1950 for some reason that few now remember or care about.

It is absolutely of no use to smile meekly at these people and offer them more tea: they are vandalizing your home! Treat them as if they had put sugar in your petrol tank or scattered moths over your best cashmere sweaters. Cement mortar can be damagingly inappropriate to old walls, while more benign lime mortar is not difficult to use. Lime was used and thoroughly understood by illiterate, superstitious people thousands of years ago: if they could do it, then we should not be frightened.

The mix and the job

Lime has its own very simple rules, but these have fallen out of mainstream knowledge and so it may seem less convenient for modern-trained trades to get to grips with lime mortar. But it is far from impossible. Some principal differences between cement and lime that affect its use on a job such as repointing including the following. It is more caustic than cement, so goggles, gloves and overalls are necessary, and a mask if handling powders (however, lime dries to calcium carbonate, a chemical formula that even appears in food additives – so while eating building materials is highly inadvisable, this might at least indicate that lime does not represent a long-term hazard once set). Lime is also extremely frost sensitive until set, so should not be used as winter approaches because a thick application can take months to set properly; the time that lime mortar takes to set and become stronger is longer and less predictable than with cement, so experience is necessary – particularly when using lime mortar in repairs that are more adventurous than pointing.

To find those who have the knowledge, the local conservation officer might be a good starting point for enquiries. The procedure for mixing and applying the mortar might look as follows – and even if you are simply observing, be sure to wear goggles, as splashes of lime can be damaging and painful. Thick lime putty (bought in tubs, or very carefully mixed up to the same consistency on site from cheaper hydrated 'bag lime' and water) is mixed with about three times its volume of clean builders' sand ('sharp' or 'soft' according to conditions) until it achieves a heavy mousse-like consistency (with no white powdery specks left if starting with the powdered lime). The raked-out joints, which should be two or three times deeper than their height, are wetted, and the mortar pressed well in without soiling the faces of the bricks or stones; the mortar is then faced up a few millimetres back from the face line of old, worn masonry, or faced up flush in new work (*see also* the drawing in the section 'Repointing', page 74), and smoothed with a pointing tool.

Later, when it has begun to set, the new mortar can be prodded with a stiff brush to close up any surface cracks. It should not be left to dry too quickly in the sun, or allowed to be washed out by rain (this causes staining of the masonry): it will need 'tending' (basically pushing back into shape to close cracks, or spraying if too dry) for some days or, in extreme cases, a week or so after applying.

This is not a complete DIY guide, and those interested in doing their own lime pointing could contact the SPAB or local authorities that run courses (*see* Further Information, page 202). A sample mix should have been made in advance and allowed to dry in order to check for colour, especially if repointing only in patches. It should tone down in time, but not by very much, and so the match should be adjusted so it is nearly right when first dry. (*See also* the drawing in this chapter 'Quick Guide to Lime' page 68, and Chapter 9: Reasons to be Careful – 'Substance abuse', page 114.)

Similar considerations apply to stone as to brick, but as there will be a greater variation in the hardness and evenness of stones found in some areas than is generally found among old brick, the lime mortar may need to be adjusted to match these qualities, and also climate conditions.

'Plastic' repairs to masonry

The term 'plastic repairs' is confusing because the phrase was invented before petrochemical plastics, which we may now first think of, became widespread; in fact it means 'mouldable'. Usually, damaged stone or brick is chipped away to provide a reasonable mechanical key (a little like large-scale dentistry), and this can be supplemented with corrosion-proof metal fixings if necessary (also like dentistry). A mix of a fine lime mortar is then packed by degrees into the cavity according to depth, the outer layers incorporating ground dust from the decayed brick or stone to give better colour. This does not work on all stone types; commonly, some sandstones are types to which

It must be a daily occurrence that someone scratches some old lime mortar like this, decides it is soft and rings the builder. But this wall is happy enough and should be left alone. The only problem is that, reading this book, you can't feel this brickwork for yourself so you need to take advice from a conservation professional. Better that, however, than waste money on an unnecessary repair that might shorten the life of the wall.

Repointing, or building new brickwork, can be done neatly but still not quite match the old mortar completely; but even if a good match is difficult to achieve, it is not impossible. Sometimes old mortar has become stained, and a decision has to be taken on whether to match the old or be honest about the new. In situations where a join is going to be noticeable it can be worth having trial areas done in advance. A discreet match depends on the joint profile and on the colour of the mix, but most importantly of all on using the same traditional mix as the original, which would usually mean lime and a local sand. If new mortar has not blended after a reasonable time then it can be possible to, carefully, tint it – but this can be laborious and risks staining the brick edges (the bricks should not be washed over with tint along with the mortar as that would change their colour, making matters worse). What these pictures happen to point out well is the bonding pattern, here Flemish bond, where the presence of regular headers (brick ends) indicates that the wall would be expected to be at least as thick as the length of a brick. This was a very popular bond for pre-modern brickwork used in housing.

This wall had some localized repointing a few years before, top left of picture, and maybe needs a little more now, centre, but the lower part is better left alone for now. In reality a wall rarely suddenly needs repointing all over at once. The brick bond here, by the way, is a variation on Flemish garden wall bond.

This original use of 'gingerbread' stone (left) is quite distinctive and is still nowadays very successfully executed in new buildings; while there is always room for novel interpretations, this new wall (right) has not started out with the right material for a convincing traditional look.

Here a new extension (right) carefully recaptures an original decorative finish (left) in chalk and brick.

it is probably less successfully applied, whereas lime-stone is more compatible since set lime mortar is chemically very similar. This type of repair has been much adapted in the recent past to repair brick and stonework, but unfortunately often using cement instead of lime mortar; the result is a 'filling' that is too hard, traps water behind it, and eventually drops out. Try again with lime next time.

Before carrying out repairs to stones or brickwork it is necessary to analyse why they have become defective in the first place. Was it trapped dampness? Has that been dealt with? If there is a crack, what caused it? Perhaps a rusting, embedded iron cramp? Frost action due to some missing protection above? Without understanding and solving the cause, the repair may be compromised for the same reason.

Cleaning masonry

As one would expect, the twentieth century came up with a lot of ideas and compounds for the cleaning, consolidation and repair of masonry. Although they seemed to be good ideas at the time, some of them only looked good for a while before going on to cause other problems, or they hastened the surface's decay by having made it too porous, too impermeable or too rough in the process. Since Britain has a particularly rich variety of stone types, it is not practical here to list the available conservation methods that are currently favoured; however, contacting the national heritage organizations (English Heritage, Historic Scotland, Cadw and so on) should produce more locally relevant information on their experiences with stone, as well as brick, cleaning methods and also repair options.

It can be worth remembering that part of the reason we love old buildings is for their patina of age. So gently does it! Sometimes, particularly with stonework, that patina is actually part of the stone's defence mechanism against weathering – which means that applying the equivalent of a thorough exfoliating scrub would leave it raw and vulnerable, not lastingly youthful and bright. It might be that some gentle scrubbing with minimal water and a softish bristle brush, in summer to avoid frost damage, is all that is sensible.

Shelter coats for stone, even brick

Stone that is crumbling, or otherwise needs gentle consolidation, can be considered for treatment with a shelter coat. This is basically a thin limewash that conservationists have sometimes augmented with ground-up stone (sometimes picked up from under the wall itself if it is falling off) and other carefully chosen natural substances. The whiter limestones are particularly suited to this treatment, which is chemically compatible with the rock, and which is reversible in that simple watered-down limewash plus stone dust wears away in time.

It is best to, as they say, 'experiment on an inconspicuous area first' to ensure that the coating dries to an acceptable colour. Sandstones and harder rocks may not be compatible. 'Lime water', the liquid forming at the top of a tub of lime putty, is sometimes brushed on to masonry in the same way, in the hope that it rejuvenates it.

OTHER STONE CONTENDERS

Cottages were a ready market for the use of building materials that did not quite come up to the mark for grander buildings, and in areas such as, for example, Norfolk, Suffolk, Essex and Kent, which are not rich in hard building stones, some borderline materials were also regularly used even for quite prestigious buildings. Stone that is little more than hard mud, and even beach pebbles were pressed into service, and very soft chalks and sandstones, too. These each need local research and careful repair, the principal common thread being, as with most traditional construction, to keep them able to stay dry by not sealing them up in a way that prevents them from 'breathing'.

Owners of cottages made from these materials, and from unfired earth (see below), are particularly close to nature as it is easy to visualize their pebbles, mud and soft rocks in a heap on the ground again after a thorough drenching. Keep them dry, let them

BELOW RIGHT: Cottages made use of beach pebbles, flint or field stones to make brick go further, or just for decoration.

BELOW: Galletting – the placing of small stones in the mortar joints – should be carefully replaced if repointing. Here, contrasting stones are used for decoration; in other walls such stones were used to balance the larger stones or to fill big gaps and protect the mortar. There are also traditions that claim this decoration excluded evil spirits.

breathe. There is usually no reason for repairs not to be undetectable on completion and stay that way, if the work is done with the correct materials and by someone who knows what they are doing. Very often repairs scream 'look at me!' for ever, so ask to see examples of work.

UNFIRED EARTH WALLS

In situ …

A basic method of construction used by pre-industrial cultures throughout the world was to press the soil into service … literally. Clay-rich soils were ideal, and these could be reinforced and bound with whatever was lying around – dung and straw, for example. In fact, where animals were used to trample and stir the mix, these additives were contributed more or less automatically. A stiff mix was then available for building up into walls; this might be a rather curvy, free-form design, as seen in some Devon cob cottages, or it might be carefully built up between timber shuttering, in a broadly similar way to the modern placement of concrete, but perhaps involving some of the fun of a children's mud pit.

… and in blocks

The same mixes were also made available by our mediaeval forbears in handy modular blocks. These were roughly the size of the thicker of the modern aerated concrete building blocks, and for similar reasons of handling and interlocking into a wall. These pre-fabricated blocks have the advantage that, instead of being laid in the building wet and drying out as the building progresses, the unfired earth blocks can be made when there is time, labour and material available, then dried over a summer and used the next year perhaps, all in one go. The time, labour and space necessary for all this was once a feature of the countryside.

Then …

Cottages, farmhouses and barns were often built with this material, and it was in continuous use up until at least the 1920s in some parts of the country. Because of the difficulties of transport before the days of the van and the crane it is often possible to still see signs of a shallow depression in a village or in a garden, where the material might have been excavated to build the cottages standing nearby.

BELOW: A typical configuration for earth-walled cottages as found in the West of England, with broad overhanging eaves to keep the rain off.

ABOVE: An East Anglian clay lump cottage; again the overhang has been extended in order to better keep the rain off. Cottages like this may once have had 'layboards' (see the drawing 'Useful Features' in Chapter 16: Bits and Pieces, page 183) that were commonly seen halfway down walls, and helped to throw rain clear.

The principal weakness now with unfired earth walls is that the quite simple knowledge of how to maintain and repair the material has not been passed on to recent generations, so repairs have tended to be in our modern-day cement, which is not compatible. The grey cement patch on the left hangs grimly on to some East Anglian clay lump (left), despite the hint on correct technology from the remains of some lime nearby. The grey cement render added (right) can be seen to be cracking over an in situ West Country earth cottage simply because cement is too brittle to survive on this 'organic' material.

... and now

As this material is air-dried rather than fired in a kiln, it is susceptible to returning to mud if it is allowed to become persistently very damp. But that only happens if it is not adequately cared for: it has to be kept reasonably sheltered from rain and allowed to 'breathe' by being coated with only gentle and permeable natural finishes. It should not be swathed in waterproofing, however, as that can trap water inside, which can also be damaging. Any vulnerability usually only becomes apparent if the original sheltering details such as broad overhanging roofs and 'layboards' have gone from the cottage, or if mistaken applications of waterproof renders or paints have been added during the twentieth century.

The strengths include solidity, thermal and acoustic insulation, and an appealing 'organic' look. Once a simple necessity – there was nothing else to use – earth walls are presently being reinvented using some novel plant binders in the name of low energy sustainability. The new additives include hemp, a durable natural fibre to do the job of straw, and lime, which can give the mix a basic 'set' instead of, say, dung, which these days is probably just too natural for some, though still an abundant resource.

Repair

Repair ought not to begin with modern materials since it is likely that the use of modern materials has in some way caused failures in the first place by trapping damp or restricting movement. Earth-walled cottages may need some careful initial research and investigation, but there is usually no reason why they should not be repaired with a similar mix to that with which they were built. That mix might need some reinforcement or some shuttering initially, and it might be applied wet or perhaps formed into blocks specifically for cutting in later as repairs. Owners of an earth-walled cottage would be wise to get any modern rendered walls examined for early signs of damage to the inner earth, as the general tendency for modern finishes to crack and admit and trap damp in walls can give rise to quite a rapid rate of decay inside earth walls, while the surface might still appear sound.

TIMBER FRAME

To many, the half-timbered cottage is the definitive English country cottage. Timber is a quick and versatile building material to use, and archaeology has demonstrated that wooden posts were used to construct the earliest huts and communal houses long before cottages existed. The 'cruck' cottage is popularly known as a very early form of individual cottage – where two trunks were inclined to meet each other at the roof's ridge and so form the complete gable of a cottage. Such cottages rarely survive now in their original simple 'tent' shape, and will often have been built around and the framework added to. There are bound to be many examples still hidden unsuspected behind later brickwork, or simply rendered over. So maybe it's time to pop outside and take another look …?

Timbers

Hardwoods and softwoods

Surviving examples are mainly native oak and elm, but it is possible that other native hardwoods were regularly pressed into service, and perhaps if they were less durable species the buildings may not have survived intact to be counted now. We know that softwood was used too, and even imported from Scandinavia and the Baltic, as it survives in both mediaeval and Georgian buildings: its origins have been confirmed by analysis of the growth rings. But as far as cottages are concerned, we would probably be safe in assuming that the timber was locally

Very little has changed in green oak woodworking for hundreds of years, other than that the craft is perhaps not as prevalent as it once was. But these skills can certainly still be found.

grown and not moved very far between felling, converting into frame members and then erection. To do anything more elaborate would have been expensive.

Timbers are very likely to have been reused in order to save money and effort, and although the idea that quite so many cottages were built from old ships' timbers is difficult to prove, it seems reasonable that some could have been. Perhaps 'seconds' and offcuts from shipbuilding filtered into building, or perhaps salesmen referred to 'ship's timber' to denote quality. It is of interest, but it is still wood. Oak can survive, even become harder, underwater in certain specific conditions, and this was even exploited as a method of preparing it for use. Being damp in the presence of air is, however, very damaging to timber and this is the principal danger found in old buildings. At first sight newly revealed timber might not live up to preconceptions: oak should be hard, softwood soft, but damp oak can be very soft while very old dry softwood can be hard enough to make driving in a nail very difficult.

Seasoning and framework

Oak is the 'gold standard' of ancient timber frame. It would have been sensible to fell it in winter to try to minimize the amount of sap moisture present in the wood, and then work it into components while still 'green', that is, unseasoned. Since natural seasoning can take several decades, the oak would have been incorporated into buildings while still green, and long before reaching a stable dimensional state. Oak will shrink slightly as the natural moisture departs and this shrinkage is more pronounced, proportionately, widthways than lengthways. This situation could have been exploited by the original craftsmen in order that their joints and structures tightened over time. A technical beauty of timber frame is that it can knit together to form a net or grid that, like modern structural grids, shares the load between several members. This useful feature can, of course, have been undermined by ancient or modern alterations such as cutting in staircases or severing roof members to allow for additional windows, and these things were not always done in a thoughtful way. (*See also* Chapter 3: Don't Bring Me Down – 'Seasonal movement' … 'and seasoning', page 40.)

DID CRUCK-FRAMED COTTAGES BEGIN SIMPLY, LIKE THIS, OR WERE THEY ALWAYS PART OF A MORE COMPLICATED CONSTRUCTION ?

IT CAN BE DIFFICULT TO TELL AS, BY THE TIME THEY HAVE REACHED US, THEY HAVE BEEN ADAPTED, RE-WORKED, REPAIRED & EXTENDED.

THE CRUCK & THE JETTY

Cerdic's weight bends floor beam downwards (deflection exaggerated)

Weight of walls on oversailing beam-ends push centre of beam up

Weight of Cerdic plus family counteract the upwards deflection

JETTIES OFFER ADVANTAGES OF SHELTERING LOWER WALLS, EXTRA SPACE ON UPPER FLOORS & EASE OF FABRICATION IN SOME CASES - SO THE STRUCTURAL ADVANTAGE, ABOVE, MIGHT NOT ALWAYS HAVE MATTERED

Black and white

Although many people still do not take kindly to the idea, it has long been established that exposed mediaeval cottage timbers were probably not routinely and universally painted black, though the north-west of England does have some spectacular black and white formal timber frame, and it is not entirely unreasonable for the custom to have rubbed off on to cottages. An application of 'boiled' linseed oil can turn oak very dark, and this treatment – which does slowly fade to look like silver, untreated timber again – might be responsible for the idea. However, cottage timbers were instead most likely to have been lime-washed along with the rest of the wall's render panels, saving laborious 'cutting in' of different finishes to different parts. So timber-framed cottages would have ended up grey and white (or grey and some colour), since limewash sticks less well to timber than to render, and once exposed, oak weathers silver.

If a building had ever been 'black and white' in the long-distant past (that is further back than any paint applied by romanticizing Victorians and their immediate descendants) there should be quite clear evidence remaining, in a number of places all over the framework, of the historic blackening substance that might have been used. A type of pitch was

A likely true mediaeval look (above left), all limewash; some experimental black removal (above right); and a colourful solution (right) that could easily have been more prevalent than black and white in real history.

Sometimes what has to be done has to be done and honestly displayed, but it is generally not a bad idea to try to maintain the appearance that everything is still working as was originally structurally intended and so avoid creating a puzzle.

routinely used on timber barns, and on clay-lump buildings, too. A possibility for the black and white look could be the trick of slightly charring timber, which is considered to have been occasionally practised in the belief that this assisted preservation and helped prevent subsequent accidental ignition. This would also be detectable on the building. Charring would probably have been done in a controlled way by moving the timber over a fire after the component was made and prior to assembly, rather than on the building. Doing this to an existing cottage now with a blowtorch, or anything else, would constitute vandalism and, of course, be unspeakably dangerous.

Further interest

If exposing timber frame during the course of repairs to an old cottage it can be interesting, though not always essential to the repair effort, to identify the timber species. It is even possible to have a dendrochronological examination of a small core sample to try to determine where and when the tree would have grown. Old joints and even old nails can be useful and interesting archaeological evidence that points to the date of construction or alterations. Such features revealed during repairs could be recorded by photographs or identified by labels if they are being unavoidably removed.

Repairs can be a fraught process, and there may not seem to be time to make such records, but later, when the wall is all patched up again, it can be interesting to be able to take more time to piece together some of the history of a cottage. Because materials, methods and ideas varied between regions in the days before instant communication, each area of the country will have slightly different traditions of design and construction. Local reference libraries and planning departments would be likely to be able to point enquirers to more detail, and to local organizations that might have more information.

Repair of timber frame

Timber can succumb to structural failure simply by becoming overstressed, but failure is more likely to be assisted by the softening due to damp and the agents of decay that thrive upon damp wood. Wood-boring insects and fungi can, if they are allowed to colonize timber for long enough, remove sufficient of its substance to render it too weak to do its job. Fortunately, the timber structures in old buildings were often (though not always) over-designed and, fortunately too, insects and fungi are not universally attracted to all types and all parts of timber – so there may be some latitude even if an attack is established. (*See also* Chapter 13: Fungus and Other Bogeymen, for first steps in how to assess whether beetle infestation is live.)

Repair with timber or steel

Timber is extremely workable and almost infinitely repairable. With an old building like a cottage that relies upon its antiquity for its interest and value, it is usually worth keeping the defective part in place and

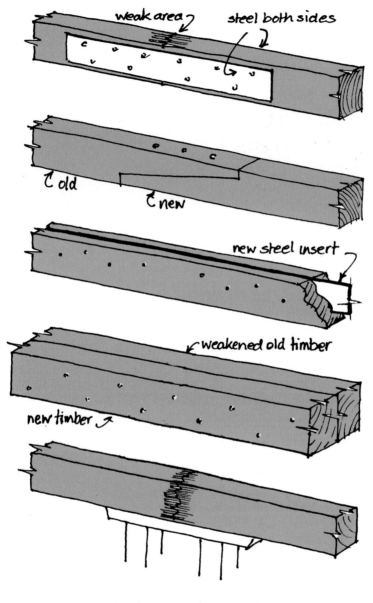

weak area

steel both sides

repair of weakened timber with steel plates either side, bolted through

old

new

scarf joints: different types for beams, posts etc can be useful eg where beam ends have rotted

new steel insert

a steel flitch-plate, requires access to cut slot in old timber

weakened old timber

new timber

side-by-side: retains original but a new timber next to it takes all the load onto walls

propping (or hanging) may be possible: eg props in a cellar can allow repair of a joist without disturbing floorboards above

TIMBER REPAIRS

AN OUTLINE OF OPTIONS FOR REPAIRING WEAKENED OR BROKEN TIMBERS - ACTUAL REPAIRS NEED STRUCTURAL DESIGN VARIOUS INGENIOUS STEEL BRACKETS MIGHT ALSO BE PROPOSED

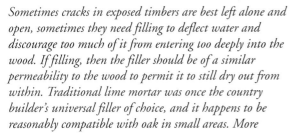

Sometimes cracks in exposed timbers are best left alone and open, sometimes they need filling to deflect water and discourage too much of it from entering too deeply into the wood. If filling, then the filler should be of a similar permeability to the wood to permit it to still dry out from within. Traditional lime mortar was once the country builder's universal filler of choice, and it happens to be reasonably compatible with oak in small areas. More recently the various fillers found on builders' vans are likely to be too waterproof for the good of the timber; this includes cement used as a filler, which also can tend to crack as it is relatively inflexible. Any waterproof fillers can harmfully trap the damp in the wood. The same applies to the infill panels between the timbers: mud daubs and lime permit breathing better than cement and plastic paints.

strapping, propping, splinting or otherwise repairing or substituting its structural function without removing the original member (*see also* the drawing 'Timber Repairs', opposite). The usual conservation philosophy of like-for-like repair implies that broken timber should be replaced with matching timber cut and jointed in the same way as the original piece, but here it may be that if we want to keep a fractured, perhaps now structurally useless, piece in place then it would be sensible to add something new alongside.

As a first option it is preferable to try not to introduce steel into an otherwise all-timber structure, since steel is a harsher material than timber and responds to movement in a different way, which might be unhelpful to the rest of the frame. However, there have been many cases in conservation where a weakened timber member has been cleverly and sensitively repaired using steel brackets, sleeves, props and various other ingenious, nameless devices. There

is no one answer other than to think first 'is preservation in situ possible?', then to work out how that can be done with minimum intervention and minimum permanent change to the rest of the fabric – and also in a way that intrudes least upon the visual whole.

New pieces of timber should ideally be matched for species and degree of seasoning, though if this means using reclaimed timber then there is the inescapable logic that another old building has had to sacrifice that material, and that may not be defensible in terms of the wider aims of building conservation. The diagrams of timber repair (opposite) show some of the basic generic repair options for timber members, but these would in most cases require a structural engineer's design and calculation unless the repair is to be a really routine and well understood carpenter's joint. (*See also* Chapter 2: The Professionals – 'Structural engineers', page 30; and Chapter 3: Don't Bring Me Down.)

Repair with fillers

With the exception of some highly specialist materials, fillers would ordinarily be regarded as cosmetic and non-structural, as their bond with old timber cannot be guaranteed under the mixture of compressive and tensile stresses that timber has to endure in most locations. Modern fillers (such as epoxy fillers, rather than the home decorator's powder mixes) do have a promising place in joinery repairs as they can avoid excessive cutting back to create a new glued joint, but fillers – as with even the glue line of a traditional timber repair – can act as a barrier to outbound water vapour.

As a simple face filler for a crack in exterior exposed timber frame, a centuries-old tradition was to use lime mortar: this has no structural function, but it can help to reinstate lost material in a way that avoids the cutting out necessary to carry out a 'proper' carpentry repair, and can also restore some of the weathering function of a piece of wood, which might keep water out of the heart of the timberwork. Lime mortar does, very importantly, seem to allow for the passage outward of water vapour from the heart of the wood at a rate that is more or less in the same league as that possessed by seasoned oak itself. However, if using a cement mix for this – as many

builders did as soon as cement came along – then water can get trapped inside the timber and start rot. Not only that, but as lime is a little more mobile than cement it can make for a more compatible filling that is less likely to crumble away at the edges.

Repair after decay

In the past, many have been frightened into unnecessary removal of failed items that have previously been attacked by insects or fungi because it was felt that they posed a risk of reinfestation. In some cases that might be true, but it is also true that there is more money at stake and less expertise necessary in assuming the worst and stripping and rebuilding part of a cottage 'just in case', rather than analysing an outbreak of decay and doing only what is necessary to repair it, and weighing up the risks of fungi or beetles returning from elsewhere by air, as they do, compared with what might or might not still be lurking in the wood. Chapter 13 Fungus and Other Bogeymen explains some of the natural limitations on the regeneration of decay, and rather than being frightened too soon into unnecessary and destructive work, instead the cottage owner should consider investing in independent advice from an expert in fungi and insect problems – one who is not tied to a

A later replacement for wattle and daub in most cases, brick was evidently felt to be a natural infill material for timber frame, however odd it may seem to us now. With mobile, breathable lime mortar this has worked reasonably well for centuries, but newer introductions of cement can be unhelpfully rigid and impermeable. There will be few such cottages that have escaped cement, however.

limited range of destructive repair options. This could save money and preserve some of the real heritage value of the cottage.

INTERNAL AND EXTERNAL FINISHES AND INFILL MATERIALS

Early finishes and wattle and daub

Over time it became desirable to keep out more and more of the wind and weather. A setting finish applied to timber or stone walls helped block the gaps. Clay, mud, animal dung and straw would have been the simplest materials to find initially, and these developed into the lime renders (*see below*) that mainly survive today. In the case of timber frame, 'wattle and daub' has become a renowned partnership, the wattle being the grid or mesh of sticks, laths or studs of one sort or another to which the daub mix was applied. This was so successful that it has not ever really been bettered in terms of compatibility with the timber frame of buildings to which it was applied.

Repairs now can adopt the same ingredients, although there may be some modern temerity over dung on health and safety grounds by those unfamiliar with farms. Courses and specialist literature are available and advisable, but basically repairs could be a matter of direct local research combined with some fun and experimentation, if properly guided for technical performance and structural appropriateness, and if the circumstances of the building and users allow.

Lime mix, direct to wall

Lime render, mixed in much the same way as for mortar (*see* 'The Care and Maintenance of Traditional Masonry' – 'Repointing', page 74), was the wall finish of choice for the latter part of the traditional building period up until the early twentieth century. Lime render was used externally, where modern buildings now use a cement render, and also internally, where modern buildings use gypsum plasters. The ability that lime has to adapt to slight movement without cracking is a distinct advantage over more modern materials, and it also permits the 'breathing' of water vapour out from the thickness of walls (if painted in a similarly 'breathable' limewash or distemper finish – *see also* Chapter 12: Paint It … Back). Internally, the modern habit of gypsum plasters can be unhelpful in an old cottage as they can have properties such as the attraction and retention of damp; these can appear to indicate failures when used in an old building that needs to shift damp around.

There is nothing mysterious about lime render (or lime plaster as it is also, confusingly, known): it was simply built up in two or three coats of decreasing thickness giving a final thickness of from about 25 to 35mm according to the irregularity of the wall that was to be covered, and whether it is being used inside or out. This would also be the basic approach to a repair, having brushed clean and wetted the wall following removal of failed plaster. As with repair of lime mortar in masonry, there is no need always to strip every last vestige of render from a complete wall if it has not all failed. Retaining anything that is still sound can save time and money. Traditional wisdom has the base coat slightly stronger (more sand, perhaps 'sharper' sand) and the final coat thinner and with more 'fat' (that is, more lime) in the mix and perhaps 'softer', finer sand so that a smoother finish can be created. Sometimes animal hair would be added to the base coats to help bind them. Between coats the surface would be scored to provide a key for the next, and left to set. Plaster of Paris might have been added to the final coat to help get a crisper finish for some special internal work (this would not be done for external work).

The almost mirror-smooth perfection that modern tradespeople can achieve with internal gypsum plasters and externally with cement is probably almost as achievable with lime, but is arguably rarely necessary or visually desirable in cottage repairs. As with lime mortar (*see* 'Repointing', page 74), it is necessary to 'tend' the mix until it has finally set, protecting it from extremes of weather such as cold, wet and sun, but especially cold: therefore work on external walls should not be carried out from autumn to spring as there is potentially a long setting time during which the work remains vulnerable.

There are basic precautions to be taken against the caustic nature of lime, such as goggles, gloves and overalls (*see also* Chapter 9: Reasons to be Careful –

'Substance abuse', page 114), and courses are run in its use by the SPAB and various other charities and local authorities: conservation officers should know the location of the nearest of these (*see* Further Information, page 202).

When repairing an old wall some enthusiasts like to grind up the old failed render and reapply it. This can save money and effort buying sand, but it should be mixed with some new lime or there will be nothing to bind the mix. Unless experimentation is acceptable, the proportions in such mixing should be supervised by someone with experience. (*See also* Chapter 9: Reasons to be Careful – 'Biological hazards', page 116.)

Lime mix on timber laths

Using a ladder-like grid of split timber laths nailed on either side of a timber-framed wall (or sometimes nailed on to studs lining the inside of an external masonry wall), a hair-reinforced lime render mix would be applied so that, crucially, little tongues of the mix hung over the gaps between the laths; these

tongues let the dry mix hold on. Otherwise the build-up of coats can be very similar to that used on masonry, as described above. Repairs can be made in lime plastering material as above, but it is necessary to ensure that the laths and their nails fixing into the main stud frame are all in good order. If not, they should be refixed or replaced locally as necessary until all are sound. In the recent past many took fright at lath and plaster and covered it in expanded metal mesh before starting all over again with new render over that. That is one way, but it is not the most economical: if the existing plaster is otherwise sound, it can be repaired. (*See also* Chapter 3: Don't Bring Me Down – 'Lath and plaster repairs', page 42; and this chapter – 'Ceilings' – 'Lath and plaster ceilings', page 95.)

Fixing to a lath and plaster wall
There are two problems that cottage owners may face when trying to put up shelves or cupboards on old lath and plaster walls: the first is that walls may not be particularly straight, which is fine for character

The, usually hidden, reverse side of a lath and plaster wall (left), and a rarely seen vertical slice through it (right) showing how the plaster tongues protrude between the laths and hang on because they are reinforced with hair. Swivel the page 90 degrees anticlockwise and you could equally be looking at a section through a ceiling.

External render on timber lath (1) has failed because the original lime undercoat has been topped with cement and a 'plastic' paint, which have trapped dampness and caused the lime plaster 'tongues' to become damp, weak and then snap off. Suitable animal hair (2) is added to a (non-hydraulic) lime putty/sand mix. The damaged section of old render is trimmed back to a sound edge (3), any broken laths replaced (screws can cause less disturbance than nailing) and other fixings checked, and the first area is dampened. The render has been mixed to a working consistency (4 and 5), and is applied in two coats here to match the original, with the base coat scratched (6) to provide a key for the top coat (7) which is then dressed, with small stones in this case, (8) to replicate the original finish.

1

2

3

4

5

6

7

8

91

Traditional boarding with and without beaded edge. Boards, traditionally, may have been limewashed long ago or painted with linseed oil 'lead' paints, each of which was 'breathable'. Since then people may have just seen 'white' and simply bought modern white paint, which might bring on the troubles discussed elsewhere in this book.

and charm but less convenient when fixing to them; the second is that conventional modern wall fixings do not offer a suitable or particularly secure anchorage to lath and plaster. A more traditional approach is therefore called for. If the vertical studs can be located, then a batten of suitable strength can be run across several stud positions and fixed securely to them, and its back surface can have been 'scribed' (profiled) appropriately to offer a level front surface for fixing the new shelf or cupboard on to. Traditionally this could be supplemented by timber brackets (for example, *see* the centre photograph on page 176) that follow the line of the studs. However, this practice is most often found in simple utility shelving or dado rails, because what furniture there was would have been free-standing: cottages were most often tenanted, and so personal items needed to be portable. Free-standing furniture would similarly avoid the problem of wall fixings today.

Electronic detectors may be able to find the studs, but the thickness of traditional plaster found in cottages can fool them (likewise those detectors that claim to locate wiring and pipes – so beware). An alternative is to drill a horizontal line of very small diameter holes into the wall and judge which are in the centre of a stud by the resistance felt over two or three adjacent holes. As a rough guide studs might be

expected to occur every 400 to 600mm (16 to 24in), and they will not necessarily be exactly or even approximately vertical and parallel: they might be little more than branches as taken from a tree.

If a single hole is required for hanging a picture, avoid banging in a nail as this can simply 'spring' the hidden lath and smash the plaster tongue that hangs over it. Instead drill a fine hole and insert a thin screw – and remember that all this is going to be fixed to is one thin lath on a small nail at either end, so the screw is just for small pictures, and not for anything heavy, valuable or dangerous (hence the existence of picture rails in period houses).

Boarded walls

A quick solution to shedding rain was to nail overlapping planks across a timber frame. The earliest would have been split quite thickly, and without sawing would have been rather unevenly shaped (as sometimes mimicked on 1930s housing and 1950s bar counters). Though the tradition is undoubtedly older, most surviving boarded walls are probably now covered in nineteenth-century timber, sawn plain (rough) or perhaps with a bead mould at the bottom. They might perhaps be 'feathered' (cut to a wedge profile) or even partially profiled to fit together, though not generally so thoroughly profiled and mechanically interlocking as the thin, modern, planed 'shiplap' boards. Fixing traditions vary with locality, but secret nailing (as with modern boarding) was not necessarily a traditional feature. (*See also* Chapter 15: Hot Love – 'Concealer', page 165.)

For internal and sheltered walls, plain, square-edged and butt-jointed boards are often used in cottages, for example as wall finishes between rooms and passageways. These are usually fixed horizontally, as with the overlapped outside versions, as like that it is easier to fix them to the upright timber posts.

FLOORS

Floorboards

Some of our cottages are old enough to have been built as a single-storey, single-roomed, small open 'hall' house. Once such a cottage was equipped with a chimney, then the upper part became ready for occupation rather than just, perhaps, being used to hang meat to smoke out of the way of domestic animals. Whether added or built in from new, upper floors came to be made from planks that were laid across timber beams for additional support. It is possible that, due to limitations in the thinness to which wood could be split (rather than sawn) in the earliest days, floorboards were once thick enough to be self-supporting, but most surviving examples have supporting 'floor joists'.

Without sophisticated mechanical saws the earliest floorboards were neither regular in width nor in thickness. Some stately homes, old houses and cottages display floorboards that are laid almost crazily zigzag, perhaps because trimming boards to be parallel was considered unnecessarily wasteful, or because there may be some structural benefit (as in cross-bracing).

Please don't try this at home
A fad of the 1980s had new owners of old houses and cottages almost automatically hiring an industrial sander and, without a thought for the centuries of patina and evidence of use they were about to obliterate, removing several millimetres from the surface of their timber floors to make it 'look new again'. The result looks as if Martians had landed and strafed the cottage with a laser: an unnaturally flat, bright timber surface with even the silvery insides of the nails on show. Why pay extra for something like a cottage because it is old, and then pay even more to make it look new? Do this to an antique table and the value plummets: the same should be true in a cottage. That was not sawdust being swept up afterwards, it was money.

Existing traditional polish finishes can usually be quite easily dissolved with regular household spirit solvents and then spruced up. Even the more aggressive stains and later, modern, varnishes can be pared back with much lighter, much more controlled stripping techniques or by manual sanding. The objective is not to reach a virgin timber surface, but only to even out any excess, crusty layers of finishes. Once that has been done, then a return to a compatible natural wax or oil finish, as appropriate to use, can wear more attractively and be much easier to retouch than a hard modern varnish. Enjoy the look of wood that has been custom worn to a unique patina over centuries: don't destroy it. If what is there is really

A common problem is where a timber floor has been stained dark around the edge of a rug in the past; the easiest solution is to leave everything as it is, get a new rug to fit, and polish up the stained area again with a suitable traditional wax or oil. If the old stain is a permanent dye that has seeped deep into the timber it is unlikely to come out anyway, even with the aggressive use of sanders – and these are definitely not recommended as heavy sanding would destroy the ages-old walked-on patina of the dark stained areas and so devalue the floor.

unbearable to you personally, then consider gently covering it up in a breathable and reversible way so that others can treasure it in the future. It could be worth more that way.

Gaps and repairs

The gaps between floorboards were once useful for fuelling open fires with oxygen, and they are still useful for ventilating a cottage to keep it dry and healthy. However, some gaps do conflict with everyday convenience, and rather than keep losing coins down them or see the same spider emerging every night, people now want them blocked up. Cork strips or papier-mâché can do this relatively harmlessly, cheaply and reversibly, and can be coloured up to match the floorboards.

In terms of conservation, the archaeological interest of a cottage is best served if things remain where they were originally put. There is also less potential for innocent structural and superficial

damage if floorboards are not removed and replaced on a whim of tidiness (floorboards can be bracing a building and keeping it square, or if not square then at least whatever shape it is). Any suspect boards can be carefully lifted (but *see below*, next paragraph, for ceilings that may be attached), while broken or weak boards can often be invisibly mended underneath using simple joinery methods, perhaps assisted by metal brackets.

CEILINGS

Direct to floorboard – the 'cottage ceiling'

In old country cottages, the idea of having a special finish under floorboards would have once seemed extravagantly foppish: why worry about a bit of light, even water, spilling from one level to another? However, sophistication did eventually take over, and a version of the lath and plaster wall described above was applied directly to the underside of the floorboards. This is the 'classic' cottage ceiling, with an undulating ceiling recessed between the 'beams' or rough joists (there is no room to get a good sweep with a trowel to smooth the plaster level).

In houses with higher ceilings there was room to span a completely flat ceiling fastened to the underside of the joists, but in cottages there was often insufficient headroom, which is why many remain with exposed timbers to this day. Beware when lifting a floorboard upstairs – if the ceiling is attached directly to the floorboards there will be no room to

Solid floors in cottages may once have been bare earth, perhaps later screeded over with a lime-ash mix or laid with brick or tile pavers (above) that vary, regionally, in size from about 100 to 300mm (4 to 12in) wide and 10 to 40mm (approx. ½ to 1½in) thick, and also with varying degrees of surface irregularity. Remnants might still remain under later concrete floors. If exposed, such tiles should only be washed rather than polished or varnished – that way any staining, and damp, should not be sealed in but can be allowed to eventually wear off from the surface. To cope with the fact that background dampness was continually drying out of the floor, kitchen table legs were kept from softening by standing in glass cups (right), and kitchens would be less likely to have a suspended wooden floor, even if the rest of the cottage did, due to spillages and to allow for cleaning by washing.

put wiring or plumbing, and in any case lifting a board will destroy part of the ceiling below!

Lath and plaster ceilings

Where a ceiling was installed beneath the level of the floor joists there would be a cavity between the ceiling and the floor above. In many cottages built from roughly cut timbers, the underside of the joists would have had to have been levelled first with an assortment of wedges and packing pieces. Originally the ceiling surface would most likely have been lath and plaster, a horizontal version of the lath and plaster walls described above.

As with the walls, it is crucial that the little nibs or tongues of plaster are hanging on to the laths, or the plaster will fall to the floor. The principal threats to this are persistent dampness, sudden copious leaks, vibration (so avoid hammering nearby – such as from re-roofing operations – and trade the hammer for nail guns or screws if possible) and general heavy-footedness. People have quite often deliberately removed these little nibs where they were visible in attics, for the sake of tidiness. This is a dangerous practice, and they subsequently had an awful lot of tidying to do in their bedrooms.

Again, as with lath and plaster walls, unfamiliarity with the material on the part of modern professionals and tradespeople means that, when faced with a repair, they resort to a complete rebuild with something they do understand, such as plasterboard or expanded metal and new plaster. That would be unfortunate, as those new methods are rather too precisely flat for a cottage, and because, arguably, lath and plaster performs better acoustically. Lath and plaster can often be repaired like for like, perhaps in a patch rather than tackling the whole ceiling: as long as all the laths are sound and firmly nailed to the joists, and the plaster is properly keyed to them and incorporates appropriate hair reinforcement, then it should be no worse than the original. (*See also* Chapter 3: Don't Bring Me Down – 'Lath and plaster repairs', page 42; and 'Lime mix on timber laths', page 90).

Downlighters

The recent fashion for downlighters that are recessed into the surface of ceilings is one that is probably best avoided with lath and plaster. These lights were designed for use in modern sheet finishes such as plasterboard. Cutting a hole in lath and plaster for even a single small fitting can leave perhaps two laths unsupported, which means weakening the ceiling. Aside from that, there are issues with heat generated by halogen and other incandescent lamps rising into the unknown voids in an old cottage floor. And if the ceiling falling down or starting a fire is not enough to worry about, there is also the risk of smoke penetration through the light fittings from one floor to another in the event of a fire elsewhere in the home.

If a cottage already has these lights they ought to be checked for these possible failings. And if it does not have them, light the room another way and accept that, sexy though they may be, downlighters are better matched to modern construction.

STAIRS

Stairs are not always the most spacious feature in a cottage, and in the case of a cottage that is an ancient conversion from a single-storey, single-roomed dwelling, any staircase would be an afterthought at best. But even in purpose-built two-storey cottages, access upstairs was originally very likely to have been little more than a ladder. Ladders, as can be inferred from the evidence of old floor openings in many cottages, were considered perfectly adequate and often remained in use right up until the twentieth century – and some to this very day. Even among cottages with 'proper' staircases, there are many examples that wind around behind fireplaces or lurk in corners in ways that require agility and nerve to use. They would certainly not find favour with a modern building inspector, but they seem to be tolerated, and it can be as well to provide whatever is sensible in terms of additional hand-holds. A rope handrail may often have been added in the past as a useful extra because it is flexible enough not to jab the hips or otherwise inflict injury in a confined space. Old, existing, cramped staircases have been tolerated in the past by incoming regulations except perhaps where a cottage is being significantly altered – then the owner could face having to find room for a much larger staircase that meets all the current requirements of height, angle and size of step.

Traditionally built stairs can be graceful, and use space cleverly in a way that is worth keeping; the alternative is to find room in the cottage for the more generous staircases stipulated by current Building Regulations, but that removes authenticity and could take up significant space.

A traditionally constructed stair may have an arcane-looking system of wedges and blocks underneath to hold it together, and these, in good condition, might prevent creaking and bowing. Balustrades and balconies in some cottages may not meet current regulations for height, strength and ability to stop small children squeezing through. Any modifications that are thought necessary should be sensitively thought through, and ideally made to be 'reversible' (*see* Introduction – 'Preserving interest: preserving value', page 15) and possibly removed when the need has passed (in the manner of a child's stair gate, for instance). As is compatible with our forbears' attitude to health and safety, a cottage balustrade might be an indication of the peril of falling, rather than prevention.

SEPARATION BETWEEN DWELLINGS

In modern building there are regulations and customs that ensure basic separation of one dwelling from another in terms of security, fire, smoke, noise and thermal insulation. These were not always seriously addressed in the past and could be to a low standard in a cottage, with separation between ownerships at living-room level being possibly as flimsy as a ½in (13mm) thick board in some cases. Noise can be a nuisance, and the first step would be to ensure that there are no direct small gaps around the edges of plaster panels in timber frame, or gaps and cracks in masonry. Gaps provide air paths to the neighbouring house that can act as conduits for sound. If there are gaps, these could be blocked with a dense and mouldable material such as hair-reinforced lime mortar, if appropriate to do so.

Security and fire issues might need more specialist advice in terms of performance of materials and remedial works, but bear in mind that, for conservation reasons, anything new applied to the cottage should ideally be 'reversible' (capable of being removed without a scar at some point in the future). (*See also* Chapter 5: A Hard Rain – 'Roofspaces and Fire', page 64, for roofspace separation; and Chapter 15: Hot Love for thermal insulation.)

Even if direct separation along boundaries is adequate, in closely packed dwellings such as cottages there are potential risks that modern regulations would have dealt with, but which history may have allowed through the net. These include neighbouring windows that have been enlarged into picture windows until they are close enough to permit the spread of fire from one dwelling to another; balanced flues installed under previous regulations (or illegally) that pose a fire and fume risk; doors that would have taken time to burn down when they were wooden, but may melt if they are now plastic. These can be referred to a professional adviser, and in any event, these days it makes sense to invest in the various electronic detectors that are intended to give some advanced warning of such risks.

Party walls

Twenty-first-century regulation has now addressed the issue of work close to boundaries, either directly to shared walls or any other excavation works close enough to possibly affect foundations. For details of the Party Wall Act search www.planningportal. gov.uk, or obtain similar information in print from the local authority.

CELLARS

Cellar walls

Cellars are not usually extensive in cottages, if they exist at all. A lot will have depended on the subsoil, and the use of the original building. Often some ground floor utility areas were at a much lower level and can be partly underground. There were no sophisticated 'tanking' materials available in the pre-modern period, so unless someone has applied a modern treatment or modern paint recently, the underground retaining wall will tend to be generally damp and will need to be kept in a 'breathable' condition. This means that, if decorating this wall, lime mortars, renders and limewash paints would be favoured for traditional damp management (and then only direct to an old masonry wall, not over modern 'waterproof' paint or render). Cement render, pointing and modern masonry paints would be avoided in a traditional regime, because they can simply bottle up the damp and drive it higher up the wall. Highly waterproof remedial modern paints also fall into this category as they, too, would try to form a waterproof skin to trap damp in the wall.

If a permanently dry inner surface is wanted, a 'dry lining' can be applied, and there are various informal and manufactured options – but for conservation purposes only those that permit a constant and thorough ventilation of the wall behind the dry lining are likely to help prevent the wall itself being saturated.

Cellar floors

If the floor is laid to a fall, it is possible that flooding was anticipated; sump tanks and pumps would be an even more telling indication. Some cottage cellars boasted their own wells and springs, which these days should be regularly tested for purity before considering drinking from them. Their content can change with variations in ground water levels, the 'water table'. In times of severe flooding be cautious about pumping out a flooded cellar over a long period; it is probable that the surrounding water table is feeding the flood anyway, and it would not be reasonable to pump out several acres worth of flooding through one cellar wall – in any case this could risk washing away the mortar from the walls.

CHAPTER SEVEN

Knock on Wood
Doors and windows

CHARACTER

The character of a cottage and most other buildings is determined in large part by doors and windows – just as we look for the individuality of a human face in eyes, nose and mouth. Some may be tempted to enlist help to try to make improvements, but in housing, at least, there are complex technical and visual issues that can have unfortunate consequences if overlooked.

Traditional doors and windows

Material limitations
Old doors and windows were made by hand from ordinary pieces of wood, as cut from trees. That was about all they had. There were no materials big enough to make a one-piece door (no plywood, no hardboard, no plastic). The glass that went into windows was expensive and only available in relatively small sheets. There were, in the past, only so many ways a door or window could be made by hand, and this helps distinguish them from modern industrialized versions that are made according to the logic of machine tools.

Doors
Doors started as a series of vertical planks (the simple design still used on sheds), and progressed to a cleverly designed frame in-filled with panels that were as big as natural wood would allow without splitting. This design has proved so attractive that fake 'panelled doors' are now in many modern homes, stamped out of one piece of modern board. If imita-

tion implies admiration, then a real panelled door is obviously worth cherishing.

Windows
Glazed windows started out as leaded lights, the glass held in lead 'cames' because the tiny squares of glass available in mediaeval times would have been almost totally obscured by the time a hefty mediaeval wooden frame was built around each. Leaded light panels were framed up in slender iron, also helping light transmission by its slenderness compared to wood. Eventually, slightly bigger, and cheaper, panes of glass allowed wooden frames to be used, framed up like doors and hung on side hinges; these would have been the cottage window of the eighteenth and nineteenth centuries.

The Georgians developed their sash windows to let in more light. Despite the availability of mouth-blown panes that were only around the size of a sheet of A4 paper (and often to the same $1:\sqrt{2}$ width:height proportion), because their sashes used the strength of cleverly designed and well seasoned timber to make for thin glazing bars between each, the panes could be joined together with minimum visual obstruction. The thinness of Georgian glass allowed the whole sashes to be light enough in weight to be built tall – and that throws extra light deep into rooms.

Later variants
Modern windows in modern houses can span large distances, made possible by steel lintels and huge sheets of modern glass – it does not matter to them that the frames around the edges of the sheets are

98

A leaded light window inside (1) and out (2), here with a timber reinforcing batten behind. A detail of another window (3) with a metal version of this internal reinforcing bar ('ferramenta'), these bars are attached to the 'H'-shaped lead 'cames' that hold the glass. The diamond pattern is not just a whim – it resists vertical 'squashing' better than a square grid if the building moves (the diagonal grid is also an ancient protective symbol and may have been comforting to those not used to being 'on view' behind glass). Leaded lights are often paired with iron frames (4), in this case showing the alternative square grid and neat in-built ferramenta.

very big and chunky. But that does matter if changing the frames in a cottage from wood, or iron, into plastic, because plastic is generally not so strong for an equivalent cross-section and so frames have to be thicker. So a change from traditional wood or iron to modern standard timber sections or plastic can produce a thicker frame. A thicker frame will potentially cut out light in a smaller window opening, and this has led to some enlargement of openings in the days before official consents were required for window alterations, often distorting the look of the building.

A traditional window frame is nearly always capable of repair, even if most of it is, genuinely, rotten. And in the rare event of all of it being rotten and beyond all repair, then it can be replaced like for like. (*See also* Chapter 15: Hot Love – 'Windows' – 'Seconday glazing', page 167.)

Cottages would probably not have had the typical Georgian vertically sliding sash window in great numbers when the box sash was first invented: they were a new luxury with all sorts of high tech accessories such as weights, pulleys and fancy catches that were probably beyond the cottagers' spending power.

Where the window technology has been changed, as in most of these windows, the original brickwork details of these cottages have been lost. The right-hand windows are a reminder of how the cottages were meant to look.

And vertical sash windows require a room height in excess of that normally found in cottages. Instead, an outward-opening multi-pane window was more likely, or a horizontally sliding sash window (no need for weights and pulleys) may have been installed to get over the problem of passers-by inconveniently walking into an open window. Vertical sliders have, however, been fitted to cottages in great numbers from later in the Georgian period, and whether that constitutes an inappropriate alteration to an historic building is a subject that conservationists will continue debating during long winter evenings for much of eternity.

Replacement windows

Cottages have lasted for a long, long time. Some can trace their origins back to the days before their occupants could afford glass, and these may still display a sliding internal shutter (to keep out bad weather) with timber bars outside (to keep out bad people). They may have had oilskin stretched over them to allow in some daylight when it was raining or windy. But the same cottage has travelled extensively through time, and later may have had dalliances with iron-framed, leaded light windows, side-hung casements and vertically sliding 'Georgian' windows among the more common historical variants.

LEFT: Two types of window from previous centuries: those on the right of the picture are similar to the unglazed openings that predated the use of glass, and here it is more interesting for us that they were only supplemented with new windows and not replaced.
RIGHT: Another example of old technology retained and providing interest. Other, even very trivial,

artefacts (even as apparently trivial as redundant old-fashioned light switches or curtain brackets inside a cottage) will be of interest in the future, so think twice before removing any features that tell the history of a cottage.

Out of time

Size-wise, windows are very important elements of a cottage: if a cottage is viewed as an antique, then having plastic windows on an old cottage is as rational as having an illuminated digital display on an old grandfather clock.

Familiarity, time and being blissfully unaware of historical details may prevent a great deal of the variety found in cottage windows from appearing too out of place to most onlookers. But modern factory-made timber, aluminium and plastic windows can seem very out of place to many people. Some early twentieth-century steel and timber factory-made windows occupy a sort of twilight zone of acceptability due, perhaps, only to having been around for longer than the people who might criticize them. However, factory-made windows are factory made, and that fact is readable in their detail and design, which separates them from all the other hand-made configurations that history has supplied.

There are other factors that should distance modern replacements from cottages: the difficulty of trimming plastic and aluminium special sections when movement occurs in the walls is one; the tendency for plastic frames to be larger in cross section (*see above*) is another. A significant difference

The difference in detail between old cottage windows in timber (left) and new PVC (right).

in appearance is also noticeable in the quality of the glass. Old glass becomes progressively less optically perfect as we travel back though time. For a long time, until the early to mid-twentieth century, all the cheaper domestic glass showed some rippling or striations as a result of the manufacturing process. This is visible in reflections outside and refractions cast inside, whether it is from some Georgian mouth-blown glass or some 1930s glass. It is part of the quality that helps identify a cottage as the genuine article rather than a fake.

As we come under pressure to better insulate all homes, there will be a need to tackle the heat loss through windows, but this does not have to mean that cottages must accept double glazing and do what new houses do to appear 'traditional', such as adopting plastic frames with fake leadwork stuck on to the glass, or with pretend glazing bars dangling inside the glass. (*See* Chapter 15: Hot Love – 'Windows', page 167, for some of the kinder insulation options.)

Replacement doors

Because a door is so big, it is unlikely ever to rot all over, so it is probably always going to be repairable. It spoils a cottage to strip it of its original door for the sake of a repair – it's like having a valuable antique teapot and chucking away the lid because of a chip. A period door is an asset and worth repairing properly, even if the repair costs slightly more than a replacement.

Period doors were mainly made from decent seasoned wood, and for most of their lives were painted with materials that did not trap damp in the timber (as, unfortunately, much modern paint can tend to do – *see* Chapter 12: Paint It … Back). Many of the replacement doors already applied to cottages do not reflect British design traditions, and are twentieth-century confections made to designs imported from Europe or the USA (for example, the ubiquitous modern design with the half-round window at the top that finds its way into cottages features regularly in a 1960s US sit-com on television, but is

Any type of external door will generally suffer most at the bottom where rain splashes up and water drains down, but timber is almost infinitely repairable; the boarded door is receiving minor reconstruction, but it is often quite reasonable to rebuild in excess of half a door if that is what is necessary to preserve some of the original. The blue door here shows the useful pattern of wear associated with traditional paints – they wear away, which permits drying, rather than hanging around and blistering, which can trap water. Cottages, being simple, would often have had the simplest boarded door, like the one shown being repaired. Each of these doors would be good for many years with simple care and traditional decoration.

Before sawing holes in old doors for pet access, there are often kinder alternatives that can be explored, which would leave less of a permanent memorial to Tiddles.

A version of the outward-opening timber casement, which is probably seen as the typical British cottage window. The size of the glass panes can be indicative of age.

Timber sliding sash windows: vertically sliding (left), here with optional shutters for security, and horizontally sliding (right), with optional dog.

extraordinarily rare in Victorian photographs of British towns and villages. It's like putting sixties American tail fins on a Morris Minor – quite interesting the first time, maybe …).

If those modern wooden doors seem alien, then some plastic doors that have been fitted do not resemble traditional doors so much as giant cat-flaps, because they were made – it seems for cheapness – with standard central panels joined with a gasket to their made-to-fit outer frame: and that's really no way to treat a hand-built cottage.

If an out-of-place modern door needs replacing, it's easy enough to find out what would really fit the

period and also add to the value and appearance of the cottage. DIY outlets and door-to-door salesmen might seem convenient, but there are other sources, so why dress a genuine hand-made antique cottage in mass-market modern features?

For both doors and windows, the owners of listed properties, or those in conservation areas or National Parks, should be consulting their local planning authority for advice on complying with planning laws – and they may also get guidance in finding craftspeople or designers who can work with period features. (Local authority web sites under 'planning' may help.)

Standardized window frames, in an industrial material, pretending to be leaded lights. The new nineteenth-century iron foundries slipped the cast-iron window on to the market before the conservation movement was around, but since it was mostly used in the newly built cottages of the time there may have been little for conservationists to object to. The makers took care that their cast iron looked as pleasing as the traditional hand-crafted windows they were in competition with.

Gently does it

It is tempting to rush to 'upgrade' a property's smartness and insulation by changing or altering doors and windows, without giving much thought to what is being sacrificed. It is in no one's interest to remove all the character from a cottage, so some serious thought needs to be done first (and do not forget that unauthorized work on a listed building could, potentially, mean spending some time languishing in prison!). Insulation and fuel efficiency are important, but there can be cheaper and easier routes to improving both, rather than using up more and more valuable materials and energy in replacing something that is probably quite repairable and adaptable.

MAINTENANCE AND REPAIR

The timber in traditional windows and doors ideally needs to be able to breathe to help keep it free from rot. If a cottage has timber joinery that has lasted even only a hundred years, then it has outperformed some of the 1960s joinery four- or five-fold. Part of the reason twentieth-century joinery failed was the quality of the timber, part was due to the characteristics of the paint.

Wood

The wood used in the fine joinery of true period windows was often relatively strong and stable hardwood, or was a slow-grown softwood, properly seasoned – that way strength and durability were assured. This is why those doors and windows have lasted hundreds of years longer than 1960s joinery made from fast grown, hurriedly seasoned timber. The timber in old boarded or panelled internal doors was fit for its purpose in the open-fire heated, well ventilated homes of past centuries, but it may split and crack in over-dry centrally heated homes today. Ordinary linseed oil putty is a useful filler for much traditional external joinery, and a small tub can be kept handy to rub into cracks in traditional glazing putty in between redecorations – it could save rot setting in, and make for less expensive preparation when the time comes for a full repainting job.

The timber window frames found in cottages are often multi-paned with quite narrow outer frames and thin glazing bars. Even if the timber is sound, the joints may have become loose or broken. To avoid damage to the glass and the general dismantling required to reglue the joints, a metal bracket repair has proved successful in many cases. To avoid further reducing the timber, these are often simply fixed to the face of the frame; they would be of brass or stainless steel to resist corrosion and staining. A bracket or metal strip might also be let in to a groove where, for example, the repair was at a place where two surfaces met. The drilling of pilot holes prior to inserting screws helps avoid splitting thin timber sections.

Sometimes a rotten section of timber needs cutting out and replacing, but where this would mean removing and risking breaking some interesting old glass, then an alternative repair might be to use a modern exterior joinery filler. In a traditional joinery repair the timber is cut back to a straight line or similar profile that permits a new piece to be fitted in – either locked in place like a jigsaw piece and glued, or otherwise screwed and glued. To get access the window might have to be dismantled, and the sawing, prising and heaving could risk glass breakage or indeed the repair might make removal of the glass a necessity, and it requires great care to remove glass in one piece. If it is reasonable instead to scour out any rot while the window is in place and use, for example, one of the newer resin joinery fillers (as opposed to the cheaper types that might be based on

Wooden windows are almost infinitely repairable; the technology is simple and the skills are widely available, it just needs the will to bring them together.

cement powder), then the repair might be easier and less risky.

The down side would be that this is not a 'like-for-like' repair, but if it permits less timber to be removed (only the rotten timber) and preserves the glass, then it is arguably more conservative than a traditional timber repair. That the fillers would not be as 'breathable' as the timber may also seem a disadvantage with this method, but then with a traditional repair the glue line is also a barrier to breathability. So until wood can be regenerated in place according to its natural structure (who knows?), then a good filler might be seen as a reasonable solution.

Metal

Wrought iron

Real wrought-iron cottage windows are a valuable link with the past. A traditional repair to, say, a joint that has rusted away might mean deglazing the window and reworking the joint at the blacksmith's forge. As with the filler repair to a timber window discussed above, a view needs to be taken on the damage that the repair itself might bring about. Sometimes a pragmatic approach can be to use a pure iron weld in situ, or, for a non-structural repair, even an epoxy filler material. Even so a blacksmith ideally ought to be involved in the decision process, if only for the understanding they have of the effects of the repair options on the other joints present in the frame. The effects on the glass ought also to be considered, according to its age and quality (*see* 'Glass', opposite), and a blacksmith's repair will almost inevitably mean prior removal of the glass.

Cast iron

Cast iron made an appearance in window frames most commonly in 'designed' estate cottages from the early eighteenth century. An iron foundry was a feature of many country towns because the material provided much of the staple agricultural equipment and machinery. Each locality will therefore have its own patterns. Structural repairs are less predictable in cast iron, and rely on the skill and ingenuity of the metalworker. A very badly corroded piece can be replicated, even using the remains of the original to make a mould in sand for casting. This is much cheaper than having a new timber pattern made to create a mould, but the result would be a fraction smaller than the original, as timber patterns were made deliberately oversized to allow for contraction of the metal as it cooled from molten back to solid.

Metal gates

Both wrought and cast iron were used, as well as timber, for gates, and similar considerations to the above apply in the repair of these.

Paint

A good paint should help external joinery last, but surprisingly, having no paint at all might be less of a problem than having a paint that is worn so that it allows water in but not out. Modern gloss paint, if it is not flexible or breathable enough – and much is not – can crack and split, letting in water and keeping it there, feeding decay. Traditional paint had some flexibility, or at least it tended to wear out in such a way that allowed the wood beneath to dry out if it should get wet through: very old doors on forgotten outbuildings can still be seen in reasonable condition, even though most of their traditional paint wore off years ago. However, traditional paints

Old glass may appear like ordinary modern glass at first sight, but it reflects and refracts light according to the minor imperfections that are a result of its 'hand-made' manufacture.

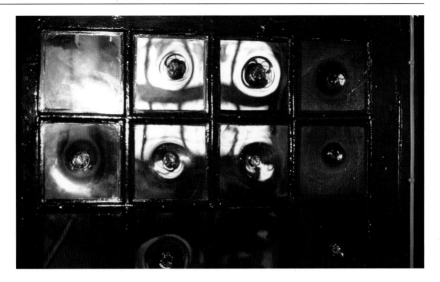

'Bulls-eye' glass might be expensive now but it was once disregarded as waste from hand-made glass – it is where the pipe was attached through which the glass was blown. As a cheap off-cut it would probably have found its way on to many cottages.

that performed more benignly were unfortunately made with lead, and were outlawed because of fears about lead's toxicity – though now some of the 'natural oil' paints mimic its qualities.

To get full benefit from breathable paint, conventional modern gloss would have to be removed, and this can involve a risk of exposure to lead dust or fumes from any underlying old lead paint layers (*see* government health and safety advice on www.hse.gov.uk). Furthermore, stripping removes all the history of the colours that are 'fossilized' in those old paint layers, along with evidence of old usage, bumps and scrapes that would be removed in preparation for a new finish. These things are part of the appeal of an old building, so paint removal needs to be weighed up carefully. (For more on paint and its removal, *see also* Chapter 12: Paint It … Back.)

Glass

Old glass is less optically perfect than modern glass. It has ripples that cast attractive reflections on the outside, and they also make for some pleasant light shows, scattering sunlight indoors. Modern glass is mirror flat, so expect no pretty light shows from that. Old glass can be less resistant to scratching and much thinner than modern glass, so care needs to be taken during redecoration, and dry abrasive papers and hot paint-stripping avoided.

In some locations modern regulations call for strengthened glass, but if this requirement applies to an old dwelling and it seems to conflict with the character of the property, then there are adhesive films or strengthened traditional-style glasses available that might be a suitable compromise (but have a word with the council's building control department or the conservation officer first to examine all options). A few moments examining old glass compared with modern should show that it is worth trying to keep the character of the old.

In certain circumstances it can be feasible to retain a mildly damaged piece of old glass, if it is not likely to leak or to break dangerously. But beware that glues and adhesive films that might assist this are not entirely foolproof, and each case would need to be assessed on its merits. In the case of terminal breakage it is now possible to obtain most historical patterns of blown, moulded, cast, rolled and polished glass, and even to have some of them toughened, laminated and coated to perform as modern glass.

Glass can be a rather seductive commodity to buy, and it is possible to get carried away, but owners interested in retaining an authentic feel to their cottage should bear in mind that, with the possible exception of mediaeval glass, most plain cottage glass would probably have been mildly imperfect, but not so crazily distorted as to resemble the view from the inside of a glacier or a themed pub.

THE PRESENT
And what the twentieth century did

Cottages had existed in a stable world for many centuries before the twentieth: the same type of occupants, same building methods, same building materials, same fuels. But by the early decades of the twentieth century all that was changing very, very fast, with different occupants with different needs, different building materials used in repairs and extensions, different methods of heating.

When we look at a cottage now, how much of what the eye can actually see is only a few years old? Very many cottages are now covered with paint, render finishes and components, some of which only first became available during our own lifetimes. In some cases absolutely everything that is on the surface is brand new and factory-made, from the roof tiles to the windows, the paint, the doorknobs … everything. Obviously things such as paint need renewing from time to time, but why shouldn't they be compatible with the cottage and of the same type, colour and texture as those used originally, instead of those designed for more modern buildings?

It is not necessary to be an antiques expert to appreciate that an eighteenth-century table would be devalued if someone stuck wood-effect plastic laminate all over it, or to see that an 'Old Master' oil painting could be made comical by some 'paint-by-numbers' additions. A cottage that has been recently covered in violently coloured plastic paint, or had factory-made plastic window frames, can be equally incongruous.

By the end of the twentieth century some unfortunate side effects became apparent in the use of modern materials and methods to restore old buildings. It is now understood that cottages were, after all, not just primitive attempts at our own 'proper'

building, but were actually based on a millennium of thorough understanding of sustainable construction that worked with the natural landscape, and with the elements, rather than fighting them. Those well tried old practices can work so differently to recent technology that to combine them both in a single building can cause problems, like a transfusion of the wrong blood type. The modern cottage owner does not have to understand all the technicalities and science involved, but they ought to be aware of where problems can lie so they can avoid the pitfalls.

The result of applying new, sometimes incompletely evaluated technology to very old buildings has often proved technically and visually damaging. The chapters in this third section start with general maintenance and examine routine problems, but they also explore some of the more common errors of the twentieth century's ways, how they are likely to affect a cottage, and what, if appropriate, might be done to restore the original balance, or at least to limit damage.

CHAPTER EIGHT

This Old House
Routine maintenance for cottages

TOO LITTLE OR TOO MUCH?

An old cottage that is correctly maintained could last for centuries more, while one that has had no maintenance at all could become uninhabitable in a decade or two. But lavished with inappropriate maintenance, the home might look pristine, yet beneath the surface it could be rotting away. This chapter examines some of the basic day-to-day maintenance tasks, and the next examines some of the general building hazards that might be found on the way. The two chapters after that address the possibilities of reversing, or coping with, past inappropriate maintenance. The final chapter of this section takes a look at the end products of trapped dampness: rot and decay. Even if not contemplating a significant repair project, day-to-day maintenance is still essential to protect one's investment, but the knowledge of the building gained through routine maintenance will help to inform any future projects.

WATER

There are many causes of building failure, but water getting into the wrong places and staying there is one of the principal culprits. It softens both timber and benign traditional mortars, and creates conditions that feed destructive insect and fungal pests. Newly built houses have the technology and materials to keep out unwelcome water. Cottages did not have this advantage when they were built, so they accepted it; nevertheless, the same materials that let the damp in, also allowed it to dry out again. The picture might have been complicated by more recent alterations to a cottage, because modern, and more and more 'waterproof' materials may have been applied during the last century.

Experience indicates that such partial conversions to 'waterproofness' are rarely totally successful, because without a total rebuild it is virtually impossible to guarantee that every pathway is sealed and that no damp can arise anywhere. Partial sealing of a structure with damp barriers may create more problems, due to damp retention, than it can solve by its partial damp exclusion.

Some homework

When thinking about repairing a cottage – whether just painting inside or out, or having the masonry repointed, or repairing plaster and render – then it can help preserve the fabric, and logically perhaps also the value of the property, if the options for traditional products are examined. Several of these traditional products happen to have been made from one

---

Shades of grey

Traditional construction used to allow a little damp in, encourage it to pass through, and ensure its departure was made easy. But trying to apply the modern 'all damp must be kept out' approach to an existing cottage building can rarely hope to be installed in a way that is sufficiently complete. The effect can be like a one-way valve: in some places damp can get in, but not out from where it finds itself. And damp feeds decay.

OPPOSITE: Many cottages are evidently well loved now and must be looking much more sophisticated than ever before, yet deep inside them there is still likely to be mediaeval technology that needs to be understood and cared for on its own terms.

very simple, ancient raw material: lime. With the right knowledge, some fairly simple but essential training, and some goggles and protective gear (as lime is quite weather sensitive and also a caustic substance until dry), a big bag of the right type of lime from a builders' merchant correctly mixed can be enough to paint the outside of a cottage by making it up into a limewash. The cost compares very favourably with the price of masonry paint.

This is fine if your cottage retains its original lime-wash finish, but sadly most cottages and older houses have already been painted over with modern 'plastic' masonry paints. It would be good to be able to return to the old finish, but limewash would only be effective if the plastic paint could be removed first – and that can be expensive in the short term, even if probably beneficial in the long term. (*See also* Chapter 12: Paint It … Back for paint, and Chapter 6: Sticks and Stones for more on lime.)

However, there are still very many unpainted old cottages still benefiting from being able to 'breathe' and to move slightly without cracking because their brick or stonework is put together using lime mortar. Lime mortar (*see also* Chapter 6: Sticks and Stones) can easily be repaired if necessary, yet every day, somewhere in the country, this kindly lime is being hacked away to be replaced by new cement pointing in the name of 'maintenance'. These misguided actions may lead to future problems with dampness or cracking, and they may also disfigure the building.

These things are not done maliciously, they are simply done by people who have not yet understood the authentic alternative offered by traditional materials. These people probably honestly believe that cement is better because it is harder (but hard is not so good if it inhibits movement) and more water-proof (again, not so good if it stops 'breathing'). They could, sadly, be wasting money and creating future problems for the cottages they are trying to look after.

GENERAL HOME CHECKS

Some of the potentially expensive, or even harmful, work done on cottages can come about through a misdiagnosis of the problems. For example, fitting new damp-proof courses or covering walls with waterproof renders and sealers has no doubt been carried out many times, when a simpler solution might have been to track down the actual source of the excess damp getting into the wall and address that. Repairing any leaking drain pipes, or shifting any soil that has built up against the wall, or removing finishes that could be sealing up a wall that needs to 'breathe' – with luck one of these, or another simple remedy, could prove effective. So before throwing money at a building solution for a damp problem, it can pay to have it properly diagnosed.

Without taking a look in bad weather, this sort of thing could go unnoticed for a long time.

Cottages with suspended timber floors need to pay attention to underfloor ventilation – keeping the air flowing should save spending money repairing a rotten floor.

Rainwater is the principal starting point of decay. Have checks carried out to see that all roof slopes are intact and still retain their full complement of sound tiles or slates. Also have checked such features as lead flashings around chimneys and rooflights and against other walls; these should all be properly lapped and not cracked or displaced, not forgetting any rooftop 'valley gutters' and 'parapet gutters', which can be well hidden high up. The more out of sight these are, the more likely they are to become dammed with leaves and debris.

All being well at high level, then make sure that all rainwater gutters and downpipes are doing their jobs properly and conducting the rainwater from the roofs to ground level. Once the water is near ground level, some of it might be saved in a water butt (ensuring that the overflow would discharge

Modern 'plastic' paints that form a waterproof skin can work well on modern buildings that are not prone to movement, but their performance on older fabric can be much less satisfactory. When a cottage flexes it can crack the film of paint, and this can allow rainwater behind it, which collects there and is trapped, along with damp from other sources. Sometimes a 'plastic' paint is not compatible with the surface – and some have even tried treatments that aim to force them to stick and probably permanently seal up the wall in the process. But ideally old buildings would be painted the way they were originally, with movement-tolerant, breathable finishes that allow damp to get out. For the many cottages that have acquired layers of modern 'plastic' masonry paint, and where stripping this off is not an option, then the modern paint has to be kept in thoroughly good order.

somewhere harmless when it is full), but probably the majority then flows into a gulley from where it should be conducted by pipes to a soakaway in the garden or straight into the public drains.

Do not just take these things for granted – get out under an umbrella and check that they look as though they are happening when it is raining hard. While at ground level (this can be when it has stopped raining) also check that any low-level iron or terracotta grilles – designed to ventilate underfloor spaces and keep them free from rot – are not blocked by soil or plants.

Tiny cracks in paintwork on windows and on walls can admit enough water to initiate decay, so keep them filled. This does not have to mean calling out decorators at once: some ordinary glazing putty can stop up cracks in joinery until the spring. Attention to cracks is particularly important on the majority of cottages if they are painted with modern non-breathing 'plastic' paints – because once water gets in it could be trapped, as in a plastic bag.

A general maintenance checklist can be found at www.oldhouse.info; this can be added to and tailored to individual homes.

PLANNED MAINTENANCE

It is worth giving an old house a check-up every so often using the services of a conservation-accredited professional. Now that some motor-car dealerships can charge more per hour for their services than do many conservation architects, engineers and surveyors, then it seems sound financial sense to give a cottage the same opportunity as a car – to be looked over by someone who has experience of likely problems and appropriate repairs. After all, a cottage is generally considered to be a better long-term investment.

With expert input owners can plan tasks that lie ahead. For example, if they think that one day they would like to strip off plastic paint from the outside and replace it with limewash, then they may need to know what, in the meantime, they should be doing about internal redecorations as well, so as ultimately to get full benefit from that future exterior stripping work. Or if there is extensive work on the horizon involving chimneys or roofs and likely to involve costly scaffolding, it could make sense to coordinate maintenance in the meantime so that perhaps some allied work could be safely delayed by some holding repairs until the full scaffolding is necessary. Other high-level work might be brought forward at that time so that all work can take advantage of the same scaffolding.

Understanding how an old cottage would have been put together can make living in one all the more rewarding. Maintenance may seem just a routine necessity, but the familiarity it brings with traditional construction and finishes can also open up choices about how the house can be decorated and presented in order to maximize its historical appeal.

CHAPTER NINE

Reasons to be Careful
Awareness of some common domestic dangers

HAZARD PERCEPTION

Past attitudes

Unfortunately the past was quite a dangerous place: with a relatively accepting attitude to physical dangers in everyday life, it also abounded in health hazards at the time as yet to be identified. Consider a schoolboy's blazer pocket from only as far back as the 1960s: this might have contained interesting things such as asbestos, mercury, lead and the results of attempts to manufacture gunpowder – all without attracting undue comment at the time, but possibly warranting a police cordon now. A whole cottage from the 1860s has potentially accumulated far worse souvenirs, so needs careful scrutiny. It is not possible to list every hazard here, but a few can be highlighted.

General building hazards

Building is a dangerous occupation, and old buildings need extra respect as they will be of unknown construction and unknowable condition in places. Assumptions based upon modern experience can be misleadingly dangerous. So apart from the general hazards of, say, using a ladder, there are the additional risks such as, for example, where is safe to lean it? Ladder safety is promoted by the government's Health and Safety Executive at www.hse.gov.uk where, for example, the booklet *The Safe Use of Ladders and Stepladders – An Employer's Guide* has been posted as a download.

Building tends to involve power tools and machinery, and for the DIY enthusiast some of this equipment can be unfamiliar and perhaps over-elaborate for ordinary tasks. People carrying out DIY and lone builders are often at greater risk because they are working alone, so someone to keep a check can be reassuring. Cottages were built without power tools, and it could be extra sustainable and extra good exercise to recreate some of that ethos in minor repairs if there is the opportunity to do so sensibly. Note that building contractors and professionals are required to adopt legislated procedures on health and safety management (*see also* Chapter 2: The Professionals – 'Other professionals', page 31).

Substance abuse

Many of the regular substances used in building can be dangerous if mishandled: this includes vapours given off by paints, toxins in fungicides and pesticides, as well as dust from the various powders going into a building and the old dust coming off it, which might contain anything. Lime and cement powders, and mixtures containing either of these substances (mortars and limewashes), can cause skin and respiratory irritation as well as being dangerous if they get in the eyes because they are caustic, and so goggles, gloves and, for the powder versions, a mask are essential. Lime when dried, however, becomes chemically equivalent to blackboard chalk, and its chemical name in its cured state, calcium carbonate, can even be found applied to food additives. So lime's aggressive stage is only a passing phase, but one which should be treated with respect.

Cottages were first built and furnished by simply reassembling nature in a more convenient way. All the ingredients for a cottage and its furniture are in this picture, and the hazards would have been familiar from everyday life at the time. Life may have become generally more survivable since then, but it is no less dangerous and we have also introduced a lot more new hazards into our homes.

Asbestos

Asbestos was once regarded only as a very useful mineral, processed into a wide range of building and general products. Then it was linked with fatal respiratory disease, and now its presence is regarded as a very serious health issue; it is considered to be most dangerous in any loose dust or powder-like form where the small fibres might enter the lungs. Its useful properties included insulation, fire resistance, fibre reinforcement and various uses in filtering and machinery.

Asbestos appeared in paints, mortars, building boards, fixings, floor and roofing tiles and sheets, plumbing and heating components, electrical insulation, lagging, seals and caulking compounds and ropes for fireplaces and ovens, domestic iron stands and countless other products and applications. It is still present in old versions of such products in homes throughout the country. It would be surprising if any house built before it was banned at the end of the twentieth century is entirely free from it in some form.

If its presence is suspected, any inhalation of its dust is absolutely to be avoided, and the immediate steps to be taken to isolate or deal with it should appear as advice on government web sites (www.hse. gov.uk). The relevant local authority department would offer advice on identification and safe removal and disposal. Certain categories of building owner have a legal duty to identify and manage asbestos, while actions such as improper disposal and fly tipping are punishable and are actively pursued.

Biological hazards

Biological hazards range from the contamination of surfaces by wildlife – with excrement from feral pigeons and rats and mice posing particular disease risks – to the theoretical possibility that the animal hair in old lime render could support anthrax spores. In the former case it is clearly sensible to wear protective clothing including gloves, and to practise scrupulous hygiene; while in the latter case it would be sensible to at least wear a suitable dust mask, and to protect others from dust if disturbing an old wall containing any unknown material (damping down can be an effective way of limiting dust, which is appropriate in some cases).

It seems inappropriate to think of embarking on wholesale demolition as a precautionary measure against any slight suspicion of anthrax, since if the wall really did contain spores, demolishing it except under the most rigorously controlled conditions would almost certainly release the spores into the environment where they could begin to do their harm.

Chemicals

There are many chemical substances that have, after years of everyday use, fallen under the suspicion of causing health problems. A cottage is likely to be old enough to have collected most of them as transient items at least, from household cleaning and gardening pesticide products to building and furnishing glues and solvents. One likely source of concern is old insecticide treatments as used for timber infestations, because these, or so their long-term guarantees imply, might remain actively toxic for several decades at least. The extent of treatment in the past and the chemicals involved should be

researched, and human contact with those timbers minimized, for example roof timbers that are likely to have been treated.

If disposing of any parts of old treated timber during future repairs, these should be subject to careful handling and appropriate disposal, which might mean avoiding burning in some cases. Preservative pre-treated building timber used to employ a mix containing arsenic until quite recently, so contact with that ought to be appropriately shielded. The government's Health and Safety Executive has details on the control of substances harmful to health: *see* www.hse.gov.uk/coshh.

Electricity

Older properties will not automatically have been upgraded to meet current levels of protection from electric shock. To take one example, the 'RCD' circuit breakers that new houses use (usually installed at the consumer unit) to protect vulnerable power sockets, such as those serving external areas, will not be present at all if the wiring has not been updated since those regulations took effect, or since the devices became available. A cottage might be found to be still running on its very first installation involving lead or rubber-sheathed cables that might be concealed behind later replacement switch plates and sockets. It is always worth having this specifically checked when moving to a property.

Furthermore, it is only relatively recently that regulations came into force to prevent those without recognized qualifications doing significant work to electrical installations, meaning that some cottages may have been entirely wired up by someone who would nowadays be considered an amateur.

All wiring would benefit from technical examination rather than relying on appearances. Old wiring is not necessarily always unsafe, but will have certain limitations and should be checked by appropriately qualified personnel who are aware of its possible limitations (and of the damage that can be done to it even by some misapplied test procedures). The findings should be explained to the owner, and any limitations that there may be in the system should be understood. Perhaps certain useful modifications can be carried out to minimize risk even if it is not

Where plain water, maybe from a hose, is not likely to be appropriate to the fire risk (ask the local fire brigade for guidance), then it can be worth taking advice on specialist extinguishers for home use, though just getting everyone out of the building quickly may be more appropriate still. Smoke detectors are considered one of the basic home safety requirements, and these can aid timely escape. Some form of reliable emergency lighting can also assist escape.

deemed absolutely necessary to revise the complete installation at the time.

Local authority building control departments should be able to direct enquirers to appropriate regulation bodies for electrical installers, while *Electrical Safety and You* is downloadable from www.hse.gov.uk. (*See also* Chapter 10: Heat, Light and Water – 'Of mice and men', page 121, regarding rodent damage and the risk of fire.)

Fire

The usual household precautions apply to cottages in respect of the risk of fire, with thatched cottages requiring additional precautions that the local fire brigade and insurers may also advise on or specify. Automatic smoke and fire detection, including in roofspaces, is sensible for older properties, and because cottages might occasionally be expected to play host to the nostalgic use of candles, lanterns or oil lamps, a scrupulous attention to the supervision and extinguishing of naked flame needs to be relearnt.

Familiarity with electric light may have made us dismissive about safety with lighting, but our ancestors were rightly paranoid about house fires and about being careful when using candles and lamps, and we should readjust to the reality of those things if we use them. After all, nowadays not all of us have their inbuilt experience about what happens to a candle when it burns down, or about how close to the ceiling it is safe to hang an oil lamp. Cottages were not built with even the rudimentary requirements of physical fire protection as are now required in a modern house. That is not to say that cottages are automatically dangerous, but any risks ought to be understood. The same would apply to a modern house since, despite regulations, people seem to remove fire doors and make holes in fire partitions without thinking – so nothing can be taken for granted. The local fire service may be able to offer specific advice to householders on enquiry, *see* www.firekills.gov.uk and www.communities.gov.uk/fire.

Gas

Country cottages do not always have the luxury of a gas supply, and those that do probably received it at a later date than in towns. Nevertheless, older underground supply pipes can be of iron, and that can rust. Within an old cottage the gas distribution pipes could be to an old technical standard and under former rules, or installed by DIY amateurs or people who were not qualified to the standards expected today. As with electricity, a gas installation should be checked by appropriately qualified personnel, and understood. Measures such as the provision of permanent ventilation in rooms containing a gas-burning appliance may have been forgotten, or deliberately or innocently removed over time, and a proper, formal report would be expected to highlight such discrepancies.

See www.gassaferegister.co.uk for details of the requirements for qualified personnel only to work on gas installations (England, Scotland, Wales and the Isle of Man; for the Channel Islands and Northern Ireland *see also* trustcorgi.com).

Lead

Water supply
For a long time lead made up a major part of the pipework supplying drinking water, and it is still present in that capacity serving many homes until it is replaced, piecemeal. It can still be present in houses, and because even lead solders have been banned from the joints in modern drinking water pipes, it can be inferred that lead pipework is not at all desirable in the supply of drinking water. It may not be apparent whether a house's supply passes through lead inside or outside the property, nor the degree of contamination that it might be giving rise to, but testing the water from the point of use ought to be possible in order to clarify this. Water standing overnight in contact with lead pipework is considered to be at extra risk of contamination (particularly in soft water areas where there is also not even the small, unreliable comfort of limescale coating the inside of the pipes).

Therefore until a test confirms the situation, some means of flushing the water through first thing in the morning, ideally without wasting it, might be devised – perhaps by flushing a WC further on the same pipe run from the kitchen sink, for example – which should draw out standing water and flush through fresh. For more information, contact your water supply company.

Before swapping metal for plastic it might be worthwhile double checking that there is no aggressive subsoil pollution on the pipe route that might chemically infiltrate the plastic pipe or its fittings.

General building
The toxic potential of lead is, however, still tolerated in many other building uses, such as for flashings and roofing accessories, because there are limited effective substitutes. Handling these items improperly presents a potential hazard (*see* www.hse.gov.uk), and leadwork will almost certainly be found somewhere on an old cottage.

Paint
Lead paint has been banned from general use for many decades, though its beneficial properties have allowed its use under special licence in a controlled way on special conservation projects to highly graded listed buildings. More importantly to cottage owners is the near certainty that at some time in the past the joinery inside and out would have been painted with lead-based paints, so care needs to be taken when stripping or preparing joinery (especially avoiding dry sanding and hot stripping to avoid raising dust or fumes: treat all dust, slurry, fumes and other residues sensibly as a hazard): *see* www.defra.gov.uk; *see also* Chapter 12: Paint It … Back – 'The "traditional" paints', page 130, and 'Some stripping techniques', page 133).

CHAPTER TEN

Heat, Light and Water
*Marrying modern building services
with ancient construction*

HAVING THE MAINS

The utility services – electricity, water and gas – came into most cottages just as they stopped being 'proper' agricultural cottages – that is, during the first half of the twentieth century when rural life was changing.

Many cottagers may have previously had their own water supply of one sort or another before mains water was available, and some of those people proudly hung on to it afterwards, even if it denied them the convenience of turning on a tap. In that lost world it was not uncommon for passers-by and workmen to ask for, or be offered water on a hot day, and this could involve using wells, pumps or ice-cold, ink-black pools in cellars. Sadly, we now have to be wary that these might now be delivering diluted agricultural chemicals, bringing a touch of regret to the memory of a glass of water offered from a covered spring one hot summer afternoon, delivered with the sprightly boast: 'I'm ninety-six you know!'

Nearly every cottage has now cemented its relationship with mains utilities, which is probably just as well otherwise conservationists would still be agonizing about the visual and physical damage that pipes and wires can do when driven into, under or across old cottages. It would be even better if at least any overhead cables were put out of sight, but that may not be an easy furrow to plough. As cottages rocketed into mini luxury homes they were also adorned with television aerials and telephone cables, to which the same complaints can be applied.

Pipes

Pipes will be involved with admitting mains water, and circulating this as well as hot water and any central heating water around the cottage. Gas, perhaps rarer in country cottages, also comes in pipes. The incoming water main is sensitive to frost, so these are almost always well buried in the ground ('two foot six' was an old rule of thumb, and further, water pipes should be insulated wherever they are exposed to the risk of freezing). They may originally have been made of lead, iron or galvanized steel, which may bring some risk of corrosion or toxicity, so these are now often replaced with plastic as the opportunity arises. (*See also* Chapter 9: Reasons to be Careful – 'Water supply', opposite.)

Original pipe installations would most often have been worn on the surface of internal walls. The idea of chopping them into the surface where they could not be seen or maintained seemed illogical to practically minded people then. The later, buried installations can be more difficult to trace, and brand new installations chopped into ancient walls and floors can be potentially very damaging to the historical fabric of a small cottage. Installations need to be considered with care and inventiveness by designers and installers – and the lightest of touches demanded by owners and planning officials in order to preserve the value of the original building.

Copper has been the pipe material of choice or necessity for much of the last century, but volatile world commodity prices have brought other materials into play from time to time. Plastics are useful

and, literally, more flexible alternatives in many ways than metals, perhaps requiring fewer joints as a result, but they might also be just as susceptible to the jaws of rodents as electric cables. Very small diameter copper pipes ('microbore') have proved useful in cottages for heating distribution as they occupy less space, cause less damage and potentially require fewer joints as they are long and need fewer corner joints – however, this needs to be coordinated with the heat source and boiler design. It may also be assumed that underfloor heating (see also Chapter 14: Future Past) is problematical to install in cottages in that it can require the removal of a lot of cottage floor first, though alternative solutions can cover an existing floor – but that is not without problems, potentially, of appearance and breathability. Future developments may be less invasive.

Drains and sewer substitutes

Drains arrived late in the countryside. There were country cottages in Britain still using a bucket in a primitive outdoor earth closet in freezing winters, while at the same time astronauts were grappling with the relative luxury of zero-gravity defecation on the international space station. An alternative for the majority of those people not connected to the mains had been a septic tank or cesspit to treat or store conventionally flushed effluent on site.

Cottages with a suitably large and appropriately drained garden might now investigate a reedbed to treat their own waste, perhaps in combination with a septic tank. Reedbeds, septic tanks and other forms of on-site treatment are much less tolerant of what is flushed into them than the mains, and cooking grease can finish them all off. However, even when connected to the main sewers, similar care is needed not to over-burden them with grease and chemical waste, and – especially important to owners of old drains – not to test old and possibly erratically designed or worn drains to their limit. Ironically, earth closets are making a comeback in a new high-technology format, and for country cottages the concentrated garden fertilizer they could produce seems a promising contribution to self-sufficiency. Rainwater disposal arrangements for modern houses with sufficient garden has for some time been to dig a soakaway pit to which rainwater pipes are connected. The same may be true of an old cottage, though the size and location may not be to the same specifications as more modern versions. In some areas (usually in towns) rainwater joins effluent in the public sewer. Very occasionally pipes just disappear into the ground. Not at all satisfactory.

Cables

Of mice and men

The problem of rats and mice chewing PVC cables (and no doubt lead and rubber before that) can be overcome by using metal conduits. Again the earliest installations in cottages would have, quite sensibly, been made this way, made possible by the unquestioning attitude to having the things on display as with early gas and water pipes.

Cottages now are most likely to be wired in twentieth-century PVC-sheathed wiring. A better alternative is, however, expensive: the use of 'MICC' ('mineral-insulated copper-covered' or '-clad') or similar cables, which, like the small bore heating pipes described above, are small diameter metal tubes (usually plastic sheathed) that can also be threaded around in a generally less damaging way, though connections at sockets and switches can be obtrusive. However, many cottages today will have skeins of plastic (or even old rubber) cables clipped to the walls. These may be on the more modern 'ring' circuits or the older individual spurs from the consumer unit or fuseboard. The actual installation would most likely be a mixture of all ages of wiring and would benefit from assessment by a properly qualified electrician (see also Chapter 9: Reasons to be Careful – 'Electricity', page 116).

When a mouse, rat or squirrel chews through the insulation of an electric cable it may or may not escape electric shock, but the bare wires can sit there with the potential to spark and ignite whatever else is

OPPOSITE: *We have learned to subconsciously edit out overhead cables and television aerials in the same way that we do not notice traffic and aircraft noise, but we do need to be prepared to draw lines somewhere, before these modern trappings become too invasive.*

Even in the more populous counties of Britain it was well into the twentieth century before basic services such as mains water and electricity had made their way into the countryside and could be taken for granted.

there under the floor, inside the wall or in the attic. It is easy to understand why early users liked to have electricity tucked up in conduits. The installations that followed through most of the twentieth century were geared more to the requirements of modern housing and used either lead, rubber or plastic-sheathed wires in combination with a fuseboard with a rewirable fuse (later a glass cartridge fuse, later still an 'MCB' switch) for each circuit that should respond to a short circuit but not, unfortunately, a leak to earth such as could easily be provided by a rodent's chewing.

If a cottage has been rewired in recent years some (but perhaps not all) of its circuits might be protected with an 'RCD' (residual current device) switch that is intended to cut off the power when such a leak to earth happens, and to keep it off until someone finds and repairs the damaged sheathing. A problem can be that RCDs were often installed to protect a group of circuits – so that group would be automatically switched off, and finding which one is damaged can take time. RCDs are supposed to reduce the risk to humans of fatal electric shock, and those that are installed for this purpose might usually be rated at '30 milliamps'. Differently rated RCDs (or ELCBs as they were once known – earth leakage circuit breaker) such as 100 milliamps are probably there for some other purpose, to do with the supply company perhaps, and should not be relied upon for shock-protection functions. It is important to understand that even though an ELCB or RCD might be identified as present on the consumer unit (what used to be the 'fuseboard'), it will very likely not be protecting every circuit, just one or just a few, so get a qualified electrician to explain the system.

Because of the danger of fire in older properties that were not built with physical fire protection in mind, some owners have had their consumer unit upgraded so that all individual circuits are each protected by their own 'RCBO' switch. An RCBO provides, in effect, a combination of the regular consumer unit 'MCB' (miniature circuit breaker) switch with its own 'RCD' for each circuit (*see above*). This combination is considered to be a better, if perhaps not foolproof, provision against fire following rodent damage, but the individual switching of each circuit is more convenient, and in addition should enable damage to be located more easily.

Many cottages have survived a great deal of time still equipped with only their very first electrical system, though upgraded, bodged and tinkered with over the years. Even though it may be fronted with the latest in shiny switches, what lies behind them is important. Owners should understand that the modern electrical accessories and appliances they may buy to connect into their system are probably designed primarily to work with the standards expected in average modern installations, and they may not actually be so satisfactory or safe if wired into an earlier or faulty system. Electricity can be instantly fatal, so arrange for a qualified electrician to help you understand it in your cottage – and this has to go beyond the 'tick-the-box' assessment that might be the basis of some forms of buyers' and sellers' surveys.

Telecommunications and electronics

Radio, television and satellite antennae

The need for big radio-receiving antennae for ordinary broadcast reception has gone, and television aerials were perhaps tolerated because it was hoped they would be ephemeral too – but at present they seem to be getting bigger, and not always out of necessity, as people seem eager to buy a new aerial even though the old pre-digital one may serve digital broadcasts adequately in many places. Satellite dishes were once proudly displayed as status symbols, and dishes are still unthinkingly installed in the places that had been used for TV aerials, on chimneys and the apexes of roofs. But satellite broadcasting is technically different from terrestrial television and does not require height to peer over the horizon at a distant transmitting mast. Satellite signals come from space, like sunshine, so until it is necessary to be bolted to a chimney to get a suntan, it is quite satisfactory to have a satellite dish tucked away in the garden: all it needs is a short post and an unobstructed view of a tiny patch of the sky. As dishes are officially frowned upon in conservation areas and on listed buildings, awareness of the garden option could save the need for a great many angry letters to council offices. Nor is there any need for residents in unlisted cottages or outside conservation areas to clutter their buildings.

The cables that join the antennae to the receivers indoors need to be installed with the same sensitivity with which owners should be viewing the rest of their property investment. The quickest, easiest route and using the colour of cable that happens to be on the installer's van is not always the best solution, so give them a chance to bring the right stuff, and discuss the installation with them in advance. Cable clips knocked into bricks and stones can irreparably disfigure and damage them, so also consider requesting in advance that fixings be limited to those suitable for mortar joints.

Broadband and fibre-optic cables

For one reason or another, the cables, pipes and sewers under streets are not always logically coordinated or mapped out. This was difficult enough to achieve when all the utilities were effectively under government control through state-owned utilities, but now there are rapidly changing companies with new mercurial technology to thread in amongst what is already there. The cottage owner in the countryside might escape most of these worries, but any new connections to mains services can risk disrupting existing supplies, and the use of convenient devices such as 'moles' to install pipes and cables without trenches is not always appropriate. Excavations alongside old cottages could risk upsetting their foundations by exceeding their depth, particularly as those carrying out the excavations may not be expecting shallow foundations, or be familiar with them.

In gardens

In a garden, the potential for damage by new excavations for any services parallels the damage done inside cottages by burying cables in the walls. Gardens may appear to be able to make a better recovery, but care should be taken in particular to protect tree roots from being severed by any kind of excavation, and tree canopies from being damaged by machinery: roots are what physically anchor a tree to the ground, so severing all of them on one side with a trench is definitely not a good idea. Roots also feed a tree and keep it healthy, and a healthy tree is more likely to remain in one piece.

Meter boxes

A big plastic box screwed to the wall of a small cottage is going to do nothing for its appeal. External meter boxes do come in more discreet patterns than the standard white, so gas meters can be situated in relatively discreet plastic boxes at ground level. Forthcoming automatic electricity metering arrangements may make access for meter reading unnecessary, so an internal meter location could be viable for the future.

HEATING AND LIGHTING

Heating

Cottages were built for open fire heating (*see* Chapter 6: Sticks and Stones – 'Chimneys' page 69, and Chapter16: Bits and Pieces – 'Light My Fire' page 179) and many have added or moved over to gas, oil or electrical systems. The sealing up and draught proofing that would kill an open fire but often goes with central heating, will have contributed to changes in the way the cottage responds to damp and movement. In particular, central heating can excessively dry timber so that doors, posts and beams may crack and twist more than in previous centuries. If introducing heating for the first time, do so gradually and gently, and when siting pipes and radiators, be aware that localized heat can cause damage so it may be appropriate to insulate or otherwise protect adjacent vulnerable surfaces. (*See also* Chapter 3: Don't Bring Me Down – 'The effects of central heating' page 42, and Chapter 14: Future Past – 'Heating and Insulation', page 156, for more on future heating prospects.)

Lighting

Artificial light was fairly modest for centuries and came in units of one candle flame for a long time. Low level lighting that is compatible with safe use of the spaces, but which leaves some dark and mysterious corners, can be appropriate in a cottage. Low ceiling heights and the unavailability of electricity for most of their existence means that cottages would be less likely to have had the central ceiling light that modern homes take for granted, so if it should be necessary to redesign the wiring in a cottage there could be an opportunity to re-examine the look of the lighting. As discussed earlier in this chapter, services' installations have the potential to damage old fabric, so it pays to be considerate about how and where these are placed. (*See also* Chapter 16: Bits and Pieces – 'Lighting' page 179, and Chapter 17: Come Outside – 'External lighting', page 196.)

CHAPTER ELEVEN

Get it Right Next Time
Addressing inappropriate past work

RIGHT FROM WRONG

Good maintenance is important, but some of the modern decorating and repair products commonly found in DIY shops and in the back of builders' vans may not be the best option for a cottage. Some modern decorating materials can be too stark looking, and some commonly used repair materials might actually harm an old property by conflicting with old-fashioned ways of dealing with damp and movement.

However, sympathetic and good-looking traditional solutions are still available, and they can even be less expensive, less trouble to use and kinder to the environment. But all cottages have journeyed through the twentieth century, and while there, they will most likely have been lavished with some of the modern repair and decoration materials that can have adversely affected the intended performance and preservation of traditional fabric. A new, enlightened owner may well want to identify any such 'mismatches' and take steps to reverse them, or at least try to minimize their adverse effects.

Some ground rules

It is reasonable to ask 'What is the difference between

Some cottages appear to have escaped the worst of the twentieth-century's misunderstanding of traditional building technology, and they look the better for it; but for every one like this there must be hundreds that are uncomfortable in their twentieth-century skin.

modern materials and the traditional ones?' These old bricks, mortars, woodwork and so on must be similar to those that make up a modern house, mustn't they? Surely they can be treated the same way? Isn't this just trying to make us spend more on special 'heritage' products when ordinary ones will do? Well, no. Actually the old, traditional materials are part of a different mechanism for dealing with damp and movement – a mechanism that helps old buildings such as cottages survive. And while traditional products can indeed be found dressed up in seductive wrappings and sold at a premium, these time-tested traditional products are usually quite simple and can also be found on sale in their basic forms.

There are sound practical reasons for trying to understand olden construction and seeing if it is possible to 'go back to basics'. Many of the true traditional products tend to be so basic, unpatented and unaccustomed to marketing budgets, that they can be much cheaper to buy than ordinary modern products. Some might even be home made, but it is always a matter of knowing what to look for.

What makes many 'ordinary' conventional modern repair products so often unsuitable for period buildings is that they have been developed, reasonably enough, to work at maximum effect on modern buildings that do not have the same need to cope with the continual cycle of damp absorption and drying that our cottages were built to tolerate. Cottages may also have to cope with a greater degree of seasonal and other minor movement than do modern houses. Old-fashioned, traditional paints, mortars and renders were able to cope with these things, whereas modern versions tend not to address them so well because the majority of newer houses, for which the modern products are largely intended, do not require it to such a degree.

Chapters 3: Don't Bring Me Down and 6: Sticks and Stones have examined how traditional materials such as lime mortars and renders can tolerate slow and minor movement without receiving or causing damage, and they can do this better than their modern equivalents made from cement. Chapters 4: The Air that I Breathe, and 12: Paint It … Back, look at how traditionally used materials – including the lime products again, as well as limewash paints and internal distempers – can deal with damp, not by

barring it completely but by accepting that whatever got in, by whatever means, had to be able to dry out effectively. But these mechanisms have to be part of a system, and unfortunately that system can have been upset by well meant but damaging alterations, maintenance and redecorations dating from the twentieth century, and still being carried out somewhere today.

What is correct maintenance, repair and decoration?

For any property in the damp UK, the top of its maintenance list should be to ensure that water, from the sky, from the ground and from the air (condensation), is shed or dried out before it begins feeding the agents of destruction. Very simple measures, such as inspecting roofs and rainwater goods and checking that soil is not building up against walls, can eventually save thousands of pounds in repairs. If the source of damp is properly diagnosed then it might be possible to eliminate it quite simply. (*See also* Chapter 4: The Air That I Breathe.)

When it comes to repairs and redecoration, those responsible for older properties need to remember that the most compatible solutions are not necessarily to be found on the shelves of a DIY store or in the back of the regular builder's van, as their stock items are likely to be appropriate to newer buildings. Older properties such as cottages must be able to let out any water that gets into them, and many modern products are simply not good at this, indeed many forbid it. For an old cottage that has not been extensively modified, correct maintenance generally means using materials and methods that are the same as, or compatible with, those with which it was built.

This is simply because cottages and other older buildings need to 'breathe', rather than be sealed up like modern houses, and also because simply built old properties such as cottages tend to shift a bit, for various reasons, rather than stay rock solid, as modern houses are assumed to do. The traditional materials from which cottages were built were developed by trial and error over the centuries to cope with this 'breathing' and movement, whereas many modern materials tend not to do this because they are intended for modern houses that do not need to breathe much, and that move relatively little.

The traditional decorative and repair materials

mentioned above and elsewhere in this book (lime mortars and renders, limewash, distempers and linseed-oil paints) are still available, though no longer mainstream. Although these are simple enough to use, many builders and decorators today may not yet have regained the experience that was once universal amongst their predecessors – the country builders who built cottages.

… and inappropriate maintenance, repair and decoration?

No maintenance at all is bad enough, but the wrong kind of maintenance can be even worse! Very often 'wrong' means the innocent or uninformed use of modern products, ones that seal up an old building and prevent it from 'breathing', or products that cannot cope with movement in a way that protects the fabric. In both cases this can lead to trapped water within the structure, which feeds decay.

Modern materials that have frequently been used on old houses in the past hundred years, and which can prove harmful, include cement mortars and renders, oil alkyd (gloss) paints for timber, vinyl and acrylic paints for walls, and 'plastic' (resin) paints for external masonry. These have become commonplace during the last century, they have often been the first things one is likely to see in a DIY shop or a builders' merchant, and in some cases they are all that is on offer. They are better suited to stable, 'non-breathing' twentieth-century house construction. On an old cottage that naturally moves a little they might crack, let in water and, being relatively impermeable, not let it out again, so setting up a pleasant habitat for rot and decay.

Similarly, anything that interferes with the original 'get wet then dry out again' philosophy of old buildings can disrupt their proper functioning. Vinyl wallpaper, for example, and waterproof sealers that are frequently sold to 'deal with' dampness, but which can only really block its path by putting a skin over it. The old, traditional way was to let the damp out, not seal it in.

So what if you own a case of inappropriate maintenance?

You are not alone. All cottages have lived through the twentieth century, and during that time most have

---

One careful owner

If a problem such as dampness is not properly diagnosed, then the solution that follows is likely to be inappropriate. It is fine to try to stop damp getting close to the cottage in the first place if at all possible (*see* Chapter 4: The Air That I Breathe, also the drawing of the French drain on page 51, and Chapter 17: Come Outside). But some damp is almost inevitable in the structure, and to try to block it with paints and sealers (and even sometimes damp-proof courses) is to imprison it where it can cause harm. It should instead be allowed to vent out. Modern paints and sealers may be good at hiding damp for a time, but eventually it could make itself known through blistering of the finishes, decay or by moving further along.

If considering buying a cottage where these 'remedial' materials and treatments are in evidence, this should perhaps be questioned in the same tone of voice that one would use if offered a car whose shiny bodywork was more bodyfiller than metal. Paint can hide a lot, but for how long?

---

been painted with plastic, rendered or pointed in cement, re-roofed over non-breathable underlays, and lovingly decorated from top to bottom in suffocating, impermeable wallpapers and paints. Not only that, they will have had fireplaces blocked, cutting down on useful ventilation, and bathrooms and kitchens installed, creating extra condensation that has nowhere to go. The more zealous owners may have proudly applied sealers and waterproof plasters to the merest hint of damp, and as if that were not enough, some building societies used to feel that anything built without a damp-proof course ought to have one whether it needed it or not.

We are lucky that we have any cottages left, as inappropriate maintenance has the potential to destroy, in that trapped damp feeds rot. Unfortunately, modern decorating products are so good at concealing defects that the damage these treatments might be doing lurks unseen until walls and roofs are opened up – then powdery insect- or

British cottages come in a very wide variety of materials, styles and locations, so it is asking a lot of any standard products to be compatible in all cases; the local traditions should be consulted before modern catalogues.

fungus-ridden pieces of timber might trickle out from where there used to be solid beams.

However, cottages can often be quite resilient. The skills to repair them may have to be relearnt, but at least these are based on reasonable common sense and basic natural materials and, originally, the use of simple tools. Unfortunately, we have to face the fact that much of the harm done innocently or out of ignorance during the last century is not practicably reversible, at least within the budgets that most householders command. Unpicking cement pointing can cause damage to bricks and stones, removing cement render is often extremely difficult, and stripping paint from joinery is time-consuming and potentially expensive, and sometimes even hazardous (*see also* Chapter 12: Paint It … Back). A much altered cottage will neither be entirely traditional nor entirely modern in function: proper conservation advice is therefore needed specific to each property in order to retune a cottage to make the best of its present situation, or to try to restore some of the beneficial features of the past.

RIGHTING WRONGS

It may be that when repairs or redecoration become necessary, there is an opportunity to go a little further in order to try to do some good to the building. If cracked exterior cement render is being replaced, advice from a conservation-accredited professional might well suggest replacing it with lime render (*see* Chapter 6: Sticks and Stones – 'Internal and external finishes'). If there is already lime render, but it has been over-coated with plastic masonry paint, then advice about the chances of successful paint removal would be useful in case 'breathable' limewash could be put back (*see* Chapter 12: Paint It…Back). If faced with a persistent damp problem, the immediate temptation may once have been to seal it up, but the better course is to find the reason why damp is accumulating and then try simple solutions first, step by step, until the problem diminishes. Such solutions would address both stopping the source of the dampness, and taking steps to permit continual ventilation of the area (*see also* Chapter 4: The Air That I Breathe).

Damage limitation

If the disruption and expense of trying to undo the excesses of the twentieth century are too much, then owners should at least be aware of the damage that could be happening, and where possible, act to reduce it. Windows and doors that are gloss painted will usually show cracks at the joints in the timber, so make sure these are filled (sometimes simple old-fashioned putty is the best filler) and kept painted. If walls have been painted with plastic masonry paint, make sure that the paint is kept in good condition and that cracks and blisters are quickly repaired and not allowed to admit the rainwater that races down the slippery plastic surface. If a roof has been re-laid under impervious underlay or over-generously stuffed around the edges with insulation so that the roofspace is airless, look into the possibilities of reintroducing some ventilation. Basically, attend to the needs of good property maintenance (for some pointers *see* Chapter 8: This Old House).

Sun and air

Take every opportunity to ventilate a cottage. Open windows when it is dry and when safe to do so. Consider having disused chimneys checked so they can be used once again for permanent controlled ventilation (a disused chimney should in any event be ventilated from top to bottom if possible to reduce dampness within the structure). Make sure the cellars and roofspaces are appropriately ventilated, and that insulation is not exceeding its remit by clogging benign, drying air paths (wire mesh might be needed to keep out opportunist birds, bats, rodents and squirrels). Learn about the 'breathable' construction and finishes introduced earlier in this book, and bit by bit, try to be sympathetic to that old regime whenever it is sensible to do so while redecorating and repairing.

Don't make it worse

Because most cottages are likely to have been modified during the twentieth century, few will still be functioning entirely as their original builders intended. They will be hybrids of old and new construction and materials, which can make deciding on repairs and conservation difficult. Is it possible to adjust the cottage to be fully 'breathing' once more, or is it already too far along an unsatisfactory road of conversion into an almost-modern house?

Before investing in building repairs and decorations it can pay to seek professional conservation advice, and get to understand how any new proposals will alter the way a particular old building is going to function in the future. Remember that there are often cheaper, simpler traditional alternatives that are worth trying, rather than rushing in with potentially harmful modern 'fixes'. Getting those traditionally based ideas tailored to your home by an expert can be a worthwhile investment. Consider starting small and simple, and working up.

CHAPTER TWELVE

Paint It ... Back
Stripping inappropriate or harmful paint

OLD TRADITIONAL PAINTS WERE RIGHT FOR OLD COTTAGES

A legacy of the twentieth century is that many old cottages up and down the country have been lovingly painted outside with 'plastic' masonry paints, and inside with plastic emulsion paints. These modern paints can look fresh and smart to the modern eye, yet cottage owners should be aware that these finishes behave in quite a different way to the traditional paints that were used for centuries beforehand, and this can affect the well-being of the building fabric underneath.

Why a cottage is different

Olden construction, which this book calls 'traditional', was based out of necessity on whatever materials the locality provided. These did not include much in the way of waterproof finishes, but did include a lot of natural materials that survive adverse weather better if they are allowed to manage their own dampness levels by continually being ventilated so as to dry afterwards. Chapter 4: The Air That I Breathe gives more information on this subject, but broadly, country cottages dating from before the early twentieth century are likely to be mainly 'traditional' in terms of construction and materials, while the houses that came after them are more likely to have turned over to our modern 'conventional' and waterproofed methods and materials – these modern finishes tend to block the ability of older materials to ventilate themselves or 'breathe'.

The changeover period was slow and perhaps subject to local pockets of resistance in out-of-the-way places, or in others perhaps to experimentation with novel products that were being processed locally. During the changeover period buildings may exhibit traces of both types of construction – the old, traditional, craft-based rural products and the new industrialized factory-made ones side by side. Such a mixture also becomes inevitable as the older cottages continued their journey into the twentieth century, and came to be repaired and redecorated by those who had not just forgotten, but had never heard of the traditional systems with which cottages protected themselves. As a result most cottages are by now effectively hybrids of both ancient and modern technology, which makes assessing and predicting their performance a difficult process.

Why traditional paints are different

The 'traditional' paints

Traditional, pre-industrial paints were made from simple materials. Typically an exterior wall might be 'whitewashed' with limewash, a simple rather caustic mixture of lime putty and water that dried to a benign, soft and slightly chalky finish (*see also* the drawing 'Quick Guide to Lime' in Chapter 6, page 68, and 'Return to Breathable Paints' – 'Limewash' below, page 136, and 'Distempers, milk paint ...' below, page 138). It could shed some rainwater, but did also allow some to seep into the fabric, though that could easily dry out later in the wind and sun. It suited old buildings because they were often built on simple foundations and from

Fade away and radiate: old soft lead paint wears away in such a way that the timber may be exposed but can at least dry out in the warmth of the sun, which is better than damp getting trapped under blisters. Even the shinier, more 'varnish-bound' later lead paints seem less inclined to turn into nasty blisters than does conventional modern gloss. These doors have been left who knows how long, yet the wood is not rotting because it is able to dry out. If anyone were to consider repainting these doors, then a breathable linseed oil paint might be a sensible place to start. Why change something that seems to work?

rather mobile materials such as mud, wood and lime render, which could shift about – and that did not matter too much because a powdery surface such as limewash is less prone to splits, cracks and tears. And any flaws would be filled at the next redecoration.

Similarly inside, walls and ceilings were typically painted with distemper, another powdery, chalky finish that may not have been very 'washable' or tough but was easy enough to repair, and which also 'breathed'. Joinery was often finished with a paint made from linseed oil with a compound of lead added for opacity and body. Like limewash and distemper it tended to a slightly powdery finish, though the oil gave it more resilience and, like the other two, repainting was usually quite easy as there was relatively little tendency for it to split or blister even when worn. Unfortunately the lead compounds in lead paint are toxic and were banned from general use; it needs to be treated with special caution when found (it is likely to remain as underlying coats on most old buildings), and government web sites now give safety advice: www.hse.gov.uk and www.defra.gov.uk.

The road from traditional to modern

From late Victorian times to the mid-twentieth century the composition and performance of paints, like many other building products, gradually changed from mainly breathable towards mainly waterproof. There are many types of paint used in building, and many reasons why each formula changed, but new features such as glossier, quicker-drying and more colourful all helped to promote the new paints among tradespeople and customers alike.

Those changes were made possible by the exploitation of new materials, many of them deriving from chemical products of the new industries such as the petro-chemical industry. It was not long before new solvents, pigments and binders ousted the traditional ones, and many of the mainstream paints that we have come to know today can, if not totally accurately, be called 'plastic' paints because they tend to dry to a plastic skin on the painted surface.

The 'conventional' modern paints

In contrast to 'breathable' traditional paints, the conventional modern paints that we now regard as ordinary tend to provide a water-resistant surface. Water resistance is usually coupled with water vapour resistance, which means that when these paints were first applied to old cottages they sealed up surfaces that for hundreds of years previously had been able to regulate their own dampness levels by 'breathing out' water vapour and 'breathing in' drier air. This protective function therefore began to be denied to old buildings.

Ordinary modern exterior wall paint, which can incorporate resins (or plastics), is matched with modern building methods: it dries faster than lime-wash, and can be used reliably for more of the year. In addition it is available in a wide variety of colours that can be reasonably uniform from tub to tub. This has made it popular with decorators and the DIY market. But one of its strengths when painted on firm new buildings is also one of its weaknesses when applied to more mobile old buildings: its waterproof-ness, or specifically its relatively high resistance to water vapour. As long as the paint film is unbroken it can shed water very well, and since modern buildings are fairly rigid, they are less likely to crack the film of paint. But old buildings are often not so rigid, and if

they shift and the paint cracks, then water gets in. Because the waterproofness is not just a one-way quality, that water can get trapped behind the rest of the paint film – and if damp then builds up amongst the soft porous fabric that makes up a cottage's walls, and any timbers inside, then decay can result.

It is a similar story with the modern versions of interior paints, vinyl emulsions for example, and joinery paints, oil or acrylic gloss, for example. They also form a 'skin', which needs to be intact to work best – but that, on an old building, is difficult to guarantee. There is a further complication with using modern paints that are effectively waterproof 'skins': they can prevent a house losing water vapour from within its fabric. Most modern houses are designed from the ground up with all kinds of barriers and devices to stop water vapour and dampness getting into the fabric in the first place. But this is almost impossible to achieve with an old house, and that dampness must be allowed out of internal and external walls, otherwise it can lurk, ready to feed rot and decay.

STRIP IT OR STICK WITH IT?

Ideally, a cottage still possessing its underlying original mobile and 'breathable' construction should be

The wear patterns of modern paint can involve blistering and peeling that traps damp. This has to be corrected immediately to avoid decay. It also seems that here, part of the problem is that underneath are traditional paints (the ones that are not peeling off) to which the new paint does not stick. The logic last century used to be to apply special primers to try to make modern paint stick to traditional paint – instead of just accepting that more traditional paint was the simplest answer.

painted with equally movement-tolerant and breathable paints. Traditional, basic 'old-fashioned' coatings would work well, but for these to be effective any modern waterproof paint coatings would have to be removed first. Not only that, but any other unhelpful modern waterproof elements of construction, such as cement renders, would have to be removed as well. This is clearly potentially a disruptive and expensive project for most householders to contemplate, though many have decided that it is worth the effort and money in order to better preserve their property.

There can also be visual benefits to making the switch back to traditional paints as they can be gentler looking, less bland and more subtly coloured, responding to the weather and resisting some cracking and generally giving the property a more authentic period quality. Stripping paint is a complex subject and any one cottage should be professionally assessed first as it is possible to cause more damage to an old house by inappropriate paint removal than by accepting and managing what is already there. One aspect that conservationists are concerned about is the stripping of joinery finishes, which, apart from the risks of exposing old toxic lead paint, can also strip the layers of old paint that are each a record of the colours and uses of the property at any time during its history. Remember that it is history and authenticity that makes old things more valuable to the market, and this is a concern that cottage owners need to take seriously.

Some stripping techniques and some pros and cons

Scraping and abrading
'Sanding' using abrasive papers is the basic removal method and one that raises dust unless accompanied by wetting. The dust might contain harmful substances such as lead and asbestos from old paint layers, while wetting can raise the gain of timber and make it look 'hairy'. Too much wetting can necessitate long and thorough drying to avoid problems with damp and with subsequently applied paint not adhering well. Abrasive papers and wire wool can damage glass – particularly old glass.

Very gentle scraping and peeling would apply when removing emulsion paint from previously

Burning off old paint is the default setting of many decorators, but it removes history as well as paint, creates a cocktail of fumes, and could risk damage to glass or even a house fire.

distempered ceilings, sometimes wetting or gentle steaming can help in those situations but beware of scraping furrows in the soft surface of the ceiling and any decorative mouldings.

Burning and hot air guns
Used to melt away paint, these methods are effective on 'plastic' and 'oil' paints; however, the fumes created, particularly with old underlying lead paint, can be a direct health hazard. In addition, the potential to ignite debris in unseen nooks and crannies on cottages and old buildings generally makes this a method to avoid in most cases. The main conservation organizations presume against this method, not out of timidity but for the hard-headed reason that there have been serious losses in fires caused by such 'hot' work.

Grit blasting

Grit blasting is a powered version of abrading, and subject to the same cautions, except that the operatives are usually dressed in protective gear (though this does not protect anyone downwind). However, this process in its basic form is usually deemed far too aggressive for the soft fabric that lies underneath paint on most cottages and old buildings – holes and fissures can be created in the paint and then the underlying cottage is blown away more effectively than the paint, since plastic paint is fairly resilient and blasted grit simply bounces off.

Patent and specialist grit blasting techniques

These techniques are a refinement of grit blasting, and require experienced operatives and specialized equipment; a jet of fine grit, with or without water, is delivered at an oblique angle by various different means. This can be a very controllable method in expert hands, and has been favoured by conservation organizations in the past, but locating those expert hands requires care. Different abrasive compounds may offer further improvements and refinements in the future.

Pressurized hot water and 'steam'

These can be appropriate to stripping 'plastic' masonry paints without directly physically abrading soft underlying fabric, but could deliver unhelpful amounts of water into that porous fabric. Again, it is usually a specialist undertaking, and one which should be carefully controlled; also allow enough time to complete the work before freezing weather, so

that trapped water has a chance to leave and any new finish has time to consolidate. Using traditional finishes, this probably means stripping no later than early spring.

Chemical strippers

These strippers need tailoring to match the paint to be dissolved, and range from DIY products in tins to processes in the hands of specialist contractors. Some firms undertake to match their strippers to paint samples, or to try a sample panel on site. Unfortunately, it is not yet possible to reliably target just the modern paint and leave the traditional lasyers intact, but who knows what the future may deliver?

The normal cautions with chemicals apply, since they are likely by definition to be caustic, and residues need thorough flushing away and neutralizing or they can undermine the new paint applied afterwards. If stripping timber using water-based preparations or when flushing with water, this can raise the grain of timber and make the wood look 'furry'; the chemicals used might also bleach or discolour timber unacceptably, which would be of particular concern if removing paint from an exposed timber-frame building.

Dipping

This is where timber components are removed from the building and immersed in a bath of chemical strippers. In addition to the above cautions, the chemical bath might also act to release the glue holding the item together and possibly attack metal fixings. Doors have often come in for this kind of

Sample panels and careful experimentation are advisable to evaluate a removal or cleaning system for optimum results. With mediaeval buildings, inside and out, there can be intricate coloured murals under later layers of paint, so care is needed to explore before stripping. Owners of listed buildings should also consult their conservation officer, as formal permission may be needed for stripping or even for a change of colour (this may also apply to other circumstances – in conservation areas and National Parks, for example).

stripping in order to expose the timber. But it needs to be remembered that in some cases paint was considered an essential part of the look of the door in past times. Without paint a door was unfinished, in which case to completely strip a door is possibly to go a step too far.

A poor show?

Stripping rarely works flawlessly and sometimes not at all ...

No good on ceilings?

For example, if emulsion paint has become thoroughly bonded to an old ceiling it may be better to give in, hope that someone invents a better method soon, and simply apply some distemper to at least get the traditional look. This can be better than making future paint removal more difficult with yet more emulsion paint. A new coat of distemper ('soft' distemper, *see below*) over old emulsion should scrub off again one day.

Partial success on external walls?

On external walls, stripping work that delivers a high percentage of removal of impermeable modern paint spread over the whole surface area can be considered a victory in most cases. The paint will most probably not all come off, but its surface should be well broken up so that no scraps remain that are greater than a few square centimetres, and so that the edges of these fragments are 'feathered' smooth and not standing up or showing as ridges. If following a strip with limewash, then the three, four or five coats of this that are necessary initially should mask the surviving scraps of modern paint if an appropriate colour is chosen – though it would be wise to pause after the first coat to make sure the limewash is sticking well to the old scraps of paint.

No point on cement

Stripping will only be appropriate for reasons of restoring a 'breathable' regime if the underlying surface is itself breathable, such as original lime render or breathable lime-pointed masonry. There is little point stripping plastic paint from cement render, because cement is also impervious. Returning to a breathable regime would require going much

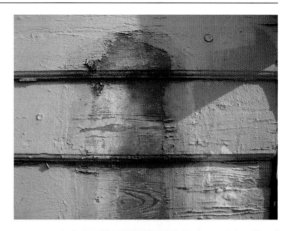

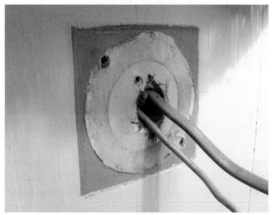

Looking behind things – in these examples a gate post and a light switch – can reveal a history of paint colours and other information. But turn off the mains first.

further and stripping off the cement, too, and replacing it with lime render.

Mainly removed, but the wall has areas of cement render

If a cottage is stripped down to mainly breathable walls but with a few patches of cement remaining, those need to be assessed to see if replacement in lime render is appropriate, or whether they can be left and overcoated with new limewash to match the rest of the cottage. Whether or not such remaining cement patches are stripped of paint, it would usually be found that limewash does not adhere well to them, so purely over these patches, it is possible to experiment with adding PVA adhesive in small quantities to the base coat of the limewash. As this additive renders the limewash effectively non-breathable, it is only for use over such cement patches and should not be allowed to cover any of the stripped lime-rendered walls, or the benefit of stripping would be lost.

If a cottage cannot be stripped successfully (it may have a pebbledash finish to which the modern paint has stuck too firmly), or the appearance of limewash is wanted without the need to strip modern plastic paint first, then this PVA additive treatment might work there, too. However, in practice it does not always last nearly as well as normal limewash does on a breathable surface, and it will make no contribution to improving the preservation of the wall.

No good at all?

If removal is not appropriate at the present time, then for exterior walls, any modern paint finishes need to be kept in good order, and any cracks and splits attended to as soon as possible. The same applies to exterior joinery. Internal walls would also benefit from a professional assessment so that a judgement can be made about the harm that might be ongoing due to any inadvertent 'sealing up' with paints there. Factors such as the existing damp management regime would have to be taken into account.

RETURN TO BREATHABLE PAINTS

Something old, something new

Following successful stripping, or if no modern paints had been applied, the cottage owner now has a greater choice of surface covering than at any time since the 1960s.

Limewash

Limewash is now available in various traditional formulations, while colours are available through traditional natural, as well as chemical, pigments. It is worth knowing that some routine modifications to make these coatings more water-resistant and less powdery can also make them less breathable, so the basic traditional product can often be the most effective for damp management. As limewash is essentially

a way of applying a liquid wearing-coat of limestone to walls, it follows that colours will usually be pastels, though quite strong colours are possible and, traditionally, natural earth pigments or vegetable dyes were used.

Limewash is simply lime putty diluted with water (*see also* Chapter 6: the drawing 'Quick Guide to Lime', page 68), coloured if necessary (traditionally with vegetable dyes or natural earths), and applied in as many coats as necessary to build up a good surface over its ideal backgrounds – lime render or traditional masonry. The mix can be textured with a little very fine sand, but this, and any pigments, should be kept to under 10 per cent of the mix ideally, and other additives avoided as some may inhibit the breathability of the mix, or otherwise weaken it. One such traditional variant was to add tallow (animal fat), which helps to create a smoother, more water-resistant finish, in much the same way as adding oil to distemper (*see below*) – but as the whole point of using limewash is usually to get the maximum breathability, adding tallow is probably too far on the road to impermeability for most 'breathing' applications.

As with lime putty, limewash is caustic until it dries, so goggles, gloves and other personal protection are necessary; however, the caustic quality can actually be an advantage, as it helps sterilize the wall of potential mould in the one application. As with other lime putty mixes, limewash can take some time (days, weeks) to dry and set firm between coats. It needs to be applied to a dampened surface, but should be kept protected from rain and sun during application and while drying, and should not be used in the months coming up to, and during winter, as it can be destroyed if still unset when there is a frost. It is, however, easy to re-coat, even repair, when the time comes, or if mistakes have been made, requiring arguably less preparation than modern masonry paint. Furthermore, limewash can be significantly cheaper to buy than modern masonry paint if using self-mixed 'bag lime' (rather than proprietary tubs of ready-coloured limewash).

If limewash is mixed on site, ensure that colour mixing is well controlled and that enough is mixed in one go to complete an elevation of the cottage – though in fact, because a natural property of lime-

Also available in plain white: extracts from the gallery of potential limewash colours and styles. The character comes from the straightforward use of the material itself, and does not require any artistic special effects during application.

wash is that its colour varies gently anyway, slight differences are not going to be too bad if managed well, or these can be deliberately dappled in by brushing on extra coats to make a feature of them.

Limewash can last as long as modern masonry paint between redecoration, even though it appears to be a softer surface; the great thing is that when it wears it does so in a way that does not endanger the wall so dramatically by trapping wet. For those interested in DIY it can be worth finding out more about limewash and how to use it properly, since the skills involved are different to, but really no more complicated than, using modern paint systems properly.

Some commercially available paints aimed at old buildings do contain lime or are based upon limewash mixes, but it can be that their other ingredients, perhaps added to make the mix feel and look more like a conventional paint, have the effect of reducing breathability. It would be a pity to have gone to all the trouble of stripping conventional paint only to replace it with an expensive and non-breathable variant of limewash. So take care when choosing limewash, and if in doubt, seek professional help. Some such paints claim that they can be used over conventional paint, in which case breathability would not be improved, of course – though if they adhered properly they might at least look a little more 'cottage' than what was there before.

Mineral paints

Instead of limewash outside, modern silicate (or 'mineral') paints are favoured by some to try to give some breathability while also facing up to extremes of exposure. Different manufacturers' formulations of mineral paints vary along with their useful degree of breathability, which of course needs to be checked. These paints can be expensive, and too tenacious for some conservationists' taste: they can be very difficult to remove, and are therefore considered to permanently change the surface.

Distempers, milk paint, low-vinyl emulsion

For inside use, the purest of the traditional paints is perhaps 'soft' distemper. Insofar as this is a way of applying chalk to walls, then this is related to lime-wash, but where limewash starts as something else and dries to chalk, distemper is (roughly speaking) powdered chalk mixed with a glue size. Used white on ceilings, the absence of built-in varnishes means it resists yellowing with age and can remain crisply snow white for many years. Also like limewash, distempers are available traditionally or chemically pigmented (pastel colours come more easily), and with additives to increase durability. These additives may reduce useful 'breathability', however.

Repainting is easy, as preparation does not have to tackle any curled edges as, again, there is no 'varnish-like' component to curl, and new coats should fill minor cracks. In addition it is kind to use, and accidental spilt spots can be brushed up from the floor even if they have dried, with less trouble than with emulsion paint. An oil-bound distemper, or one bound with casein as in milk ('milk paint' – milk can dry to form a plastic-like skin: try it in the fridge) is an alternative for areas where continual rubbing of the chalky distemper surface might prove inconvenient – although these are less breathable than 'regular', 'soft' distemper. (The wear issue might be addressed locally in other inventive ways where breathability is of prime importance, such as by providing a ventilated dado that keeps the wall behind fresh while presenting a wearable surface to the room or corridor.)

In the 'less breathable' category are the 'low vinyl' or 'obliterating' emulsions that are modern trade paints used in conventional modern construction to permit decoration when a newly plastered wall is still drying out – not ideal for a fully breathing old building, but in some circumstances a useful compromise to have available. These low-vinyl paints can be coloured to a greater range than normally offered, using the same machines that colour regular modern emulsion, but as they may start from a slightly different 'base' version, customers need to accept that the result could be a bit of a lottery, and sometimes retailers are reluctant to experiment.

Paints for joinery

Lead paint, once the 'gold standard' for joinery, is now reserved only for use under special licence terms for conservation uses on certain listed buildings. Even then the more recent formulations can seem a rather glossy and quite different product from the matt, almost powdery film still seen surviving on very old doors in the countryside. But lead paint has close modern relatives also based on linseed, and on other natural oils that use substances other than lead to try to bring back many of the traditional advantages of lead paint to old houses. A natural oil paint can be quicker and easier to prepare for redecoration as there should be less tendency for it to blister and curl, and less need for repeat undercoats or primers beyond an initial treatment of oil to the timber. However, drying times can be longer.

A good quality conventional modern paint system might read 'aluminium wood primer, undercoat and gloss top coat' (probably two coats of each); the alternative might be a linseed oil paint system, which is a coat of linseed oil followed by two or three of top coat. Subsequent recoats could be just one coat of linseed oil paint where a conventional system is likely to require at least two, since undercoat and top coat seem always to be specified. But it is important to check with manufacturers and suppliers, as each product will have different requirements in different locations and for different degrees of exposure.

Water-based paints are not always good news

A misconception has developed that water-based paints are generally breathable and therefore benign for old houses; however, while some modern water-based paints are indeed breathable, sadly some others are not usefully breathable at all. Although water-

138

based paints are gradually replacing the oil-based undercoats, semi-gloss, eggshell and even gloss paints familiar to modern DIY, in order to cut down on 'volatile organic compounds' (VOCs – being phased out for environmental reasons) in their make-up, they seem to be retaining the established modern 'dry-to-a-skin' water vapour-resisting characteristics.

'Boiled' linseed oil for bare oak

Where joinery is bare wood that has perhaps just been stripped of some flaky polyurethane varnish, or simply the carpentry of an oak frame that has perhaps been released from its bondage under 'blackboard' paint, the simplest traditional treatment can be 'boiled' linseed oil (traditionally diluted with turpentine as necessary) – the name indicates how it has been processed, and does not involve the user in any heating. This oil deflects rain without sealing up the timber harmfully; it is an almost colourless finish, but its presence turns the timber a rich, dark colour initially, then gradually wears back to show oak's naturally weathered, silver colour again. It can be applied at the regular redecoration intervals needed for the rest of the cottage; as there are no binders to give it 'body' it would not crack, but an intermediate application can be beneficial and, apart from access, is relatively easy to do.

'Boiled' linseed oil is being applied to the oak at the top of this picture; it may also have been applied to this post years before, but it wears away completely after several decades. This single application pictured went on to retain its colour for over six years – like other traditional finishes, it does not crack and blister and suddenly become a liability: it simply and gradually fades away.

CONVENTIONAL MODERN PAINTS

Selective uses

For joinery

Although it can be harmful to seal up joinery with conventional modern oil alkyd or water-based 'plastic' gloss paints, not every last modern paint is inappropriate for joinery, and there are some modern formulations of paint that can be useful. Modern opaque stains that can be more 'breathable' than gloss paint, and paints that claim to be 'vapour permeable', have been around for a long time – though for some reason their potential advantages have often been overlooked on old buildings, perhaps because of their cost. But breathability and vapour permeability are relative terms and, pending some meaningful standard measurement of them appearing on the pack-

aging, owners should take professional advice to weigh up actual long-term cost and breathability with the traditional-style natural oil alternatives.

Where conventional modern paint is not being stripped from existing painted joinery, then repainting with a good quality and reasonably 'flexible' modern conventional paint is usually sensible. But this has to be kept in very good order, and cracks should be dealt with immediately between decorations in order to stop damp becoming trapped. That is not always possible, which is why traditional, more breathable paints can offer a more relaxed alternative where they can be used.

For ironwork

The robust ironwork that forms, for example, the gates and rainwater goods that come with cottages, can be protected by starting with a modern 'zinc' metal primer that has a protective chemical action on iron. This has to be applied to clean, dry, grease-free bare metal using the number of coats specified by the manufacturer. That may be followed by a couple of coats of the marine quality coating known as mica-

Above is conventional modern masonry paint over pebbledash; beneath is new limewash on lime render. Where significant repairs are made to an old wall it can make sense to revert to traditional finishes – even if only as an experiment against future stripping of the full wall. Where stripping of modern masonry paint is not appropriate, perhaps because there are cement finishes under the paint that cannot be changed for now, then conventional modern masonry paint needs to be reapplied and kept in good order so as to minimize water ingress.

ceous iron oxide paint (MIO), checking the compatibility of this and other coats with the manufacturer. If a matt micaceous finish is used, this can be followed by ordinary oil gloss paint to give the desired finish colour, otherwise a self-coloured glossy micaceous finish may be satisfactory – and that smooth finish would be more appropriate as a wearing surface inside gutters and hoppers.

It is important that the initial paint job is thorough, and in the case of rainwater goods, that the back of pipes and the underside of gutters are very thoroughly painted. In most cases this would mean dismantling: reassembling traditional gutters with new, special, non-hardening mastic for gutters and stainless steel bolts should make the next round of redecoration that much easier. And that could be some time ahead, as the decorative regime described above has been known to work effectively for a satisfyingly long period of years, with only local chip repair and a new top coat at the time of each general household redecoration in between times.

Actual results will depend not only on the quality of work and exposure, but in future on the make-up of the paint, as it is likely that such high performance paints will have to be significantly reformulated to meet environmental requirements on 'volatile organic compound' (VOC) content. It is wise always to check for compatibility between primer, intermediate and top coats with the respective manufacturers to ensure there would be no adverse reaction between

the coats; this can be doubly important once the composition of the paints changes.

COLOUR

There are paint ranges marketed for their traditional, period or heritage colours that are not necessarily offering the traditional formulations of the paint itself that should offer traditional benefits such as breathability – this means they could just be modern, non-breathable paints in colours selected from a traditional palette. Cottage owners need to ask if the paint is really traditional and breathable, or just conventionally modern and impervious. Genuinely traditional paints, traditionally pigmented, tend to have to come in colours that would have been possible in the past. Limewashes and distempers are basically liquid limestone or chalk, and so these start from white and work up through pastel shades.

Traditionally in many historical paints, some pigments, blue for example, were rare and expensive for a long time, while others, some shades of purple, were more or less unattainable until chemical dyes appeared popularly (from the late nineteenth century). This may account for planning authorities' resistance to the over-use of those colours in conservation areas (colour changes can require formal consent in such areas and on a listed building, and it can save trouble to ask the conservation officer first).

Limewash and distempers would have been

coloured with 'natural earths' as used by artists, though we can assume these would have been too expensive for cottagers unless they were freely and locally available. Cottage colours may have been from the local minerals or an abundant plant. In many areas an appropriate colour can be found by a little historical research. If a locality has become famous for one colour it is probable that modern paint manufacturers latched on to that long ago as a marketing tool, and the colour may have transmuted into something that no local vegetable substance could reasonably be capable of. If in doubt, start from a subtle shade.

When using limewash for the first time, the base coats do not really need to be coloured at all (they can anyway look almost transparent until dry) as there could yet be several finishing coats on top, depending on conditions. So colour can be gradually applied experimentally coat by coat until something satisfying results. But remember that with limewash the colour will change in time on drying and subsequent re-wetting by rain, and also in mixing, between batches.

There has been a tendency for limewash to be quite deeply coloured in recent years, and this is probably more a reflection of the influence of

If I could turn back time

If owners are fortunate enough to have an old cottage that has never had modern paints and finishes, they should still be aware that even amongst traditional paints there are varieties that are more, and less, breathable than others; therefore correct advice is always appropriate when selecting paints. At the present time there is increasing variety in the types of traditional paints on offer, and the days of 'no choice but modern' are probably over for good as many traditionally formulated paints may also still promise sustainability benefits. However, do not expect to be able to find the right paint in ordinary shops or DIY stores yet, though it may not be long.

Removing inappropriate paints – those that are unhelpfully sealing up an old cottage, retaining damp and preventing it from 'breathing' – can be very beneficial. However, as the processes are expensive it can pay to have the cottage professionally assessed first to see if any other factors might make stripping less worthwhile than other measures that might reopen the fabric to breathability. There are plenty of things other than paint that can have altered the original make-up of a cottage over the years, and it might be in some cases that paint removal will make no real difference. But where circumstances are right, the difference can be as refreshing as the coming of spring.

The removal of modern paint layers that are deemed unhelpful cannot yet be reliably achieved without also removing the original

'benign' layers underneath. (Note, too, that both the traditional and more recent layers might contain harmful substances, which will affect the choice of stripping method.) This might be a pity, because each layer contains interesting forensic information about the colour of the cottage at different times in its past, and the hidden marks and stains can reveal something of its usage. That interest is part of what makes a cottage valuable. Paint stripping wipes away that archaeology for ever, and that is something to bear in mind when making the decision. At the very least some patches ought to be left undisturbed and labelled for future preservation. But some very careful investigation is often also required, because what looks like a cottage today might have been part of a richer building in the past, or home to some special type of use. It is quite common for the internal and external walls of humble-looking cottages to have been painted in the Middle Ages with garish mediaeval colours, or even to have patterns and portraits and heraldry still hidden under later layers of paint.

Paint removal on an old building is only doing any technical good it if is followed by the application of a traditionally breathable quality of paint. Stripping all the old paint just to replace it with modern paint again will have taken away history and then reinstated the potential for long-tem decay, so is probably a complete waste of money.

modern paint colours, or perhaps middle-aged memories of the 1970s, rather than representing the Middle Ages. Heavily coloured limewash can shed its pigment in an unsightly way over timbers and joinery due to rain washing, causing staining (plain white limewash may also 'run', but that should wear off).

These colours happen to sit together well, even if the paints and tints may not all be traditional. Sometimes agreement needs to be reached so that colours do not clash, sometimes a whole block really benefits from being a uniform colour, and sometimes there will be traditional colour ranges that are locally preferred. As cottages become more valued for their antiquity we may see a return to more authentic paints and colours in the near future that could leave some of these modern finishes looking a little more brash than perhaps they do to people at present.

CHAPTER THIRTEEN

Fungus and Other Bogeymen
Putting rot into perspective

BE AFRAID, BUT BE REASONABLY AFRAID

Most cottages have timber roofs, internal walls, floors and staircases, and in a good many the whole structural frame is made of wood. Timber is a natural material, and nature has devised thousands of special plants and animals whose function is to help recycle dead trees from forests – by eating them. Unfortunately, some of these creatures became bored with forests and are instead intent on the disposal of the dead trees that make up our homes. Worse still, climate change threatens to unleash a new wave of timber-hungry pests that are waiting just across the Channel.

Some of the changes made to cottages in the twentieth century – ones that resulted in sealing in dampness, reducing ventilation and increasing internal temperatures – could have increased the likelihood of colonization by fungus and insects by creating the perfect environment for them. Then some of the twentieth century's favourite remedies for insect and fungal attack could have brought about even more destruction by requiring the frantic cutting out and burning of anything in the immediate vicinity that might possibly be perceived to one day threaten to invoke any written guarantees.

Know thine enemy

Established timber threats in the UK include fungi and insects, notably beetles. The beetles are often called 'woodworm' because in the larval stages of their lives they burrow tunnels inside wood. The furniture beetle (*Anobium punctatum*) and deathwatch beetle (*Xestobium rufovillosum*) are perhaps the most commonly known. Of the fungi, dry rot (*Serpula lacrymans*) has the most melodramatic reputation. There are many other species of insects and fungi that can drain the substance from timber in houses, too many to list here, but the methods of coping with them have much in common.

Drastic measures

The twentieth-century solution to insect and fungal pests was to try to kill them, comprehensively and with all the subtlety of twentieth-century warfare. This might have involved spraying or fumigating whole areas of houses against insects using highly toxic chemicals, and at one time there was apparently little thought about the effect on human occupants in the long term. Chemical spraying did not address the fact that deathwatch beetle larvae can spend years safely inside the timber munching wood, and that when they emerge as adult flying insects, they can reuse old exit holes, avoiding altogether the poisons laid for them.

In the case of dry rot, vast chunks of the fabric around the infection site were routinely chopped out and burnt, so destroying parts of the building that was supposed to be under preservation. That was last century's approach, yet there are still those eager to do more of the same today, so it does make sense to seek out professional advisers and contractors who are in touch with present-day thinking – not least because a more conservative approach could be less expensive.

Current thinking

Building conservationists queried the poisonous and destructive methods of treatment devised in the last century, and wanted lower-key methods of control. There were also general health concerns about toxic spraying and a general dislike of the 'just in case' ripping out of nearby fabric that had not yet been affected. Some of the older, destructive treatment regimes were, regrettably, sold on the back of ignorance and fear. The newer treatments tend to be more scientific, exploiting particular weaknesses in pest species that can enable the development, for example, of insect traps, the exploitation of natural predators, or the generation of conditions in the fabric on a permanent or temporary basis that, while harmless to humans, are discouraging or lethal to the pests. The latest generation of toxic sprays are still used if absolutely necessary, even by conservationists, but in a controlled and targeted way. But there are simple practical first steps that anyone can take. First of all, more about how the troublemakers operate.

Mainly about beetles

Beetle attack

There is no doubt that, given time, timber-consuming fungi and insects can reduce a piece of wood to a dangerously frail shadow of its former self. But particularly with beetles, not all species of timber are susceptible to all forms of attack, and of those species at risk it is often only a part of the timber (for example the softer 'sapwood') that is particularly attractive to the pests.

If the signs of insect attack are identified it makes sense to establish whether the infestation is still active (beetle colonies that died out years ago never bothered to hang up a 'gone away' sign by filling in their flight holes and sweeping up after themselves), and whether the damage done so far has actually compromised the structural integrity of the cottage in any way. This information needs to come from an impartial expert on timber decay, and perhaps also a conservation-accredited structural engineer, each of whom might possibly be able to offer reassurance, or low-key solutions that are more attractive than launching into costly 'gung-ho' remedial work that may not strictly be necessary.

Furniture beetle and deathwatch beetle

Householders can themselves look out for some of the signs that an expert would need to know about: is there dust around the flight holes (up to 2mm diameter) of furniture beetles in spring and summer? Can deathwatch beetles be heard tapping at those same times? Are their flight holes (around 3mm) reopened the following year? (that is, if they have been deliberately blocked by householders with paper or wax). Can the carcasses of deathwatch be found lying around in summer? Deathwatch colonies are sometimes accompanied by smaller, shiny blue-black beetles (*Korynetes caeruleus*) that are supposed to feed on deathwatch larvae; these predators may be found more often than the deathwatch themselves and are, naturally, useful. Spiders, if you can stand them, are another useful predator.

There is logic in conservative treatments for insect attacks. Wood-boring beetles such as the deathwatch have wings and fly about freely all over the house looking for another beetle to mate with, so they are not going to be hanging about looking for poisoned wood to die on. It seems more reasonable to ensure that timbers are dry enough to be unattractive to them for egg-laying purposes, rather than poison every other insect that comes into contact with sprayed timber. Sprayed insecticides are considered to be of limited use against deathwatch beetles (*see above*), but unfortunately sprayed timber can kill the spiders that might otherwise catch and eat the beetles in flight, and can kill the other predator beetles that have developed a taste for their young.

Ensuring that timber dries out is a very gradual process. It may be tedious for someone who owns a cottage not to be able to deal with it in five minutes and have a piece of paper to wave at the next purchaser to prove an end to the problem. But that may only ever be a paper exercise and not a realistic option. In the lifespan of the cottage a decade or so is not long to wait, provided there is enough substance left in the timber and the colony is in decline. Because wood-boring beetles have wings, even if it were possible to somehow sterilize a cottage completely, a new colony of beetles could fly in the window at any time.

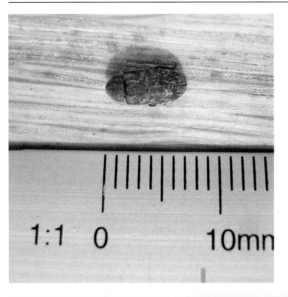

Wood-boring beetles include the deathwatch (top left), about 6mm long and with 2–3mm relatively clean flight holes, and the furniture beetle which is a little smaller and with 1–2mm flight holes accompanied by piles of wood dust (top right, lower left). Deathwatch beetles make a rapid tapping noise in spring, which is also when furniture beetles make their dusty piles. They are both then flying about looking for a mate, and both have dull brown wing cases. The beetle shown with the shiny blue-black livery (Korynetes caeruleus) (lower right) is thought to attack the deathwatch's young, and borrows its tunnels to do so. Talk nicely to these ones, they seem to be on your side.

Mainly about fungi

Gardeners who have tried growing edible mushrooms will know that this is possible, but not necessarily easy: if the conditions are not right they just won't happen. The same is true of the problem fungi that threaten houses: they are only there because the conditions are just right. Mess up those ideal conditions and, logically, the fungi should wither and die.

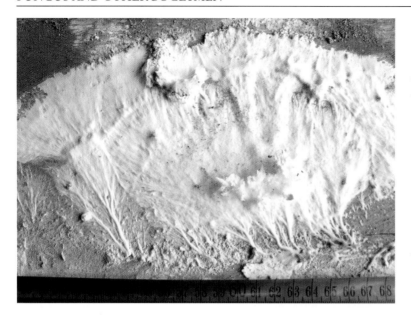

If a fungus is found that is soft and squashy, then it is being nurtured rather too freely with water. Remove the fungi by all means, but taking away the water is the way to kill them, and that may mean turning your attention to roof leaks and to providing proper ventilation. The same wet, warm conditions also encourage wood-boring beetles either directly, or as a result of the fungi having pre-digested the timber for them.

Usually that means stopping their water supply, since fungi, like insects, thrive on timber that has been made extra digestible by being moist. This is why a lot of 'wet rots' occur in cellars. Improving ventilation, stopping leaks and keeping other vulnerable organic materials out of damp places will help discourage the growth of fungi.

Dry rot

Dry rot got its name because it was thought to tolerate slightly lower levels of (nevertheless excess) dampness, and because it can cross barren, apparently dry territory in search of more water. It was this creeping, B movie-like behaviour that so frightened people and caused so much destructive 'repair' in the past. But a common-sense approach that is gaining ground is to cut off the water supply and rely on nature to do the rest. Anyone who regularly forgets to water houseplants should understand this. Some maintain that leaving tendrils and spores in the fabric risks future outbreaks, and this idea can lead to all sorts of destruction in the name of 'cleansing'. But a new outbreak could happen in any case whenever there is enough damp, because the air contains numerous opportunist fungal spores, and it does not seem possible to eradicate those.

More on fungi

The identification of fungi is not straightforward, since each may have a different form, according to the stage at which it is found. Some of the signs of dry rot are difficult to distinguish from other fungi, and this can, innocently or otherwise, lead to unnecessary and extreme remedies being sold to householders. Dry rot has engendered rather emotional reactions, and this probably has something to do with it being cited in the demolition of stately homes in the 1950s. There were probably other reasons at the time that such drastic action was taken, and the idea of a fungus consuming a whole stately home beyond reasonable repair may not be so sustainable today.

Asking an independent timber decay consultant if they offer an assessment service for samples may prove a cost-effective first step. The classic dry rot 'fruiting body' is supposed to be about the size of a dinner plate with a whitish rim and a rust-red powdery centre, but nature is not always so obliging as to reproduce textbook examples, and other stages in its life look radically different. Signs that fungi, including dry rot, may be present can also include timber that is crazed on its surface or appears to be cracking into cubes, due to the substance – that is, the body or 'goodness' – having been leeched from the wood. The same experts may be able to propose a sensible course of action, which is likely to begin with drying the fungus's habitat.

THE FUTURE

It has been suggested that one English beetle pest, the house longhorn beetle, owes its existence in the UK to hitching a ride in nineteenth-century seamen's chests, and that once in the country, it has been restricted by climate from spreading much beyond its adopted home counties habitat. But climate change could be responsible for a redistribution of such insect pests in the future. Deathwatch beetle has not been thought a big problem in Scotland so far, but what about in a warmer future? Termites are said to be spreading north in France and are reputed to have made at least temporary bridgeheads around some southern English ports. It may not be long before established patterns of infestation are upset, and the future of the UK's historic buildings depends on some fast and inventive thinking.

It is probably just as well that we have learned some of the lessons of the twentieth century, and also that our neighbours have come to terms with the problem ahead of us, or all our cottages might be demolished in a frenzy of termite fear.

Things not to do

Paradoxically, many modern paints, plasters, renders and mortars that are routinely used to 'improve' old houses can actually seal them up and trap the moisture that attracts rot and insects, while central heating increases their chances of survival. Appropriate conservation care all round is a way to ensure a healthy future for an old house, and traditional 'breathable' finishes can give the fabric of an old house a real chance of getting rid of excess moisture that would otherwise invite pests to take up residence. Central heating applied too indiscrimi-

nately can raise the temperature of the naturally damper extremities of the house – cellars, roof-spaces and exterior walls – to a level that is the perfect environment for wood-consuming insects and fungi.

Things to do

Having one's home slowly and unnecessarily destroyed by insects and fungi is not pleasant, but it is important not to be panicked into overkill, which could result in even more parts of the house being destroyed, expensively and unnecessarily, by contractors. At least the insects and fungi do it for free. Get conservation-based, impartial advice to find out if there is a problem, how serious it really is, and what all the current options are for reducing or eliminating it. Too much moisture is the root cause of most of these problems, so the causes of excess dampness need to be addressed in any solution (*see* Chapter 4: The Air That I Breathe, for more on this). Sustained, gentle (not fast and furious) drying and ventilation would normally be part of the whole remedy.

Once any structural issues have been established and dealt with, then be prepared for today's more intelligent solutions to take time to work. Sites where fungi had grown should of course be cleaned and monitored, along with other at-risk areas, and signs of beetle infestation checked in anticipation of a gradual decline in evidence over the years.

Part of the reason for over-reaction in the past was perhaps the pursuit of certainty in a solution. With the benefit of experience we can see that even some of those over-the-top solutions have not always been effective, so it requires a more balanced attitude to reach a solution that is a good compromise between effectiveness and reasonableness. This might involve step-by-step exploratory treatments, or the building owner accepting less than 100 per cent annihilation from gentler or more experimental methods, while welcoming any improvement that has been bought without extreme sacrifice.

IN THE YEAR 2525
Preparing for the future

Plenty of cottages claim to have survived for five hundred years already, if the dates inscribed on their walls are all to be believed. Many can be identified as having done so by analysis of their construction. It is a sad fact that some misplaced twentieth-century maintenance will have accelerated decay in some, but provided those lessons are acted upon, then with proper care most of our cottages might reasonably expect to survive the next five hundred years. But how much will cottages have to change to earn a useful place in the far future? Or can they only survive as museum pieces? Perhaps technology will fix all the environmental and energy problems we are now faced with, and cottages will continue their voyage through time as romantic lifestyle accessories? Or perhaps country cottages will all be drafted back to their original purpose for housing farm workers, as rising sea levels shrink our islands and the pressure on new, low technology food production increases?

It is quite possible, as we face an uncertain beginning to the twenty-first century, that the dwindling of fuel and fertilizers derived from oil, and the rising cost of transporting food from overseas, will force some return of agricultural labour to the British countryside. Perhaps this will happen along with the adoption of some low cost 'intermediate' technology. Whether or not your heart misses a beat at the prospect of little red tractors and morris dancers everywhere, this is not likely to be a romantic, theme-park turning back of the clock.

There are some serious issues to be faced, and to help solve them, our old cottages can teach us much about how sustainability was handled in buildings in the past – at a time when those skills were important for survival. Old cottages could find themselves acting as templates for a new era of locally sourced building that does not damage the environment and blends with its surroundings: old technology applied to new buildings. We would certainly be stupid not to pay attention to the lessons of a thousand years of sustainable building.

Whatever the future holds, we have to cope with the present, and that means making sure that existing cottages are run as efficiently as possible. We can certainly try to leave behind the wasteful habits picked up last century. But what else is reasonable in this changeover period? The chapters in this fourth section examine some of the practical limitations to be faced when trying to 'green' a cottage according to today's understanding of sustainability.

Chapter 14 Future Past – *Understanding sustainability*
Chapter 15 Hot Love – *Home insulation pros and cons*

CHAPTER FOURTEEN

Future Past
Understanding sustainability

ENERGY IN COTTAGES

Cottages have long been way ahead of our present attempts at sustainable building. Few, if any, of the modern templates for sustainable mass housing can free themselves from dependence in some way on energy and material supplies that are intrinsically unsustainable. The world that allowed cottages to be built totally sustainably might have gone now too, but cottages have a lead in having been truly sustainably built, and they have the potential to keep returning that investment for centuries. If a cottage is to stay ahead of the game, it will need its occupants to address some of the environmentally questionable energy consumption that they have brought into the cottage – in particular those high levels of heating using fossil fuels. Part of that challenge is to find ways of adapting cottages towards the twenty-first century's idea of low energy living, without robbing them of their history and beauty.

These cottages are about a dozen miles apart and it would not be unreasonable to suppose that they might have looked much more similar when they were first built. The renewals, replacements and redecorations that are inevitable over time mean that little of what we see on the surface is likely actually to be as old as the first build, and we don't really know what that first build looked like in detail. Would the original builders recognize their cottages? Might the present occupants recognize their cottages if they saw them in 200 years? How will future developments and needs alter such cottages, and who will decide whether their character is being lost or enhanced with each step?

Frugal or wasteful?

There was usually little option but for cottages to be entirely sustainably built. They used strictly local materials, and most were strangers to any kind of fossil fuel for a long time. That was a matter of necessity, not choice. The degree of sustainability and energy self-sufficiency represented by a mediaeval cottage in its heyday can only be dreamed about by the designers of today's green housing who are tied to factories, transport and remotely sourced components. Given also that a cottage might have lasted five hundred years or more, then it can hardly be accused of squandering the 'embodied' energy in the materials that it contains. Few are likely to claim that a modern 'green' home has a design life of five hundred years, so it appears that in the war on waste, cottages proudly wear a chestful of medals.

But heating is the big issue now: old housing stock is sometimes condemned for being poorly insulated and liable to use more fuel. But if they were built at a time when total sustainability was the only option, how can they stand accused of breaking the rules of sustainability now? It is not our cottages that have changed and suddenly become unsustainable, it is our own society's behaviour that has become unsustainable, its love of convenient automatic heating and its desire to dress for summer even in winter. Over the years, owners of old properties have abandoned the original open hearth 'carbon-neutral' wood fires in favour of fossil-fuel central heating … and then turned up the thermostat.

Open fires were also a vital part of the mechanism that ventilated a cottage, whereas central heating prefers to be sealed up, as in modern houses, and this might generate decay in a cottage and cause extra resources to be used up in repairs. But open wood fires, or even modern log-burning boilers, need reasonably constant attention, so it is also a matter of lifestyle: we don't want to be chained to a cottage, but we want it to be instantly warm when we turn up. Cottages were built sustainably by people who lived sustainably. Evidently we do not live sustainably, so which of us is going to have to change?

Compromises

To avoid damp-induced decay, old buildings need to 'breathe' rather than be sealed up like a modern building. This is not just having airy rooms, it means ensuring that water vapour can migrate out through finishes and walls, even floors and ceilings. Limiting ventilation is one of the tricks that new housing uses to appear 'leakproof', but this can be harmful to a cottage (let alone us, the occupants). Also there is often limited scope for applying high levels of insulation in a cottage because there is simply no space, with current insulating technology, to allow for it without blocking ventilation paths or masking the original features that make a cottage a cottage. On top of this, measures such as ordinary double glazing would also strip a cottage of much of the character and authenticity that makes it desirable.

The measures that may be appropriate to upgrade a more modern house to suit our relatively pampered twenty-first-century ways could bring about the instant disfigurement and long-term destruction of cottages and other old buildings. This is not a win-win solution. So if the big issue is fuel consumption, then maybe can that be limited in other ways? It is possible to live in a slightly draughty, minimally modernized cottage and to spend no more on heating than a family in a small and highly insulated modern house. It is possible, and a lot of people do it already: they cope by accepting that they are not going to be so warm in winter. But that just isn't likely to be everybody's cup of tea.

A possible future

However, we could meet half way. The idea that we can lounge around indoors in a British winter while dressed only for the tropics is unsustainable, and might soon become very unfashionable. To avoid the numbing cold and potential price increases of fossil fuel, our cottage family of the near future may have converted their oil boiler to vegetable-sourced oils, or have installed an automatic boiler that burns processed 'biomass' (biomass is the name given to anything organic and replenishable that burns well, from wood chips to processed chicken droppings …). Such fuels are closer to the goal of being 'carbon neutral', which here means their use as fuel would not create a net increase in the amount of the greenhouse gas carbon dioxide, the exhaust gas that comes from our bodies and our machines that is accused of climate change.

The woodpile could be making a return to Britain's cottages if this carbon-neutral fuel is exploited once more for regular domestic heating. Cottages do, after all, generally have the chimneys that many modern homes lack.

Carbon-neutral fuel may be fine in theory, but there are other problems, in that growing and processing some of these 'biomass' fuels displaces food production, and also these 'substitute' fuels are unlikely to be all that cheap if everyone in the world is clamouring for them. Perhaps these fuels might end up reserved for use by older buildings to maintain a balance of heating, cost and environmental protection that is equivalent to modern properties.

In preparing for low energy living there would also be lofts to insulate, and possibly some discreet internal secondary glazing to install – all carefully designed to maintain the cottage's essential 'breathability' and to be as inconspicuous as possible. Curtains, blinds and shutters would all be used to

Cottages were originally never plugged into any mains or plumbed in to sewers (some may still not be to this day) and so they are well used to being independent. It is up to us to come up with solutions with our technology, which match the ingenuity of the solutions our forbears created with theirs. Cottages have been waiting for us to catch up with their lead in self-sufficiency.

their maximum heat-retaining potential, and perhaps soon, solar collectors may sprout in quiet, sunny corners of gardens rather than adorning rooftops, where they might not only attract the disapproval of planning authorities but also devalue a cottage's appeal.

Can technology help?

Potentially, technology could help us get much of our household energy from renewable resources, and assist our design, use and repair of artefacts for maximum total efficiency – but not overnight. The technologies – such as panels to generate electricity from sunlight, or domestic wind turbines – are still being refined, and at present may struggle to pay back the financial outlay – not to mention the environmental costs of manufacture, installation and maintenance – through generated electricity. That will surely change, helped by the momentum of people prepared to buy the products at this early stage without realistically expecting much of a financial return perhaps.

We should be very wary of making irreversible adaptations to old properties while these technologies develop, since today's clumsy, ugly solution may easily develop into something more graceful in the near future. We may have become an unsustainable society but we can still be quite inventive. What is perhaps more difficult to change is our society's economy, which appears to involve a desire for continual growth fuelled by obsolescence and replacement rather than adaptation and repair. Without finding other planets to sell things to, and

perhaps another one to mine for raw materials, and another to use for landfill, this obsession with ever-increasing growth seems ultimately a bubble that must burst, and this means that as a global society we are going to have to start living within our means. The way cottage dwellers did.

There are many things that manufacturers can do to adjust to a future where resources are more highly valued, but arguably the most important include making products long lasting, adaptable, and easy and economical to repair with local skills. Cottages were designed for this, and that is why we should be learning from them, not knocking them about until their lessons are unreadable.

Self help

While it may be novel to some, the idea of sustainability has been aired quite thoroughly before, during the 1970s when concerns were also felt over fuel shortages and the environment. The 1970s was a time when much mainstream industry did not seem to take up the sustainability challenge seriously (maybe it held its breath until the 1980s?), and also a time when people would more often engage in DIY out of economic necessity or in dogged pursuit of personal achievement. As a result the 1970s and early 1980s saw a number of enthusiasts writing books and articles about how to gather and conserve natural energy through home-engineered projects. These would now need to be viewed through a twenty-first-century filter of awareness and sensitivities in those things that have changed significantly since the 1970s (for example, building conservation, official building regulations, and health and safety).

But such pioneers showed that it was, for example, technically possible to build one's own solar water-heating system out of old plumbing components, long before mainstream industry had seen any profit in making mass-market purpose-built equipment. Or how about a windmill that turns wind into electricity using a second-hand alternator from a bus? The advantages of DIY remain, that labour is freely given and recycled 'junk' parts are cheap-ish too, which means that running repairs will not necessarily involve waiting three months for a specialist part to be delivered and a hefty call-out charge. Of course, junk is dependent upon a consumer society and is

not inexhaustible itself, but like so many green initiatives, it could all be a useful start.

The technology behind a basic solar hot water system is not complex; there were kits being sold in Australia and the United States around a hundred years ago to exploit their sunny climates. A modern householder would need to be careful to work within their personal DIY capabilities and to research the design in a modern context, but they could find that sustainability need not always mean an expensive outlay, with the economic and environmental break-even point a receding speck on the horizon.

Similar self-help ventures are no doubt possible in the newly fashionable greywater recycling and in the rediscovered backwaters of rainwater harvesting – providing that the trouble is taken to research and understand the technicalities and hazards, and that experimenters do not become over-ambitious and flout common sense and regulation. But if all this sounds as if it will cast a post-apocalyptic shadow on the cottage dream and involve too much time in the shed, then there are other things that we can all do – starting with understanding the problems and separating out the hype.

Greenwash, fashion and bandwagons

Confusion

The causes of global warming are confusing and evidently not yet entirely agreed upon even by experts, but governments seem generally to have decided to point the finger at carbon dioxide emissions from burning fossil fuels. Allied to this is the logic that fossil fuels, which are in practical terms a one-off and non-renewable resource, must eventually run out if we keep using them at present rates. In the meantime they are likely to become increasingly more expensive to obtain and use. Many of the officially sponsored responses to the climate change crisis are therefore aimed squarely at reducing fossil fuel use and finding alternatives.

What constitutes 'sustainable' behaviour is not easy to define. Day by day, the type of questions that consumers regularly ask seem to get different answers as all the implications of the problem sink in. Is it best to get a new energy-efficient product and scrap the old one, or is it better to keep the old one in use

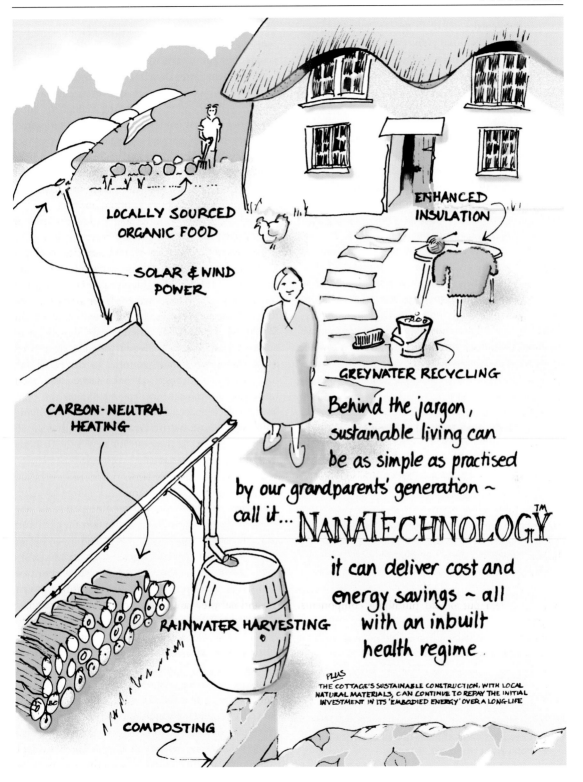

LOCALLY SOURCED
ORGANIC FOOD

SOLAR & WIND
POWER

ENHANCED
INSULATION

GREYWATER RECYCLING

CARBON · NEUTRAL
HEATING

Behind the jargon,
sustainable living can
be as simple as practised
by our grandparents' generation ~
call it... NANATECHNOLOGY™

it can deliver cost and
energy savings ~ all
with an inbuilt
health regime

RAINWATER HARVESTING

PLUS
THE COTTAGE'S SUSTAINABLE CONSTRUCTION, WITH LOCAL
NATURAL MATERIALS, CAN CONTINUE TO REPAY THE INITIAL
INVESTMENT IN ITS 'EMBODIED ENERGY' OVER A LONG LIFE

COMPOSTING

153

and get the best use out of all the 'embodied' energy and transport costs that went into making it? Is a simpler, repairable artefact better or worse for the environment than a more efficient, but more complex one that is not ever going to be practically repairable? Is it rational to pin too much hope for future home-building on 'sustainable' products that are really waste products of, perhaps, a flawed system? For example, the inventive uses of straw bales and old tyres for building 'green' housing are evidently dependent for their economy on their availability as waste or by-products of a farming, industrial and transport system that is apparently not operating efficiently enough to reabsorb them itself.

Logically, if over-enthusiastic consumption of goods, materials and transport has somehow led to global warming, then a sensible response would be to reduce that consumption, eliminate waste and to ensure efficient use and longer life from the products we already have. This could, however, be unattractive to industry and to governments, and could alter countries' economies. In the building industry new 'bolt on' energy-efficient products and technologies

are being promoted that certainly appear to enable buildings to operate more efficiently, for example by generating 'free' electricity from sun and wind.

A problem with these new technologies is that some are complex, and are unproven over a long period: will they give service long enough to repay their financial and environmental cost? What exactly was that cost in energy, transport and those rare minerals involved? Do we care that global competition for these resources may place people, who are already in a political kind of power vacuum, in a more literal kind of power vacuum?

A proportionate response

It will probably be some time before the problem facing the planet is clearly understood, alternative responses thoroughly analysed, technological responses proven, and clear guidance given on how the ordinary householder can cope with this big but ill-defined issue. Governments will doubtless be giving a lead, and it is hoped they are to be well informed from balanced sources. In the meantime the owners of cottages can take some inspiration from the attitudes of earlier inhabitants of their homes who managed 100 per cent sustainable living quite well. Those old-timers might wonder what all the fuss is about, as some of our new 'eco' ideas are really their everyday habits … recycled.

Avoidance of waste and recycling
The need to recycle too many things outside the home or consign them to landfill is to some extent an admission of defeat. Food waste is comparable to energy waste, and morally worse. It can be avoided by good planning, then inedible waste can be composted and containers reused for home-grown food. Unrepairable manufactured goods can be deconstructed for parts, and worn out clothing and worn fabrics might be cut down for other uses. Working artefacts and sound clothing can be donated to charity or sold at car boot sales, where interesting incoming recycling opportunities may be found. Only the last option did not exist in the Middle Ages, but putting aside for a moment the 'car' bit, car boot sales seem to have rekindled some of the zest of a mediaeval market, and they must keep no end of stuff out of landfill.

Dedicated follower of fashion

It is now cool to be green. Being green is really about consuming less and conserving more, as environmentalists have been saying for a long time. Now others, who enjoy consuming, also want to be seen to be doing something green. There can be valid applications of the new energy-saving technology, but there can also be unproductive uses: buying wind turbines that are unsuitable for crowded-in rooftops, or investing in costly photovoltaic panels to generate electricity if they are only used to offset wasteful use, are examples of personal applications that would be missing the point. These are merely consuming valuable materials and manufacturing effort in a way that gives no net benefit to the planet or its people. Arguably, it is conspicuous consumption that has brought about the problem, so to lash out with more conspicuous consumption does not seem at all cool. Not even tepid.

Flood plains were well understood by our forbears, who were better connected with nature, and so their buildings are less likely to be built where there was a frequent risk. Whether or not mankind has forced climate change now, there has evidently always been variety in climate, to which our ancestors simply had to adapt, as we shall have to, too.

Reduction of energy use and conservation of water

These are well publicized ideas, and the various household energy and water conserving techniques do not need restating here. A cottage existed without services 'laid on', so the modern cottager can reflect that their home was once viable without them, and that all use of them is a luxury. Without stinting oneself, or freezing, it can be useful to remember that once upon a time the use of the fire for cooking or heating water had to be planned so that it was used immediately, that lights would only be used in occupied rooms, that drinking water would be drawn as needed, and rainwater collected for gardens and laundry.

Journeys beyond the village boundary were planned so as to carry out several tasks at once if possible. Housework and the cultivation of fruit and vegetables, in addition to manual work to earn a living, were enough exercise to keep most people reasonably fit without the need for exercise machines. A mediaeval person did not have the option to leave a tap running or to make four return trips a day to the nearest town, and because we have the option to do these things easily, we have to stop ourselves and think to avoid such waste.

New machinery

If a cottager in history were considering investing in some new equipment it is probable that, having little disposable income, its potential benefits would be very thoroughly explored before the decision to buy was made. People nowadays may feel able to follow fashion or to buy things they do not really need on a whim, and while these purchases might keep the economy turning, they also keep the carbon dioxide pumping out of factories and transport.

As mentioned above, new energy-generating devices come with an initial outlay to repay – not just of money, but also in terms of the materials, energy and transport that went into creating them. Just as the old-time cottager would have considered whether a new scythe or a new harness was going to improve productivity, so the modern cottager needs to assess whether new domestic machinery will pay back the initial investment of money and resources with interest, or whether it is just a yearning for something that looks novel.

155

HEATING AND INSULATION

Cottages can be very sustainable, but what if they are also very cold?

Insulation and its effect on breathability

Insulation has to be sensibly applied to suit the circumstances of each surface in an old property; one of those circumstances is 'appearance', which can be lost under new finishes. The familiar cry for 'breathability' in old buildings should not be forgotten, because sealing them up with misapplied insulation could quickly lead to stagnant dampness followed by rot. Unaided, the innocent householder can be tempted into buying reasonable-sounding products that might have unfortunate side effects.

Anywhere in the house, owners should be very wary of anything that is sprayed on to, wraps, or otherwise encapsulates timber (or most of the other traditional building materials), depriving it of ventilation. The various foams, sprayed insulations and sheets of foil and plastic might have their place in new construction, but expert guidance is needed with older property. Insulating an older property in ways that will not interfere with other essential aspects of its performance is not simple.

As with the twentieth century's dalliance with plastic paints and cement mortars on old buildings, things can look fairly stable on the surface, but it is behind that, out of sight, that the damage could be occurring.

The breathability of insulation

Since cottage owners have an expensive investment to protect, it is perfectly reasonable for them, as consumers, to demand to know how 'breathable' any insulation product really is. In scientific terms just about everything must be breathable at some atomic level but for old houses one might usefully start with the theoretical question: 'If a person were tightly wrapped head to toe in this product after breakfast would they still be with us for lunch?' If the answer looks like being no, express your regrets to the salesperson and move on. And do not try this at home! The following chapter (Chapter 15: Hot Love) looks at some home insulation measures as applicable to cottages.

Insulation and ventilation

Cottages originally came with hundreds of tiny, accidental-on-purpose draughts that once fed open fires and helped to keep the fabric ventilated. In recent times, without open fires, some of these have been seen as a nuisance and blocked up. It may be reasonable to reduce them with ordinary DIY measures that will not permanently alter the fabric or detail of the building (and that are 'reversible'). But resist the temptation to completely eliminate every draught, since they still do contribute usefully to a cottage's ventilation. Even brand new houses have to have ventilation panels by law in certain walls and in window frames so that occupants have the old-fashioned opportunity to breathe fresh air.

There are also regulations, and sound life-preserving reasons, which would require the retention of those vents that are designed to serve heating appliances – to avoid suffocation and carbon monoxide poisoning, and to enable the appliances to work properly and efficiently.

Heating – some sustainable possibilities

New or different fuels for existing systems

A reasonably insulated, but still well ventilated cottage will always need some winter heating, unless global warming is more pronounced than is presently imagined. Recently the most popular choices of central-heating fuels have been gas, oil and electricity in that order, for reasons of relative cost. Wood has often tended to be used for effect in wood-burning stoves in cottages. After a recent official push for more efficient gas and oil boilers (some of which can have a shorter service life than older models because of their complexity), we might now be encouraged to switch to another generation of boilers that run on wood or perhaps oils sourced from farmed crops. The wood-fired central heating boiler choices presently are to burn large logs (this can be suitable for country folk who are around to feed the logs in) or alternatively wood chips or specially formed pellets that are processed and delivered by lorry to a hopper in homes for automatic feed into boilers (also adaptable to town conditions; a special pellet might mean being tied to a particular supplier).

Wood storage takes up more space than coal or oil per unit of heat output so adequate storage space may simply not be available in a small cottage. Oils from organic sources ('bio-diesels') may promise similar convenience to mineral fuel oils. With new vegetable-sourced oils and with wood there is the question of where in the world these are to be grown, and what is to happen to the displaced food production. A choice between cold and hunger?

Heat pumps
Heat pumps have been teetering on the balance of viability for several decades in Britain, probably held back by the relative cheapness of our lucky access to natural gas. But they have been taken up with gusto in other parts of Europe. The devices that are presently on the starting blocks here would turn low-grade heat – from the garden sub-soil, or a borehole, or the air, or even a stream – into higher-grade heat to release indoors.

The process concentrates heat that is extracted from those places using electricity, in the same way that a domestic refrigerator extracts heat from the food inside it and dumps the heat into the kitchen. Like a fridge, a heat pump uses electricity to do this job and, like a fridge, there is a cost involved in that power and there is the need to insulate cold areas from warm ones to a high standard. That last part of the equation can be difficult in an old cottage, in which case a heat pump might cost more in electricity (or any back-up boiler fuel used alongside the system) than is compatible with the cost of installation when compared with a 'conventional' heating system.

Nevertheless, some cottages may have big enough gardens for the necessary underground pipes (archaeology permitting), boreholes (which take less room) or perhaps suitable locations for other extraction devices (such as air-sourced), so there are hopes that this technology will adapt. A heat pump as discussed here does not draw heat already at high temperatures from deep in the earth, although such reservoirs of 'free' heat do exist in the world. The heat pumps under consideration in Britain most often are using electricity (which may or may not be sustainably generated) to 'concentrate' natural low grade heat and, if they are able to work well, they can make the

electricity 'go further' than simply using it directly for heat.

Underfloor heating and iron radiators
Underfloor pipes are often used to distribute the heat provided by heat pumps in new houses because the hot water generated is at a slightly lower temperature than radiators in a conventional system and so a greater surface area is required. A floor makes a comfortable radiator at those temperatures. That is fine for a new house built from scratch, but this could easily be a disastrous intrusion in an old cottage if it involved excavation for a replacement ground subfloor. Such excavation could easily be deeper than the foundations of many cottages, and could also interfere with its damp management, while on upper floors it could involve removing, covering or otherwise interfering with venerable old timber boards and beams.

If that sounds like bad news, then the good news is that attractive, old-fashioned cast-iron radiators are supposed to work better than modern steel ones with the water temperatures involved in heat pump systems. For a cottage, however, those radiators can occupy more space – and there is also the potential damage involved in threading the pipework around it, as with any 'wet' system of heating (*see* Chapter 10: Heat, Light and Water – 'Pipes', page 119).

A QUESTION OF BALANCE

In meeting regulations
There are likely to be more and more initiatives to insulate and to 'green' older properties. Recent moves indicate that the ideas that seem to tick all the boxes for politicians and legislators can sometimes be less than satisfactory to apply to real old properties, since old buildings can be so individual. Rather than be forced to adopt standard solutions, it would seem better to tailor solutions inventively to suit actual conditions.

Heritage organizations in the UK have for some time sought a degree of tolerance in applying new statutory energy-efficiency measures that might adversely affect the important visual and historic role of old buildings, or compromise their survival. On a local level, a council's conservation officer would be a

Blessed are the meek

An old country cottage is very likely to have been sustainably built from entirely local materials by local people living sustainable lives, without the availability of mechanized tools or transport. A cottage could originally have been designed to be occupied, maintained, heated and lit without the use of a speck of coal, a drop of oil or a watt of electricity. An old cottage has nurtured its 'embodied' energy and materials for its centuries-long life and is capable of continuing to do so for centuries more if we do not undermine its performance by badly understood alterations. These features of cottages are not just carbon friendly, they are right at the top of the 'good' end of the scale.

Could a modern sustainable dwelling even begin to hope to equal these standards? Unsustainability comes in at the cottage door when people move in with unsustainable demands involving excess energy use and unnecessary alterations. Now that cottages can be expensive lifestyle choices, and no longer take-it-or-leave-it housing, if someone has elected to live in a cottage for its period style, should twenty-first-century performance always be taken for granted? Is doing London to Brighton at 70mph the point of running a veteran car?

first step towards ironing out problems where new regulations seem to conflict with appropriate care of a cottage. When dealing with Building Regulations through the local authority there has always been an understanding that regulations ought not to adversely affect existing buildings, and building control officers can have some discretion.

Looking at the total impact of decisions

Being sustainable is not just about what new 'green' gadgets people are persuaded to go out and buy, it is about how everything is made and used and whether it is appropriate and used wisely. Anything that is old and still working adequately is not automatically environmentally inferior, since the act of destroying it and creating something to replace it might cost much more in extra material and energy than any extra energy consumption in keeping the old one going.

Replacing something unnecessarily for other reasons, maybe just because someone says it has become 'unfashionable', can show a lack of imagination and a lack of confidence in our own past judgements that as a society we can ill afford. In the race to save the planet an old cottage has a good head start over newer energy-efficient homes because of its long life and more sustainable original construction. We need to find ways to build on this lead rather than build over it.

Hot Love
Home insulation pros and cons

A LITTLE BIT MORE

Perhaps the most significant drive in improvements for existing homes in the near future will continue to be the promotion of insulation. This is being sold on the ideas of saving heating bills as well as saving the planet. While these are totally noble aims, the cottage owner needs to understand that many cottages have already received a technical and visual battering from the misapplied home improvement fashions of the twentieth century – and while this is hardly a matter of fashion, applying too much insulation without addressing its other implications could, in certain circumstances, be the last straw in bringing some cottages to their knees. It simply may not be reasonable to try to insulate a cottage in every way that

Some traditional materials, such as thatch, are considered good thermal insulation, and other types of roof can be relatively easy to insulate; some thick stone walls are even considered able to store a useful 'buffer' of heat. But whatever a cottage is built from, it is going to be difficult to add insulation to many old walls without covering up everything that makes a cottage special, or risking upsetting the mechanisms that preserve its fabric.

equals the current recommendations for new houses. Heat and energy conservation will have to be managed in other ways, and they can – by careful husbandry and common sense, by proper use of automatic controls, and by accepting that warmer clothes have to be worn indoors in winter.

If you want the thrill of living in an old property, then taking such steps goes with the territory, in the same way as wearing leathers and a helmet goes with riding a motorbike.

What insulation does

Limits the convection of heated air

Most insulation products work by trapping air within small pockets or between fibres so that it cannot easily circulate and waft away the heat that we want to keep. It is the same principle that has been used in clothes from string vests to quilted jackets. But having got this far in the book, the reader will understand that the wafting of air is one of the benign features that help cottages to dismiss harmful dampness from within their structure. So we need to be very, very careful about how insulation is applied if it is going to act to stop any beneficial air movement. In terms of clothes, the ones we wear full time need to allow our skin to breathe. Those clothes that do not do this – a heavy plastic or rubberized raincoat, for example, or a wetsuit – we have to remove from time to time to avoid unpleasantness. It is not possible to keep undressing a cottage, however, so insulation has to be breathable.

Reflect radiant heat

A few other building insulation products work by reflecting radiant heat back using metallic foils. These need care too, however, because an unbroken sheet of metal or metallized plastic can block air movement, nor is it notably vapour permeable, so it has the potential to trap dampness, or perhaps even become a focus for condensation, if misapplied.

When applied in modern houses

In modern buildings, diminished air movement is not seen as a problem because modern houses, built on the twentieth-century model, have been able to prohibit virtually all damp entering the building from outside. They do not seem to need any of the air movement that old houses do in order to get rid of such damp – although there have been a few scares where dampness generated by occupation, such as from breathing, showers and cooking, has caused mould growth and so has had to be shown out by fans.

Now built as virtually water- and vapour-proof boxes, modern houses are supposed to have adequate ventilation built in to walls and to windows, although this is sometimes rather disingenuously sealed up in order to prevent leakages spoiling their heat-retaining performance (with possible dangers to health as a result, due to oxygen starvation and the build-up of combustion gases from heating appliances). But modern construction has not solved all the problems, as human beings retain an inconvenient primitive need to breathe, and will generate moisture when they do this. A cottage, however, was built to need air movement to survive and to help its human occupants, and their heating fires, to function properly.

Sealing draughts

Air movement has always been part of the defence mechanism that dried out dampness in cottages. This was of no consequence to our tougher forbears because they themselves did not have the technology to build a draught-proof house easily – and if they did, then their open wood fires would not have worked properly because they would have been starved of oxygen. The drawing of air from countless tiny gaps around cottage walls, doors and windows, all helped dry out damp and feed the fire with oxygen, the fire radiated back heat and everyone was happy, as long as they had a seat by the fire. Draughts were coped with by the design of clothing and furniture – tall collars and nightcaps, high-backed chairs and curtained beds for example.

Now that most cottages have blocked up the chimney for most of the year and rely upon central heating, the temptation has been to seal up these draughts with foams and fillers. This was understandable, but unfortunately it was also likely to create a reservoir of damp within the fabric of the cottage. This dampness is a friend to rot and to the insect attack of timber.

160

Under pressure

Like all owners of period dwellings, cottage owners are going to come under increased pressure to provide higher levels of modern insulation material in their homes. Insulation works to keep generated heat inside the dwelling, and it is the generation of that heat by unsustainable means that has become a political and environmental issue. It could be argued that a cottage, used as it was intended with all its useful and protective draughts, could burn as much of what we now consider to be 'carbon neutral' wood as it takes to keep it as warm as toast without contributing one little bit to global warming. But not all cottages are still used that way, even though they probably could be.

The previous chapter (14: Future Past) sets out some of the factors affecting cottage heating: the balance of beneficial ventilation versus suffocating sealing up, the possibility of achieving a better environmental performance at modern levels of heating by adopting 'carbon neutral fuels', and the more direct route of simply accepting lower temperatures and wearing more clothes. These are, in fact, the sorts of measures that our ancestors unconsciously adopted in their own highly sustainable lives – not forgetting that they did not aspire to modern levels of heating, as their 'room temperature' was tolerated 10°C or so below modern expectations.

So the requirements for living in a cottage might extend from the necessary tolerance of enhanced numbers of spiders, mice and creepy crawlies to the necessity to wear woollens half the year. Still, this is not such a bad deal for such special surroundings. But extra insulation is still possible to roofs, floors and walls, even if it has to be considered very carefully.

INSULATION ON OFFER

Traditional thermal insulation materials

Timber finishes, mud walls and thatch roofs have long been admired for their insulation properties. The insulating and damp-reducing properties of purpose-designed cavities in walls have also long been understood, with historic examples of brick cavities and internal lath-and-plaster dry linings going back some time. Straw and reed matting has been used beneath roof tiles in some areas, partly as a second line of defence against drips, but also offering some insulation.

Inside, but usually limited to the homes of the very wealthy, tapestries were an application of the idea that a wall covering with a higher surface temperature would mask the 'cold radiator' effect of a masonry wall. Direct insulation of heat-producing appliances had been practised as far back as Victorian times, with some of their boilers and iron heating pipes being lagged (but often with asbestos, *see* Chapter 9: Reasons to be Careful).

Conventional modern insulation products

Mineral fibres of glass and rock
The 1960s may not have invented insulation, but it was the time when, following the arrival of central heating, there was an aspiration to have warmer homes. That was tempered by the first in a series of concerns about the future of fuel supplies, making some degree of heat conservation an insurance against rising prices. The idea of conserving heat took off, technology stepped in, and a 50mm quilt made up from glass fibres was perhaps the first mass-market product aimed at the DIY consumer. A rival product was a similar 'wool' spun from volcanic rock, and side by side, these two developed into the mainstay of quilted, blown and board-shaped insulation for several decades. In their basic form, and also some of their other variants, these products can be used within a 'breathable' system if applied properly. Some variants of the rock-based products are also used in fire-separation roles.

Plastic foams
Later on, foamed plastic appeared, and this has been the mainstay of under-floor insulation that came into prominence due to regulations in the 1980s for new-build housing. Loose polystyrene beads might be found in some attics. Sprayed-on foamed plastic has also been sold, on claims that if directly applied to the inside of an old roof it both insulates and helps stop the roof tiles from becoming dislodged – but

conservationists are very wary of sealing up tiling battens and other timbers, which these systems would imply that they do. They are also concerned that if tiles and slates are covered in adhesive plastic foam it could put difficulties in the way of subsequently reusing them.

Drawbacks and properties

Each of the conventional products has been subject to criticism on various environmental grounds due to manufacturing processes or ingredients, and there have also been other criticisms in use. Perhaps the most troublesome of the latter is respiratory irritation from the fibre materials, which has been addressed to some extent by the creation of bonded or encapsulated versions. Then there are concerns about plastic foams, that they may melt in a house fire and perhaps drop hot molten plastic and emit fumes, complicating escape and rescue, or even be flammable themselves if not adequately treated.

However, in a fire some of the rock-based fibre materials can, with professional design, be used as passive protection to inhibit the spread of flames and smoke due to the relatively high melting point of the material, and this can be usefully exploited in roofspaces in older properties in the hope of containing fire spread.

Even more recent insulation materials

New kids on the block

Newer, 'green' insulation products have come to the fore in recent years (even if some of these have perhaps been around for a long time), warmly welcomed by sustainability buffs. Most claim to have avoided the itching, the fumes and in some cases the breathability issues that might be a problem with some of the conventional insulation materials. Products such as animal wool insulation quilts and recycled paper and plastic might be expected to have had some treatment to protect from moth or to reduce flammability, and so users would be wise to ask how long-lasting, effective and safe to touch and inhale those treatments are. If a treatment for, say, moths involves insecticides, then what exactly are they? If a treatment against fire or insect infestation is

supposed to last for, say, ten years, will anyone bother to replace the insulation then?

A thinner newcomer

Thin insulating sheets, made up from layers of foams and reflective foils, claim to provide equivalent insulation to a considerably thicker quilt of fibre insulation. An appealing idea, it does require careful design and understanding of the physics involved to install this effectively. They would also need installing in association with appropriate permanent ventilation, because foams and foils are not intrinsically breathable and unless such products can be made to offer the standards of breathability necessary in an old building, then they may risk creating barriers to that breathability that is vital to protect a traditionally built cottage.

But still look for breathability

It is still necessary for the cottage owner to consider the breathability and other performance of insulation materials, even if they do have impeccable 'green' credentials. For example, there may be some recycled products with eminent environmental credentials that can be blown into roof spaces, but if they encapsulate or adhere too tightly to timber and stop it 'breathing', then they could potentially be harmful to that timber. More insulation products will certainly appear, and these may seem on the surface to solve all the applications that consumers may face, but it is technically a very difficult thing to achieve insulation in the context of an old building, and quite an easy thing to compromise an old building by misapplied insulation, so professional advice is very worthwhile here.

PLACES TO INSULATE

Loft insulation

If the loft is not used then it makes no sense to insulate at the line of the tiles because that would mean pointlessly heating the roofspace while depriving all the roof timbers of the free flow of fresh air that keeps decay at bay. The top of the first floor ceiling would then be a more sensible plane for the insulation. In any case, because heat rises, it is very sensible to start here, at the top of the cottage's living areas.

INSULATING SLOPING CEILINGS

SOME GENERAL CONSIDERATIONS

applying insulation outside implies moving the tile-line out, altering shape of roof

insulation in here is restricted for space - especially as room should be left for proper ventilation

rafter

lath-and-plaster

conventional loft insulation usually fits here and can be well ventilated

applying insulation inside obscures original surfaces and makes the room smaller

traditional construction has relied upon good ventilation in here to disperse water vapour

⚠ risk of 'interstitial condensation' needs to be understood

163

Look after yourself

The thicknesses of insulation recommended today will, inconveniently, cover all signs of the ceiling joists and of where it might be safer to tread, so it is essential to create a raised, boarded, safe walking area, or to map one out in some foolproof way. Neither old lath and plaster ceilings nor new plasterboard ones are able to take the weight of a person walking directly on them.

Whatever material is used to insulate a loft space it is sensible to wear gloves, a mask and goggles while working amongst it. (*See also* Chapter 5: A Hard Rain – 'Insulation' page 61, and 'Underlay' page 62.)

Give electric cables space

Swathing electric cables in insulation material puts them at risk of overheating because like that they lose a percentage of their current-carrying capacity: they should not therefore be buried in insulation material. Similar cautions apply to any recessed light fittings: these might require special fireproof hoods. Inset light fittings can seriously destabilize lath and plaster ceilings and are probably best avoided in cottages and older properties because of the risk of fire; they are obviously potentially hazardous under a thatched roof (*see also* Chapter 6: Sticks and Stones – 'Ceilings' – 'Downlighters' page 95).

Lag pipes and tanks

Pipes and tanks in a roofspace above the level of insulation will be at extra risk of freezing so should be well insulated themselves. A gap can also sometimes be contrived in the insulation under tanks so that heat seeps through to keep them warmer.

Don't block ventilation

At the eaves the insulation should not be allowed to block the flow of air that should be keeping the roof timbers aired, so it ought to be kept back a little – using rolled chicken wire can achieve this, and can also act as a barrier to birds, rats and squirrels. Even modern house regulations had to back-pedal on this issue, with requirements introduced to ventilate roof spaces rather than seal them up as had been practised during the twentieth century (with bad results).

Sloping walls that are also ceilings

Very common in cottages, the room in the roof – a similar configuration appears in modern housing under the heading 'chalet bungalow' or 'attic conversion' – presents particular problems when insulating because there is usually too little space in which to insert enough insulation to keep properly warm, while simultaneously ensuring enough ventilation to prevent the roof structure quickly developing decay. Alternative approaches of moving the external tile line outwards or moving the internal surface inwards to accommodate insulation are theoretically possible, but unfortunately usually far too ungainly in practice (besides which, such alterations would probably require official planning and Building Regulation consents as for walls, *below*).

In the end a compromise might be possible offering some insulation and some ventilation within the existing space, but breathability must come first and professional design is essential to try to minimize the risks in what is, in most cases, going to be an experiment. Modern installations in modern houses might draw on scientifically examined trial installations to assess things such as condensation risk and efficiency, but a cottage installation will have to rely to some extent on instinct in the absence of a one-off identical laboratory simulation. The more informed and experienced that instinct, the better. The diagram 'Insulating Sloping Ceilings' on page 163 attempts to put the problem into visual perspective.

Walls

There are many types of wall, and many types of insulation solution on offer. In a cottage that is still traditionally constructed then all those solutions that severely limit its breathability can normally be ruled out. If the cottage is a listed building then permission would be required for any thickening of the wall inside or out, and likewise externally in a conservation area or other designated area such as a National Park. Planning permission may also apply if altering the appearance of the building. Cottages being small inside and aspiring to prettiness inside and out are not ideal candidates for the application of the 'wonder materials' that promise to improve insulation: 'wonder material' is probably rather less attractive to look at than cottage.

In most circumstances it would be hoped that a cottage would not need to have quite so much surgery as exposes what is shown here, but this illustrates two situations that might arise: in a reasonably squarely built brick cottage it can sometimes be appropriate (as on the left) to dry line thin exterior walls, perhaps introducing a modest thickness of insulation behind without unduly altering the internal appearance. Ventilation of the cavity so created is important, and this requires some clever detailing (and subsequently remembering not to block the vents or slots). If (as right) a cottage has previously lost its original lath and plaster ceilings then there may be the opportunity, if replacing the modern sheet finishes, to examine any existing remedial insulation behind for dampness, or to experiment with new insulation behind the sloping parts of ceilings. But there should be about 50mm of air space left either side of the insulation (chicken wire can be useful restraint for the fibrous breathable types) for ventilation in case it ever becomes wet. If the lath and plaster ceilings do remain in place it would not normally be appropriate to remove them for this purpose, but it might be possible to slide some thinner boards of an appropriate and breathable insulating material down into this area from the roofspace above – again ensuring adequate ventilation each side. Otherwise insulation of this area would need to wait until access was available during any future re-roofing – and in the meantime maybe some more portable and breathable insulation could be gently attached to the inner sloping ceiling surface as a temporary measure.

Softly, softly

Insulation does not have to involve heavy duty engineering work, and using modern insulating soft furnishing and curtain-lining fabrics (if breathable and also not a fire risk) it is possible to create a better performing version of the insulating tapestries that once cheered up stately homes and castles. These are ideal candidates for reversibility, which means that their installation causes minimum physical disruption to the original wall and is capable of removal without leaving a scar. The other meaning of reversibility, namely a summer and a winter side, might not be a bad idea either.

Concealer

Many cottages have unfortunate grim utility extensions left over from the 1950s and 1960s, which were tacked on to provide a quick kitchen or bathroom. They would probably be poorly insulated, in accordance with the standards of their time, and owners tend to want to knock them down and start again. But they are likely to have workmanlike solid foundations, floors and walls, so a more sustainable, economical approach might be to keep as much as is useful, and clad it externally in a material that is both more 'cottagey' and which will accommodate extra insulation underneath. Traditional timber boarding sits well in most parts of the country as a material long used for 'outhouses', but talk to the local conservation officer about the details or any alternatives.

Beware of filling cavities

The brickwork cavity wall came into being a little too late for most cottages, but some are built with a

An existing extension can be tamed and its insulation improved under a covering of traditionally detailed softwood cladding. New extensions can be similarly treated. Note that this cladding would not be 1960s-style profiled 'shiplap', but simple square or feathered sawn boards that can be treated with a 'microporous' stain or linseed oil breathable paint for longevity and to permit any added insulation inside to 'breathe'. There is also the opportunity in some cases to add a pitched roof to cover an old ugly, or leaking flat one.

primitive version called 'rat trap' bond that was probably devised more to economize on bricks. Filling brick cavities with foam has been a standard measure for insulating the walls of mid-twentieth-century homes, though many regard this as foolhardy since the purpose of a cavity was to be unfilled so that damp could not so easily be transmitted from outside to in. Another concern is that if damp takes up residence in all this new foam then it would be held closely against the iron or steel ties that bind the inner and outer brickwork together in a cavity-built house, eventually rusting them away.

Cottage walls that have a cavity are more likely to be of timber frame construction with simply a lath and plaster finish both inside and out, and lots of voids between the frame members. If these voids were simply filled with insulation, there is none of the back-up found on a modern house to keep damp out from all possible angles, and so there is a real danger that the insulation could harbour damp, and decay the timber frame. If for some reason the wall is being stripped of its plaster on one side then it could be possible to insert an insulating material while allowing ventilation paths on either side, but this, too, would be subject to an assessment of the risk of 'insterstitial condensation' (see below).

The insulating material chosen needs to be one

that is going to be intrinsically fire and vermin resistant rather than relying on treatments that may wear off after a time. Some success has been claimed with rock-based insulation boards, but as a cottage is full of unknown construction, the act of insulating it is an act of faith rather than science and should be approached in a spirit of experimentation.

Interstitial condensation

It is a cold day and you wrap a scarf over your nose and mouth. Quickly the scarf becomes wet because your breath contains moisture, which condenses into water drops when it hits the cold temperatures outside your body and reaches its 'dew point'. For 'nose and mouth' read 'kitchen, bathroom and living room', and for 'scarf' read 'wall'. Interstitial condensation is where warm air reaches its 'dew point' inside a wall, causing dampness there.

Modern houses are built swathed in plastic 'vapour barriers', damp-proof courses and all sorts of belt-and-braces waterproof finishes, seals and mastics so that warm, moist air is considered not to be able to get into a wall for this to happen. It is not reasonable for vapour barriers and all the other necessary paraphernalia to be retrospectively applied to a cottage – it would be as difficult as trying to turn a flower pot into a vacuum flask, and then on a greater scale. Firstly because to do so would mean virtually dismantling the cottage, and secondly because a cottage was built to rely absolutely on the ability for water vapour to pass through unhindered so it could get out, along with all the other moisture that comes and goes.

Water that has reached its dew point and condensed out inside an airy void in a cottage wall is a problem, but it should be able to get out – as long as nobody has painted outside in plastic paint or rendered the wall in cement (*see also* Chapters 4: The Air That I Breathe, and 12: Paint It ... Back). But water that has condensed out into tightly packed insulation material in that void is more of a problem since there is now little air movement available to shift it, so it may hang around long enough to do damage by fostering decay.

And that is the big problem with insulating existing old buildings: there is a significant risk of generating decay and still not being warm, because if the insulation does get sopping wet then its effectiveness is compromised. A misguidedly insulated wall may provide a structure that, instead of being cold and dry and of no interest to fungi and woodworm, suddenly becomes wet and warm and like an incubator for them. This does not mean that it is impossible to insulate a cottage, but it does mean that anyone who pretends that it is as simple as buying something and slapping it on is very likely not the person you should be listening to.

Behind radiators

Metallic foil sheets, sometimes on insulating backing pads, are sold for applying to the wall behind water-filled radiators that are mounted on the inside of external walls, in order to reflect back heat that might otherwise be lost into the wall. The benefit of these has to be balanced with the 'sealing up' effect on a wall, but that might be reduced if these reflective pads were to be installed on spacers so the wall was still vented behind (naturally the foil or pad should not touch the radiator or it would reduce the heat output). Some types of wall construction – the thicker, heavier masonry ones – can act as a useful 'thermal store' so that heat might not be being wasted after all.

Windows

The subject of windows can make the conserva-tionist's blood boil! Old windows have charm, character and life; the frames would have been hand made, in timber or iron, and the glass likewise, shot through with ripply imperfections that dance on walls and gently warp the reflected world. To remove them and replace them with factory-made double glazing risks reducing the cottage to a comical mess, like having a clown's glasses daubed on the Mona Lisa. Even if someone had previously replaced all the hand-made old windows, then this is no excuse for repeating the mistake one more time. It ought to be put right. There are gentler solutions, as described below, starting from original-style hand-made windows.

Secondary glazing

Secondary glazing is simply another glazed frame inside the existing window. It only has to be reasonably draughtproof, not waterproof, and it can be removable in summer. If properly designed it should be invisible from the outside and safely openable or removable. In order to respect the original building its installation should be designed to avoid cutting and altering the original building, and with only those fixing points necessary to ensure a proper and secure fixing.

Secondary glazing acquired a shaky reputation from the wobbly self-assembly kits of years ago that were difficult to operate and rarely matched the glazing bars of the original frame. A bespoke installation is still likely to be best for a cottage, as DIY kits will probably be aimed at the straighter, more standard-sized windows to be found in mass-market housing from the 1960s. Safety glass or even plastic might be advisable rather than wielding fragile sheets of glass, but if frames can be sufficiently robust without dominating the window then there would be the opportunity to use special insulating glass.

Try before you buy

There are DIY temporary secondary glazing kits that use thin, flexible plastic film applied to double-sided tape, and the film is stretched taut with a hair drier. Not everyone is good at practical DIY, but those people who as children were adept enough to make model aircraft kits without getting glue all over the pilot's canopy might easily make a virtually invisible

Secondary glazing is almost certain to improve insulation and it can be considered visually successful if it is necessary to look twice to notice it from outside.

installation that should see them happily through at least one winter, probably more. This can help in assessing whether permanently investing in doubling up on glazing will ever make a sufficient difference to pay back the investment in a reasonable time. This temporary system might last several years.

The down sides are a possible increase in condensation either within the window, or shunted from the window to the next coldest surface in the room (this effect would also be likely with a permanent installation); there is also a tendency for the film to trap spiders and insects. It is necessary to try to stop up all gaps with something reversible such as foam draught excluder before making the installation, but a complete seal is impossible and the window could become something of a terrarium until such time as courage is summoned to peel back an edge. Needless to say, sealing a principal route of the cottage's 'breathing' ventilation with plastic film is quite a serious step away from conservation common sense, and this sort of installation should be monitored for side effects – summer removal may help limit those.

Alternatives and extras
If a trial of temporary plastic film secondary glazing was inconclusive (*see above*), or if the trouble, expense

Full internal shutters can be used with traditional single-glazed windows to provide insulation, which might exceed that of modern double glazing; in addition they offer some security.

and visual intrusion of permanent secondary glazing does not appeal, then there are other routes that of course can be tried first. If internal shutters exist then these can be brought out of retirement and used regularly in winter, at night and whenever the room is unoccupied. The same goes for curtains, which can be made with insulating and even heat-reflective lining material. If a window faces full sun then it can be worth experimenting with keeping shutters and curtains open even when unoccupied to accumulate solar heat, making sure to close down when the sun disappears.

Cottages were mostly built at a time when people were much more connected with nature for the pursuit of their comfort; therefore pantries, larders and staircases are often on a north-facing wall, while living rooms face the sun. Trees may offer summer shade, and hedges planted to shield against persistent winds. These things can make a significant difference, and they are being rediscovered in modern 'green' housing; they also cost little to run.

Double glazing

Pending any new breakthrough in glazing technology, modern double glazing is much thicker and heavier than the single glazing that cottages were originally likely to have had. This means that even if the characterful original glass were to be sacrificed, new double-glazed units could not fit properly directly in their place, and the glazing bars may not be wide enough or strong enough to carry it. (This is one of the reasons for considering secondary glazing, *see above*.)

Sometimes, however, a new window in a new extension might call for new glazing to meet current regulations, in which case one can either be totally honest and have a plain all-glass opening without glazing bars, or fake glazing bars can be planted each side of the sheet of double glazing in a carefully designed replica of existing frames so that from a distance the window appears more or less traditional. That illusion is not perfect, but should be all the better for being in traditional materials using traditional profiles and mouldings; wood is infinitely versatile in that respect.

Should anyone still be entertaining the idea of new window frames in materials that are non-traditional,

consider what happens when the cottage moves a little (most old buildings do) and the window needs adjusting. Easy enough in wood – but how to shave a complex factory-extruded section of frame with all its special gaskets so that it still functions afterwards? Of course listed buildings and those in some conservation areas and National Parks are unlikely to be able to consider replacement double glazing, so kinder and more attractive alternatives – such as secondary glazing – would have to be considered.

Draught strips

Without altering windows and even before resorting to secondary glazing, reasonable draught-proofing measures in conjunction with the use of curtains, blinds and shutters to keep heat in can be very effective (*see* 'Alternatives and extras', above). Simple self-adhesive foam strips can be just as effective as proprietary systems, and can be preferable as they are more likely to be 'reversible' (not alter the building permanently), and also removable for repainting the frame. The object is not to try to make the window airtight enough to be fit for duty in a submarine or in outer space, but to reduce the big, nuisance draughts – perhaps in conjunction with other measures. People still need to breathe, and even modern house windows are required to have ventilators.

Doors

Cottage doors are special and often originally quite simple vertically boarded affairs. A flashy modern replacement would look out of place on the British cottage, especially if it owes its design to another part of the world. The simplest measure to equal, or perhaps even to surpass the insulation of a modern door, is a door curtain, and the more overlap and better lined this is, the better for keeping the cold out.

By the Edwardian period some clever and simple ironmongery was commonplace that lifted a curtain rail off the ground to allow the whole curtain to swing with the door as well as lift; this can be replicated with some DIY effort and head scratching, or purchased new. On the floor the knitted 'sausage' or old stocking stuffed with fabric offcuts is a bit of a cliché perhaps, but it is a quick and effective way to stop an awkward draught across a worn threshold. As

Features like this were almost certainly put there to air hidden timbers to prevent them from rotting, not just to make people cold, so they should not be blocked, and any insulation that is installed inside the cottage should not inhibit this ventilation. That may be difficult to organize, but it is worth the effort as there is no point trying to save fuel bills by blocking a few draughts if the end result is a bigger repair bill for the floor. More modern-looking versions of such grilles may serve heating appliances, in which case they are there to keep the occupants safe from suffocation by combustion gases, so no reason to block those, either.

for windows, draught strips (*see above*) can be applied to doors.

Floors

Timber

Internal timber floors over cellars, external passages and 'flying freeholds' might need to be carefully insulated in a way that does not inhibit the ventilation against the timber surfaces that is necessary to keep the wood sound. Ground floors to some cottages may have suspended timber floors, and these would be likely to be accompanied by external air vents to keep the underfloor void fresh and dry. In the days of open fires these vents were known to be useful, but now they can be misunderstood as sources of draught and wrongly blocked up, leading to dampness and decay of the timber floor.

Naturally it is going to be difficult to insulate under such a floor without reducing the essential ventilation. Insulation quilt should not be tightly packed against timbers, and ideally a 50mm air gap should exist around them, again a difficult balance. Some additional benefit can be gained by filling gaps between and around the floorboards with cork or papier mâché – unless, of course, there is still an open fire in the room, in which case the draughts may still be serving their original purpose.

Solid earth, brick or stone

An original cottage floor would probably have been direct to earth, or a brick or stone surface applied to the earth. Over the years these could have been replaced or overlaid with a screed of lime-ash or, later, concrete. More recent concrete versions perhaps incorporate a damp-proof membrane, which might in fact encourage ground dampness to seek an alternative outlet in the walls. Digging up an original floor goes against the grain in conservation terms, and should not be attempted unless there is a pressing and thoroughly understood need – and then not without professional advice since the wall's foundations were often only as deep as the floor and risk being terminally disturbed. If the underlying earth is habitually dry, then there is possibly little to be gained by replacing a solid floor in terms of insulation when the cost and upheaval is factored in.

If replacement is absolutely necessary (and listed building consent would be required for protected buildings), then it could be appropriate to consider a breathable lime concrete-based version, which can perhaps be insulated with natural granular 'breathable' materials rather than the plastic foam favoured by modern building. Introducing a completely damp-proof floor into an otherwise fully breathable building can send ground dampness elsewhere in the structure, so the 'solution' to a damp floor may simply create other problems. In traditional use, floors direct to ground would have been understood to be slightly damp and used with breathable mats and finishes. Nowadays, people who are used to modern houses might expect to be able to lay a foam-backed carpet on them, and then be puzzled as to why it goes mouldy underneath.

STYLE COUNSEL
Keeping the look alive

About fifteen minutes in a gallery showing eighteenth- and nineteenth-century paintings of cottage interiors should be enough to convince anyone that the native décor for a country cottage was not rich in fitted carpets, easy chairs, skeins of horse brasses or coach lamps. Those images seem only to go back to the 1950s. Not that cottages were not romanticized in past centuries. Old paintings wouldn't have shown bathrooms or WCs because they did not exist (perhaps by the late nineteenth century a portable bathtub if you were lucky, and an earth closet somewhere in the garden). Cooking very often remained a function of the fireplace in the main living room right into the twentieth century.

No one, except perhaps the curator of a folk museum, expects a cottage now to be as sparse as it was when it was first built and as first occupied by rural workers. Even up until the 1960s there were great numbers of both rural and urban homes with no bathrooms. It has to be accepted that there will be compromises when fitting modern life into a cottage – and sometimes the juxtaposition of ancient and modern can be thrilling – though having chosen a cottage it would seem odd to want the interior to look deliberately modern, particularly as 'modern' implies so many things that cottages are often just not very good at, such as straight, level, precise, smooth, rigid … and so on. To inflict these qualities on a cottage would mean destroying what makes it a cottage.

Yet there have been plenty of examples of people paying a premium for a country cottage, then paying out even more money to 'modernize' it and finding themselves left with something that has had all the character ironed out of it. In the worst cases the cottage ends up looking less like a cottage and more like a poorly built modern house (you can sometimes tell by looking at the chimneys: for some reason the modernizers often forget to buff those up). Probably no one has actually said to their builder 'Please make this sweet-looking cottage look rather plain and boring by straightening everything and making sure it is decorated as blandly as possible'.

Part of the reason that precisely this happens, though, could be due to the way in which architects and surveyors have judged the results of builders' work on modern buildings. Builders have come to feel that 'perfectly straight' has to be acceptable, and that there can never be any argument about 'mirror smooth'. There is usually no box on a snagging list to tick for 'imperfectly lined up but nevertheless quite pleasing' or 'not quite the same colour all over yet curiously engaging'. Therefore modern judgements have become applied to work to cottages, robbing them of some of their charm. This needs rethinking for cottages.

It is not a question of working to modern standards, then roughing it up a bit. An appropriate 'cottage' look ought to be easier to achieve straight off simply by adopting (or adapting) some of the more traditional materials and methods, such as described in this book, that should naturally look right. Professional conservation advice should help apply these sensibly, and increase the chances of the result looking right and not devaluing the cottage.

The chapters in this final section offer reasons to do some things and not others, reasons that would provide a helpful framework for people to fill in with

171

their own individuality. For example, reasons why traditional finishes might be used to benefit a traditionally functioning cottage's performance, and because they would naturally offer a traditional look; reasons to use free-standing furniture, rather than fitted furniture in a 'wobbly walled' cottage; and reasons to use rugs without foam backing rather than fitted carpets in some cases. But, sorry, there are going to be no pictures of how your cottage 'must' look and what colour the bathroom should be; those you have to work out for yourself.

Traditional cottage style owed much to local geology and to historical ways of earning a living; however, today's onlookers can easily be confused by what has come along later – and from far away.

CHAPTER SIXTEEN

Bits and Pieces
Interiors and accessories

COTTAGE STYLE

Cottage interiors, judging by the photographs in recent glossy magazines, have settled down either to a 1950s 'take' on the 'well upholstered Victorian' look, or a more spartan 1970s folk revival look with herbs dangling from the ceiling. In more extreme cases they can look like a furniture showroom. There is always going to be a large amount of historical licence applied to cottage interiors since the reality in their time as proper country cottages was shockingly austere, even if maybe charming. We like a little more comfort nowadays.

Do what you want to do?

This book has tried to convey some of the logic of using traditional methods and materials. That is in order to preserve the functioning of the old building fabric for the preservation of the cottage as a whole, and also as the most honest way to regain an authentic look. Those ideas are applicable inside as well as out. Chapter 6: Sticks and Stones looks at some of the practicalities of walls, floors and ceilings that help determine the way they used to look, and how they have come down to us now.

As far as colour choices go, in the privacy of your own home, if purple is your thing and the local planning authority won't let you have it outside, then provided it is a paint appropriate to the structure, which allows the fabric to work properly (*see* Chapter 12: Paint It ... Back), the entire interior might provide an outlet. But generally pastel shades were favoured in the past because traditional 'chalk-based' paints were basically white, pigments were often expensive, and cottagers were often poor.

Someone who has bought a cottage has usually consciously bought into a period property, so it should be recognized that some of the interior style ought to match the architecture and be true to the history of the cottage. Elsewhere in this book it has been discussed how traditional paint finishes could help a cottage survive by allowing it to 'breathe', while foam-backed carpets could self-destruct on some original cottage floors; and how recessed down-lighters can destabilize a lath and plaster ceiling and possibly be a fire hazard; and how plastic double glazing on a cottage can make people stop in the street and stare in disbelief ... and so on. Such starting points may help put a cottage owner on a reasonable course. But if not, here are some further ideas ...

Be true to your cottage

A cottage is difficult to occupy in an authentically period way because the material life of a cottager was so very different to our own, more fortunate material experience. And there is no point imagining what a real cottager from the past would do with the wealth and opportunity of today if suddenly faced with it – the place might easily become enthusiastically over-stuffed. 'Expensive' in a cottage can quickly equal uncomfortably tasteless: gold taps and two marble basins in a room where six children once had to share a bed and a single china washbowl? Perhaps not. A cottage is, by definition, small and not flashy. It is humble, even, and self-effacing – so while style has no rules, there are some ideas that could inform the modern country cottage dweller.

An unfussy interpretation of a cottage interior typical in the 1960s and 1970s; note the high-backed chair close to the fireplace – this acknowledges that draughts are necessary to fuel the fire, as it is designed to shield the occupant's head and neck from them. Though an 1860s version of this chair may not have been upholstered, the principle would have been the same.

Remember you're a human

As a visitor in a dripping raincoat and wet shoes, standing on the threshold of many a modern home can be a rather embarrassing experience since one step inside will forever stain the near-white carpet and exotic woven grass wallpaper. A country cottage needs to be robust enough to cope with owners and visitors who have actively engaged with the countryside. There is mud there. If there is only one entrance door, then it needs to be able to cope with hats, gloves, boots, wet coats, wet paws and wagging tails, variously attached to some who have been disoriented by an evening in the village pub, or excited by rabbits. A back door would offer a degree of segregation, if available – but will anyone actually bother to go round?

Be true to yourself

Hard, wooden painted chairs, things from the garden drying over the range, and just a bakelite telephone for technology may look good in a colour supple-

OPPOSITE: Country cottage style comes from the cottage itself and its equally simple accessories – these are fragile charms that can be outshone by too much surrounding sophistication or modern glitz.

ment's photo-shoot of a cottage, but in a cottage that is a full-time home and not a celebrity's hideaway, this kind of hair shirt novelty could soon wear off. Nor is there any reason to become over-elaborate: a cottage is by definition a rather small house, and unless the cottage owner really is a modern-day version of those wealthy Georgian ladies who got their kicks dressing up as shepherdesses for the afternoon, then no one is going to expect a cottage interior to be loudly expensive. There is scope to be original, inventive, and even to indulge in some individuality through crafty recycling. But space is probably going to be limited, so it is necessary to decide what is important for comfort, and to balance those things with what is important to keep the place in good physical shape.

Keep it simple ...

Modern life guarantees that there will be some anachronisms in any cottage interior. It can look silly, even in bigger houses, to try to dress up light switches, televisions and suchlike as antique accessories, but in a cottage where does one go in search of style hints? Some manufacturers have borrowed design ideas from brass door handles to make light switches for Georgian and Victorian houses – but if the original surviving door latch in a cottage is a

175

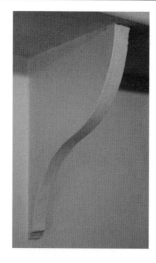

The features of a cottage interior are likely to be simple, even crude, and sometimes, as this latch (right), pickled under lots of paint. New owners are likely to want to tackle some improvements. To carefully remove the paint from the latch might be an improvement as that is undoing some careless decorating that gummed it up. To varnish or paint the stairs (left) would be unfortunate if they have been bare wood ever since they were built. Crudeness and simplicity can be what gives a cottage charm, and makes it worth more money and more interesting to live in. Misapplied neatening and smartening have the potential to destroy cottage charm.

wooden peg and a piece of string, then what? It is arguable that a light switch should be just a light switch – the simplest, most self-effacing, honest modern design that is on offer. Alternatively, it might be some people's preference to have a faithful (rather than fanciful) regulation-compliant reproduction of the very first type of light switch that was likely to have been in the cottage.

Old designs can be researched in museums, libraries and online, but beware of creating what conservationists call a 'conjectural restoration', where the cottage could turn into a dishonest jumble of period styles and fake fittings that bear no relation to the building's actual journey through time. Reproductions can be unsatisfying.

... Or just keep it

A cottage is a time traveller. It has been a long, one-way journey that has resulted in a great many acquisitions, losses and scars. Some of these may be harmful and need addressing to protect the fabric from decay; some may be harmless. All are an honest record of that journey through time, which will be of interest to someone. Some judgement is needed, but those

old fittings that are now redundant, do they really need unscrewing and chucking out, or can they be left for future generations to see? (A future conversation piece: 'Do you know that once all telephones were attached to one of these things on the wall with a wire?' 'No, you don't say!') That nasty 1930s fireplace with the cracked tiles, if it were prised off the wall, would it reveal a magical inglenook all intact, which could be filled again with holly boughs and beaming rustics by Christmas? Or would it reveal a frightening black hole that has to be propped up by seriously complex and expensive metalwork, having sat there for months smelling of soot? Perhaps 1930s tiled fireplaces will make a come-back.

Distressing

It has been suggested that centuries ago, when sugar was exotic and expensive, socialites would have blackened their teeth to make it look as though they were in the habit of eating lots of this luxury item. In the twenty-first century people can buy new furniture that has had holes made in it especially to look as though it has an infestation of woodworm. It seems that Britons have always had this very highly developed sense of irony. At least the faking of woodworm

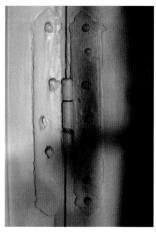

RIGHT: There is no shame in not being able to run to real stone for a new piece of work, and an honest, plain piece of traditional render would probably be less conspicuous than drawing attention to the difference. This is an outside wall, but

the same sort of attempted cover-up has often happened inside cottages.

ABOVE: A modern door hinge is neater and so much more precise than this, but if you like cottages then you are likely to think that this is much more interesting.

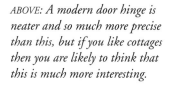

RIGHT: Another more modern custom that also appears internally, is the deep desire for exposed timbers, which can sometimes be pursued in ways that perhaps do not show all the traditional detailing.

holes is often done quite convincingly – unlike the gouges made in 'beams' and the trowel marks (modern-shaped trowels) deliberately left in new plasterwork that is supposed to transport us back to the time of Henry V. If it does, then it is only as far as one of the film versions, made when this kind of 'stick-on' mediaeval fakery was in vogue.

If you have a real cottage made with genuine period materials it needs no fakery. And if you are introducing non-original antique, reproduction or other ambiguous items into the cottage for fun or

decoration ('reversibly', of course), then it is a good idea to mark their provenance by discreet labelling, so as not to mislead future owners.

More distressing still

A 1980s fashion that still reappears from time to time is the complete stripping of early lime plaster finishes from cottage walls and ceilings in order to expose the 'rustic' brickwork, stonework or 'beams' behind. The exposed surfaces might, unaccountably, then be varnished – which is extra damaging from a

Sometimes the need for an extension can be lessened by making better use of the existing internal space, such as inserting a lobby to create separate access for two previously joined bedrooms. The necessary work ought ideally to be 'reversible' (removable without leaving a scar), honest and respectful to the existing style and materials.

breathability point of view – *see* Chapter 4: The Air that I Breathe. The human equivalent to this form of stripping is to take someone in their very best outfit and then attempt to infer the look of their everyday working clothes by getting them to strip to their underclothes, and then to wrap them in clingfilm. (Floors suffer similar privations, *see also* Chapter 6: Sticks and Stones – 'Floorboards', 'Please don't try this at home' page 93.)

Stimulate crafts

Instead of going to enormous lengths to deconstruct something, or to have something modern pretend to be something old, why not have something new made using traditional methods and get the real look? There are plenty of craftspeople who work in traditional ways with timber, iron, brick, plaster and all the materials of history. If one takes the view that the industrialization of the twentieth century unnaturally halted the evolution of design in handcrafts that had been around for thousands of years, then it can be a very exciting prospect to be able to allow someone working in such a craft to develop that skill and produce a modern design. Ideally, it would be a

Television and reality

Few can have been unaware of the home 'makeover' television programmes of recent decades. It is easy to imagine a presenter turning up to see a couple who have just lovingly extended and 'restored a ruined old cottage to its former glory'. The exterior shot might show, behind the presenter's 4×4, a crisply painted cottage nestling against its new extension. Inside, the misty and apparently candle-lit sweep around the living space looks like … any modern interior, straight out of a department store or kitchen showroom. Cottage features? … In the corner perhaps a scrap of stone poking out of the new plasterwork or, up in the ceiling, among a constellation of downlights, a heavily varnished 'beam'.

Television likes a dramatic 'before and after', you can't blame it, and sometimes it wants to sell us things as well. But real life involves more dimensions than a brief screen image. If television is like a sweet-shop window with viewers' noses pressed eagerly against it, then perhaps there needs to be someone saying, 'Come along now, if you eat all that you'll be sick!' And so here it is: conservation and sustainability are not about forcing passing fashions into old homes, nor about copycat consumption. A cottage can benefit from a light touch that is entirely individual to the property and to the owner.

modern design for something that replaces a missing component: a missing fire surround perhaps that takes account of modern function and safety requirements, but is traditionally made in appropriate traditional materials, the design having evolved from those of the past without necessarily copying them.

Lighting

Being homely places, cottages would usually benefit from general lighting that uses the part of the colour spectrum that we still, perhaps subconsciously, associate with the flames of fire and candles. This version of white (yellowish) is about the same as the incandescent tungsten filament bulbs that are being phased out. Some of the replacement compact fluorescent (energy-saving) lamps make a reasonable attempt at copying this warm white light, others can tend towards green – such as old-fashioned fluorescent lights – or towards blue – (like daylight) halogen, and some white LED (light-emitting diode) lamps.

Not all the new generation of lower energy lamps fit properly in old lamp holders, and as yet, few work with older dimmer switches or with automatic timers or light-sensitive switches. But these deficiencies – along with the colour of the light, slow warm-up times, over-long size and a tendency to flicker in some lamps – should be addressed quite quickly as the products adapt. It may therefore be worth waiting and shopping around, rather than dismissing existing fittings and well loved lampshades too hastily.

Halogen lamps are being marketed as energy saving, and they tend to be usefully interchangeable with old incandescent bulbs; watt for watt they appear brighter than the equivalent 'ordinary' light bulb, but are not as efficient as the compact fluorescents. LEDs are gaining ground as replacement for ordinary lighting, and promise to be more energy efficient in use than any of the above; they can mimic colours easily, and can even be adjusted to change colour within a single array. LEDs are probably the future, though there can be a certain harshness about some incarnations of this light source at present, as may be noticed in traffic and vehicle applications.

The potential hazards of installing downlighters in a traditional cottage ceiling are mentioned in Chapter 6: Sticks and Stones – 'Lath and Plaster Ceilings', 'Downlighters' page 95.

LIGHT MY FIRE

Second only to 'beams' in the estate agents' mantra of cottage charms is the 'inglenook', a term often misapplied to any large fireplace. An inglenook is usually taken to be a fairly substantial thing with space to sit and to store dry goods alongside a large fire opening. In practice such a large fireplace may have become filled by an iron range in many cottages as they travelled through the nineteenth century, and then later still perhaps a 1950s tiled fire surround. But there are still ample photographs of old men in faded suits and with clay pipes, sitting roasting one side of themselves in the inglenooks of old pubs, for us to get the picture – and to want it for ourselves. But beware: there can have been very sound reasons why a big old fireplace was reduced, and, of course, those later alterations are now old enough to count as history in their own right. Listed buildings require permission for such alterations and investigations, and there will almost inevitably be structural implications (and a risk of discovering asbestos somewhere along the timeline – *see* Chapter 9: Reasons to be Careful).

Some fireplace practicalities

Sweeping
Whether or not they have a true inglenook, the older country cottages are highly likely to have a quite sizeable open fireplace. This may now be behind a later insertion that is more practical to use – but it could still be there. Very old chimneys were made large to burn logs and accommodate cooking and the curing of meat, but by the time the twentieth century was in full swing and coal was being burned, many fireplaces had been reduced in size.

This means that a cottage might have a fireplace behind which are hidden ledges and voids that can collect a pile of soot and tar, and if this escapes the attention of the sweep, the soot pile could ignite and cause a chimney fire. A cottage's chimney should be swept thoroughly enough to deal with such deposits, and in some cases only determined vacuuming of the hidden insides after general sweeping will come anywhere near doing a thorough enough job in removing the potential for a chimney fire. (For more on parging *see* Chapter 6: Sticks and Stones – 'Chimneys', page 69; for thatch and flues *see* Chapter 5: A Hard Rain – 'Roofspaces and Fire', page 64).

Tuning and using a fireplace

To burn well a chimney needs to be relatively warm, quite smooth internally, tall enough to generate a pressure difference between top and bottom, free from gusts and eddies caused by neighbouring obstructions at roof level, and at ground level to be fed by a reasonably vigorous network of draughts flowing into the hearth to provide oxygen. Modern occupants may expect to light a fire and have it burn properly immediately, but they will be lucky if it does. Obviously, if it smokes there may be some blockage or other physical problem that needs to be checked, but even smoking can be the result of bad 'draw' where there is insufficient air feeding in the bottom and insufficient warmth in an otherwise sound flue. Sometimes a fire will respond well once it is established and the chimney has become warm, which would have been fine for mediaeval people who were going to leave it burning more or less constantly for months on end. But we tend not to live like that, so various methods of tuning an old fireplace have become established, which might involve, depending on the circumstances:

- A fire hood, to tame some of the smoke and direct the flow up the chimney.
- A register plate – a horizontal sheet of steel (usually) that restricts the opening from the top of the fireplace into the chimney (this would also be where any modern flue liner would be likely to begin if there was one), and this plate would also need scrupulous cleaning to prevent soot build-up.
- A ducted air supply serving the hearth immediately in front of the grate to compensate for blocked draughts from elsewhere in the room.
- Raising or lowering the grate, or the fire basket, to adjust the distance between the fire and the top of the fire opening.

These measures would not pre-warm a cold chimney, so only patience can solve that. Or, perhaps, lining a chimney would help it warm more quickly: if straight

and wide enough, a cottage chimney might accept a prefabricated insulated liner in metal, clayware or a cement-based product. But *see also* Chapter 6: Sticks and Stones – 'Chimneys', page 69.

Now that open fires have become unfamiliar 'luxuries' rather than a common household necessity, users need to remember that they are potentially hazardous and that they can spit burning embers, so a mesh guard is necessary. Also burning logs and coals can roll off, so a fireproof hearth and fender (a kerb to the hearth) is useful. Fuel such as logs might look neat if stacked close by, but they will be just as flammable outside the fireplace as in, and stray sparks or conducted heat can ignite them. Some fuels, damp wood or certain species of tree, can burn sending a lot of tar into the chimney or spit sparks. Fireguards need to be appropriate to their task: protection from things spitting out of the fire is a different task to protecting things from accidentally getting into the fire. And then there is the constant supervision of the activities of dependants such as pets and children.

KITCHENS AND BATHROOMS

A quart into a pint pot

There is very little historical precedent for kitchens and bathrooms in a cottage, so they are mainly relatively new insertions or located in mid-twentieth-century extensions. Until then, many, if not most cottages would have had no inside toilet, no bathroom, and the kitchen may have been converted from a former 'scullery' or wash-house. The original cooking space – the living-room fireplace – had been tamed with a new fireplace after the old cooking range was removed.

Having a bath

If seeking some kind of visual reinterpretation of the past in a cottage bathroom, there is not much that can be done to reinvent the look of the 'tin' bath that would have been brought in from the shed on bath nights. Therefore reproduction antique cottage bathrooms have not much to reproduce, and cottage sanitaryware has tended to be simple, practical and modern – and small, as many are still confined to modest ground floor extensions if a first floor space was not available for conversion or extension.

Existing installations

If the positions of kitchen appliances and sanitary fittings have been established, then it can be easier to try to live with them (the positions, if not the actual appliances) as all the head-scratching about pipe runs and falls will have been done beforehand, and with luck everything is working. Changing layouts can involve lifting floors beyond the bathroom and nego-tiating hidden obstacles, and sometimes it will be realized, too late, that there was only ever one possible layout after all.

New installations

If installing a bathroom or kitchen for the first time in a room in an old cottage, then it would be consid-erate to the cottage to avoid irreversible alterations. Should features such as old fireplaces not be required in the new layout, then they might be boxed in rather than removed from the cottage altogether. Routing pipe runs (*see* Chapter 10: Heat, Light and Water – 'Pipes', page 119) in a cottage is a matter for some sensitivity, and these should be planned in advance with a commitment to take the least damaging path.

If a bathroom in a traditional 'breathing' cottage needs to be tiled, then it can make sense to install the tiles on boards that are spaced from the walls on battens, as here, and with a deliberately ventilated air gap behind. The old iron high-level cistern was to remain because it is part of the history of the cottage, and also these are capable of simple adaptation to work more efficiently than a modern low-level arrangement. This cottage appears to be undergoing quite extensive rebuilding for what is a conservation project, and that is because most of its finishes and some interior walls and ceilings had previously been taken away – back in the 1960s when it was thought groovy to have an open-plan, stripped-down cottage. The times they are a-changing.

Because of the confined spaces in most cottage rooms it is usually less frustrating to plan a layout starting from the possibilities dictated by how the plumbing meshes with limiting factors such as existing ancient floor joists and beams, rather than trying to squeeze in a layout that is 'against the grain'.

Fitted or unfitted

Fitted bathrooms and kitchens can be made difficult in a cottage by the uneven nature of walls, floors and ceilings – not such a big problem in a nineteenth-century brick cottage or in a relatively new extension perhaps, but potentially a considerable problem in a sixteenth-century wattle-and-daub cottage. As above, if the problems appear to have been addressed already in an existing layout, then it can pay to learn from that and perhaps live with it or adapt it only a little. Otherwise the problem of fitting units might be avoided by having free-standing items. This can often be successfully coupled with the honest exposing of pipes (carefully crafted and polished metal would look more purposeful than plastic), which is less damaging to the cottage than burrowing them away inside the walls.

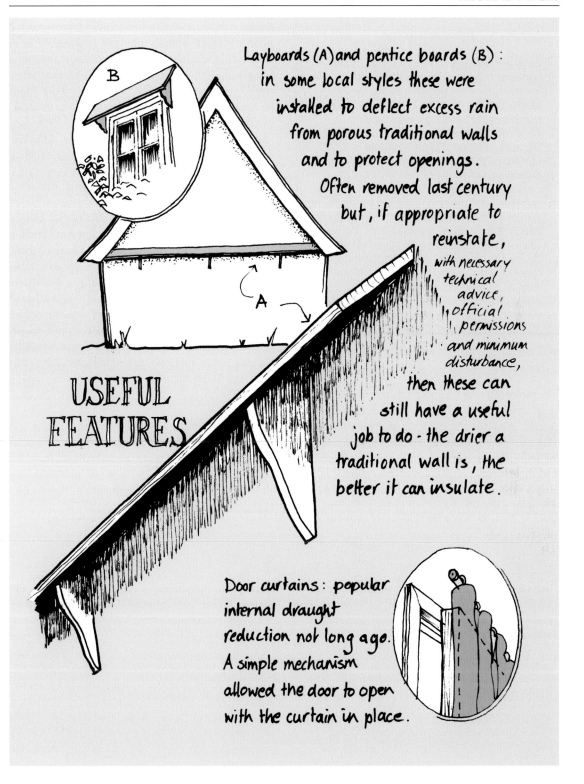

Layboards (A) and pentice boards (B): in some local styles these were installed to deflect excess rain from porous traditional walls and to protect openings. Often removed last century but, if appropriate to reinstate, with necessary technical advice, official permissions and minimum disturbance, then these can still have a useful job to do - the drier a traditional wall is, the better it can insulate.

USEFUL FEATURES

Door curtains: popular internal draught reduction not long ago. A simple mechanism allowed the door to open with the curtain in place.

Too much loving

Of all our heritage buildings, cottages are perhaps among the most vulnerable to innocent damage: because of the slow attrition of DIY, because of their small size, because occupants may have other priorities than heritage preservation, and because of modern short spans of ownership that cause a regular churning of redecoration and alteration.

Because cottages may seem so commonplace they might appear to be secure as a national asset. But take a good look in the countryside: how far do you have to travel before seeing a cottage that is not covered in bland and potentially harmful 'plastic' paint and chubbily framed plastic windows? Being an abundant and accessible object of consumer desire is no guarantee of survival at all: ask a dodo.

The shower and the tiled wall

The shower and the tiled wall arguably do not belong in a cottage because they can cause trouble, the one because it pumps water at walls that are probably at odds with damp already, the other because it requires the wall to be straightened and it also seals it up, not always perfectly enough to stop water getting in, but usually well enough to stop it getting out. But you will never persuade people not to have showers. So a shower cabinet might be free standing, provided the floor is properly able to cope and is protected from water; or it might be perhaps curtained in over a free-standing bath if that is going to be used effectively by all members of the household. Tiles might be applied to a board that is applied over the wall, but thoroughly ventilated between its back face and the original wall surface. The success, or otherwise, of these ideas is in the way they are detailed, built and used.

Windows

If converting an existing room, then the existing windows may be, for example, too low for a kitchen worktop, or they may need obscuring for a bathroom or toilet. Of course it would be regrettable to alter an old window, also expensive, and also unnecessary: with a little ingenuity there are usually ways to avoid changing existing windows to get around difficulties with internal heights. And obscured glass is not an absolute necessity as curtains, blinds and even self-clinging plastic film offer reasonable alternatives that allow interesting old plain glass to remain in place.

Consent

For a listed cottage, all such changes internally and externally require listed building consent. External changes in a conservation area or National Park, for example, may also require consent, and plumbing alterations could require a Building Regulations application or notification.

CHAPTER SEVENTEEN

Come Outside
Site and garden, animals and trees, porches and outbuildings

STAND BACK

A cottage rarely stands in complete isolation: it will be affected by its site, and technically it cannot be properly assessed without knowing what is happening in and around its garden. Visually the view could be made or broken by the look of the garden – but a garden will have a life of its own, and some practical issues can affect the cottage.

Underground, overground

The subsoil helps determine how much dampness there may be lurking underground, which, when underneath a cottage, might either be 'wicked' relatively harmlessly away through totally 'breathing' traditional fabric and finishes, or trapped inside the fabric by modern impermeable barriers and paints, where it might feed decay. To give the cottage the best chance of coping with its allocation of damp it is best not to encourage more to come its way through mismanaging the garden: thus soil and leaves should not be allowed to build up against outside walls, nor obscure air vents that were intended to keep the undersides of timber floors dry. Paths and lawns should be examined to see if they are channelling rainwater towards the house. Even perfectly level,

Cottages have become accepted as part of the landscape, which is helped by the fact that they are usually built out of materials the landscape delivered and are contained by mature gardens.

hard landscaping finishes such as concrete paths that abut the cottage's walls can cause rain to splash up and over-wet the walls, and also prevent damp from evaporating from the ground adjacent to the wall – a gravel strip can be kinder on both these counts (and *see also* the French drain drawing in Chapter 4: The Air That I Breathe, page 51).

Cottage gardens might contain some rudimentary archaeological remains of old greenhouses, garden frames, privies and compost heaps. Rubbish used to be buried or burned, so each cottage may have its

own stash of interesting old bottles, cans and broken crockery. Sometimes cottages will have been built on the site of much older settlements, and the local authority may keep records of neighbouring finds and perhaps be able to give advice on what to look out for if digging or excavating in the garden. Aerial photography and specialized equipment to reveal archaeology is not available to most people, but a dry summer can produce interesting patterns on a lawn that might hint at former paths or buildings.

GARDENING

Newcomers to an old house are often tempted to wade into the garden and make their changes straightaway. But just as with the house itself, the garden will be full of surprises and at different seasons, and these each need time to make themselves known – some of them are very subtle and beautiful, and are all too easily extinguished. Not even an expert gardener can always predict everything a newly discovered garden is going to offer throughout the year.

A garden attached to an old cottage will very likely have seen many uses, planting schemes and fashions in its lifetime, and there may be some fruiting or specimen plants and trees that have taken a long time to reach maturity: these may need taming, but they deserve to be given a chance. Though no garden is likely to have stayed as it was first planted, it can be interesting to look at what plant and flower varieties were available and popular when the cottage was occupied by families dependent on the soil. Back gardens particularly could have been given over to any of the staple vegetables such as parsnips, potatoes, turnips, peas and beans according to period. Medicinal plants and cooking herbs would also have been grown.

When it comes to more decorative plants, a tip for predicting which types of plant might do well in any one garden is to look at which weeds thrive naturally, and then to choose their cultivated relations. Apart from fruit and vegetables, cottage gardens are very likely to have hosted goats, chickens or pigs – again according to the period in history. Lawnmowers were accessories of the relatively well off until early in the last century, so lawns in cottage gardens, unless grazed by animals, would once not have been as popular as they have now become.

Garden walls, fences, hedges and gates

Many old gardens have been subdivided over time to provide additional building plots, or homes have been demolished and rebuilt within an existing garden. This can mean that boundary walls might be much older than the dwellings inside them. Like the walls of old buildings, old garden walls tended to be built with minimal footings but with lime mortar (or even dry stone – unmortared – in some areas), which tolerates a degree of movement without having to fracture the bricks or stones. Due to the forgiving nature of lime, it can be possible for an imaginative and conservation-friendly engineer to suggest ways of repairing or stabilizing a leaning wall that may appear to others to be on a one-way path to collapse. Walls can hold clues to past uses of gardens: traces of lean-to greenhouses perhaps, or the fixings for guide-wires that once supported trained fruit trees.

Walls and fences can be covered by the planning provisions attached to conservation areas and similar designated areas, and in rural areas, what might appear to be just an overgrown hedge could be a remnant of a very old hedgerow and would be likely to have statutory protection (*see* The Hedgerow Regulations www.opsi.gov.uk and www.defra.gov.uk). If appropriate, it might be interesting to consider traditional hedgerow species for any new hedges – some of them even produce usable fruit.

Gates – if there were any to a cottage garden – would likely be of timber or simple wrought iron, and were perhaps intended to keep out livestock (for some of the repair considerations of these materials *see* Chapter 7: Knock on Wood – 'Maintenance and Repair', page 104). Old photographs can illustrate what types of gate may have been attached to different types of property in any one area. By definition a cottage is unlikely to have had quite the same need to provide vehicle access as we like for our cars, though an associated barn or cart shed may have necessitated a wide 'field gate'. Adding vehicle gates now, to give access to parking, needs to be handled with sensitivity, otherwise the result can look pretentious. Simple is often best assimilated.

RIGHT: Simple, non-waterproof and inexpensive surfaces and accessories would traditionally have been associated with a cottage garden. These also have the advantage of allowing rainwater to seep into the soil and replenish it, rather than be whisked away in sewers if there is mains drainage.

OPPOSITE: Perfectly charming, and all without a perfectly straight line.

The paling or picket fence is a definitive cottage accessory, next to roses around the door, and it doesn't matter if it isn't quite straight. Generally timber features are capable of weathering informally. In some parts of the country a wooden fence would not be considered tough enough, and the art of drystone walling lives on.

190

A cottage photographed in the mid 1970s (opposite, top), and what seems to be the same cottage more recently – 'seems to be' because local landmarks have changed over the years, as apparently have the immediate surroundings to the cottage, and this can change the perception of the building.

Trees

Problems and health

Trees are frequently, but often unfairly, perceived to threaten foundations and drains with their roots, or to be about to fall down. They might occasionally present a hazard or otherwise stand in the way of some more urgent need, and some combinations of position, ground conditions and species are more likely to cause trouble than others, but there are, nevertheless, very many trees that can be seen to have coexisted in very close proximity to buildings for very many years without a problem. In some cases the act of removing a tree can potentially destabilize established ground conditions and so perhaps upset any adjacent property's foundations. Leaf fall can block gutters and downpipes, and trees from a wide area can contribute to this, as leaves are carried on the wind.

Local authorities usually have the services of a tree officer or landscape officer who can advise on specific situations: trees in conservation areas and many other specially designated areas are automatically protected, and outside those areas, any tree could be protected by a tree preservation order. Trees may appear big and tough but they can be adversely affected by excavations, changes to paving and ground-loading, and insensitive trimming of their branches, or pruning work at the wrong time of year. It is better to have a healthy tree nearby than a sick one, so it can pay to seek whatever advice the local authority or a properly qualified tree surgeon is able to give.

Benefits

Every living tree helps the planet by soaking up atmospheric carbon dioxide (the 'greenhouse gas' that everyone is now concerned about) and generating vital oxygen (for us to breathe). When considering making a country cottage your home, there are very likely to be trees close by, and they are likely to

193

have been there for some considerable time: some people hate trees for blocking views, where others see only that views are enhanced by them. If you belong to the former group and a particular tree is likely to be a particular source of concern, then, rather than deplete the planet of a little more oxygen and generally upset your neighbours by petitioning for it to be removed, it can be better to avoid the problem and buy a different property more suited to your views. The remainder can enjoy the fact that trees can be beautiful in themselves and can help screen gardens: for example, trees that encourage birds can concentrate birdsong in a way that can usefully mask the distant drone from a motorway, while the leaves can block the unnatural orange light that comes from the motorway's lamp posts at night.

A BIT ON THE SIDE

Existing outbuildings

An outbuilding may be either detached from the cottage or attached to it, but it would obviously not be a part of the original living accommodation, in other words a workshop, coal store, shed, or even a greenhouse. Cottage outbuildings can be an evocative part of the cottage scene and, like the cottages themselves, require careful self-restraint from their owners to prevent them becoming so smart and straight that they become unattractive.

Existing outbuildings can offer, in the right circumstances, space into which to extend the cottage. This might sometimes be acceptable (to planners, conservation officers and the owners themselves) if what was in the outbuilding is genuinely of little merit or interest, or it can be retained in the new plan without being over-sanitized. For example, consider shunting utility functions such as a larder, 'utility room', boot room, perhaps a shower cubicle or a WC into such a space so that it can legitimately retain some of its basic wall and floor finishes.

If the outbuilding is large enough, these new functions can occupy 'pods' that are separate from the original structure. And even if the inside of the outbuilding has been 'upgraded', there is absolutely no reason that the outside has to be primped and suburbanized: it can be gently repaired if necessary,

but it could stay looking like a lean-to shed to the outside world.

Existing extensions

Existing cottage extensions can range from a corrugated iron, lean-to 'scullery' to a 1960s flat-roofed kitchen and bathroom, up to a hefty, more recent affair. The first might or might not be substantial enough to be reincorporated as modern living accommodation, but it could perhaps qualify for the treatment suggested above. The second could be improved and insulated as suggested in Chapter 15: Hot Love – 'Walls' – 'Concealer', page 165 and its accompanying photograph. The third type can, unfortunately, often be rather overbearing (if built, as many were in the 1980s, as if extending a modern house instead of a cottage) – but they might be candidates for ivy. (*See also* Chapter 16: Bits and Pieces – 'Kitchens and Bathrooms', page 180.)

New outbuildings and extensions

To move into a cottage and immediately have to build an extension is an indication that maybe the wrong property has been chosen and, worse, this could mean the end of the cottage as a proper cottage. To want to strap suburban 'must haves' such as plastic conservatories on to a cottage implies that the point of cottage living has been missed somewhere. Particularly as everyone knows that, despite the attempts of regulations to prevent conservatories being used as living rooms, many are – and in winter this can lead to excessive heat loss. A cottage may well have had a conservatory, but more as a lean-to greenhouse for growing tomatoes.

There is always the occasional exception to every prejudice, and to stay true to the cottage idea we have to ask what sort of addition could be appropriate if domestic circumstances did change and the owners did not want to move? An 'original' cottager might have opted for something like the corrugated iron lean-to mentioned above, or a tiny single room extension, probably in the same materials as the original build or whatever was affordable at the time. 'Tiny' is more likely to be appropriate to a cottage extension, and that means not only in its 'footprint' but also in its scale.

With modern regulation and custom requiring particular room heights and facilities, it can be a challenge for the designer to achieve the required accommodation inside an extension that remains subservient to the original cottage. But it is a challenge that can and should be met.

Extensions and planning permission

Many planning authorities have tended to resist the idea of adding more to the end of a cottage in a way that matches its original shape and colours, so that it looks as if some giant handle has been turned and more building extruded. The reason that this approach is unpopular is that it can make it difficult to 'read' the original size of the cottage, and so the cottage is lost and becomes a house instead. Unfortunately the response to this is often to make such a jarring break between old and new that, while it is still possible to read the original building, the whole composition becomes painful.

Cottages, being so small, certainly do need to retain their integrity and still be able to convey their original size after being extended. Being small also means that the cottage needs to have any extension sensitively and cleverly designed so as not to upstage the original and so as to create an overall composition that is still pleasant to look at. (*See also* Chapter 2: The Professionals – 'Some Red Tape', page 34, for more on the designing and building process and listed building consent.)

Some extension suggestions

Every cottage will demand an individual solution: there are no books big enough to contain examples of every possible contingency. But remember that a cottage demands that any extension is small and much less conspicuous than the cottage itself. Remember, too, that extending a cottage risks undermining its 'cottageness'. It's rather like asking for a powerful 600cc engine to be attached to a faithful moped – maybe things won't be the same between you again.

- Start with a sensitive conservation-accredited architect who understands and loves old buildings.

- Stick to local traditional roof pitches (usually 45 degrees) as a priority.
- Favour the use of original local materials, or if there is an established pattern of historic extensions (a stone area that converted to brick in Victorian times perhaps) seek inspiration there.
- Consider dressing an extension as if it were an outhouse (timber boarding, properly traditional and not modern 'shiplap', is good at this – *see* Chapter 15: Hot Love – 'Concealer', page 165).
- Remember that there are other options apart from those run-of-the-mill extensions in clunky blockwork on massive concrete footings: there are alternative and inventive lightweight solutions possible that can be designed to be suitable for first floor extensions or for placing on archaeologically sensitive ground.
- Insist on traditional window frames and doors (no, not traditional style, but real traditional) – the windows can be secondarily glazed (*see* Chapter 15 again: 'Secondary glazing', page 167); although sometimes a plain sheet of glass, cottage window size, can be less conspicuous and more honest.
- Don't be afraid of genuine traditional materials that are new, such as clay roof tiles, because if used on one clearly defined extension they should weather down much more honestly from, say, natural red than from 'red-with-something-stuck-to-them-to-look-old'.
- Think about using traditional materials in an 'holistic' way if at all possible, meaning as part of a totally traditional construction (for example, by building a 'breathable' wall compatible with the rest of the cottage – *see also* Chapters 4: The Air That I Breathe, and 6: Sticks and Stones) so that their use is honest and as intended rather than 'stick on'.
- There is no need to strain to incorporate every last period detail if they are not appropriate (though most had a useful purpose); the design discipline imposed by traditional materials ought to generate a result that, even if honestly modern in interpretation, should automatically fit in scale, shape, colour and texture.
- Do consider the quality of the details. Because a cottage is so small, so its extension should be even

smaller, and then anachronistic things such as grey plastic rainwater pipes, cast aluminium 'coach lamps' and lacquered brass door handles can assume a jarring prominence. Iron, wrought or cast, was probably the more usual cottage option for these features.

Doing all this should help to ensure a design for the extension that is sympathetic to the cottage. But if the builders who build it are rather too deeply immersed in the modern tradition of building to the nearest nanometre, then you may have to consider sneaking out and hiding their plumb lines and spirit levels – or at least threaten to do it, they should get the point. But, equally, don't let them get carried too far the other way and start 'distressing' things artificially.

THERE'S A LOVELY MOON OUT THERE

External lighting

Nowadays light pollution is not only unpopular with traditionalists and stargazers, it also counts against sustainability, since much external lighting is unnecessarily over-used. So on houses and cottages there is likely to be a trend away from really bright and expensive-to-run floodlights, and towards the localized low-level lighting of features that would eliminate dark corners. These can be switched automatically when needed. Townspeople have had street lighting for some time, but in the distant past country folk would have carried a meagre candle with them, or relied on the moon to light their visits to more distant neighbours.

External lighting for most old cottages and houses would only have become really widespread once electricity was established, and then only when that was regarded as cheap. So the coach lamps and mini lamp posts that so many think of as being traditional are often largely artificial features of the 1960s onwards. Traditional gas and oil lanterns did exist, and a little research comparing old photographs and specialist manufacturers' catalogues can produce some authentic-looking electric examples. But don't forget that a real cottager would have been less able to afford these luxuries, so it might be as well to introduce light from clever and unseen modern sources, so as to wear our twenty-first century wealth discreetly.

THE BIRDS AND THE BEES

Of the wild animals frequently associated with buildings, rats, mice and grey squirrels are considered pests, while most wild birds and bats are among those species that have special legal protection. Feral pigeons have fallen from favour, and while once eaten as a delicacy in the country and fed crumbs by children in cities, these are now considered a pest and a health hazard, though their disposal requires a licence.

If more space is absolutely necessary, the impact on an existing cottage can sometimes be reduced by placing utility rooms in a linked, rather than attached, extension.

PORCHES

Modern building lore can produce
a heavy-handed extension that
burrows into the original fabric (a),
whereas a light 1920s style porch
in timber and glass can enclose
the same useful space (b);
but as shelter while finding keys
or ringing the bell, a simple
canopy - lightly attached - can
be a very good solution (c);
b and c can also be
'reversible' solutions.

Mice

Mice, particularly, are frequent chewers of electric wiring as they can be small enough to fit through the holes drilled in joists, beams and studwork walls to admit cables. The mouse that finds the hole just a little too small, or who feels the need to exercise its teeth, can gnaw through the plastic insulation, expose the live conductor, and bring about a short circuit and possibly a house fire. A qualified electrician can probably suggest various forms of circuit-breaker that upgrade existing installations and which are supposed to shut down more quickly in the event of such a fault (*see also* Chapter 9: Reasons to be Careful – 'Electricity' page 116, and Chapter 10: Heat, Light and Water – 'Of mice and men', page 121, regarding rodent damage and the risk of fire). Rats and mice are hard to exclude from old houses as these have so many hidden voids and spaces, and neither cats, the pre-eminent natural deterrent, nor electronic acoustic scarers, can usually reach inside these secret cavities.

Birds, squirrels and bats

Birds and squirrels can find roof insulation useful nesting material, and old houses are often badly protected at the eaves, so they can get in. Chicken wire is probably the kindest way to exclude them, while retaining the ventilation essential to keep old roof timbers in good order. Most wild birds may not be disturbed while nesting by law (the RSPB would have details www.rspb.co.uk), and are also specifically protected at other times. Red squirrels are also protected by law, as their populations are threatened. Grey squirrels, however, although arguably as graceful, are considered an alien species and a pest.

It is illegal to disturb or handle bats in most cases, a protected animal whose numbers are feared to be declining. Bats often roost in old roof spaces, and can access tiny crevices at lightning speed. Although they perhaps look alarmingly large if met in full wingspan on the stairs of an evening, they can be smaller than a mouse when folded up, and if it were legal to stroke them, some might purr like a cat, so they are not all as alarming as vampires. Re-roofing work needs to be programmed to avoid bats' breeding times, which can vary with type, so if bats are there, or even if they might only be expected to be in residence, then it is better to check with the authorities in advance. The Bat Conservation Trust web site (www.bats.org.uk) and the local council should have up-to-date information.

Birds can get indoors through surprisingly small gaps in old roofs and flues, but apparently it is beneath their dignity to crawl out the same way, and windows have to be opened.

A bat may look a little frightening in flight or when hanging upside down, but seen the 'right way up' they are much more appealing

Bees, wasps and hornets

Wild bees, wasps and hornets can find old houses compelling nesting places. Wasps and hornets have their own place in the ecosystem, though few friends in houses. Bee swarms might be especially attractive to amateur or professional bee-keepers if they are reasonably accessible for capture. Bees were traditionally kept in many gardens from the Middle Ages and well into the twentieth century for their usefulness not only in providing honey (and beeswax, a useful indoor timber finish) but for their work in pollinating food crops. Bee numbers have recently been under threat, in Britain and other parts of the world, which has highlighted their importance – they are said to contribute to the production of about a third of our food. People living in the town or country can try to help sustain the bee population by taking some simple steps to encourage and help them, and might even consider learning about becoming bee-keepers themselves (*see* www.britishbee.org.uk). No cottage garden would be complete without bees.

Postscript

ABOUT CONSERVATION

This book might, in places, seem to take a harsh view of some of the twentieth century's ways – for that period's apparent carelessness of the planet's future and frequent mistreatment of old buildings. Like the twentieth-century parent who realizes that a lifetime of smoking and feeding their children harmful fats was a big mistake, the building industry has emerged into the new century bearing some guilt. Or at least it ought to, but there is still a great deal that needs to be done to spread the message to all its parts.

If you are the sort of person who, say, likes to repair old things rather than replace them with a flimsier modern version, or who considers the ingredients in food before buying it, or who takes care to change the oil in the car regularly, then you probably need no encouragement to learn how to look after

your cottage well and maintain its value for the future. If you do not care at all about such things, then please consider that, while none of us (nor most of our possessions) is likely to last into the twenty-sixth century to influence our descendants, a cottage has the potential to do so. But it depends upon your help now.

ABOUT COUNTRY COTTAGES

The words 'country cottage' are much more specific than 'house', and conjure up a particular, often romantic image. Even if real country life in the days of working cottages was far from the cosy, rosy life that many now like to imagine, people still want to buy into something that promises to be more personal and more satisfying than modern housing. Yet to want 'country' implies that some urban slick-ness and convenience will have to be left behind, and to want 'cottage' means that an owner has to be prepared to bond with a small, old, primitive building.

To think otherwise may simply result in trying to turn country into town, and trying to turn a cottage into just another modern house. So many cottages have already been assimilated into that kind of suburban conformity that the survivors now deserve much more sympathetic treatment in order to preserve their distinctiveness. And arguably, the cottage should now be much more robustly defended than it has been, both as a symbol of Britain's hard-working past and as a template for sustainable building in its future.

Mediaeval people, even some Victorians, would find the idea of wagons bigger than their homes terrifyingly unnatural. To us it is normal. It can help from time to time to imagine ourselves into the mindset of the world that cottages came from, and this can remind us that they need special treatment in the modern world.

Further Information

This book features photographs of cottages seen on village streets up and down the country. Some have retained their informal cottage charm, some have been neatened and straightened with more modern materials. A few of the former group pictured here are in the care of the National Trust, and those are, of course, more likely to show a strong bias towards traditional and 'conservative' repair methods. Deliberately, no distinction has been made here about such ownership, since it could invite some cottage owners to say 'That's all very well for them, they have the resources'. But in practice, traditional repair need not be complicated, nor even expensive, because a conservation approach to historic building maintenance can be cheaper in the short term since it favours minimum intervention – less work, less money.

The use of traditional materials can also be more efficient in the long term, where they are less likely to upset the working of the cottage by, for example, trapping dampness – so less decay, fewer repair bills for the future. And traditional finishes can often be simpler to redecorate, on a traditionally built cottage, than some of our modern 'convenience' products, because traditional finishes are made for old construction and so tend not to fail so dramatically when put together with it. So rather than be seen as a specialist enterprise for conservation organizations only, building conservation techniques can be practised by the wider ownership of all old buildings.

To take the subjects introduced in this book further, there is a broad range of organizations, some listed below, which should be found eager to share their knowledge in the hope that we all may benefit. It is not necessary to become a building expert, or a historian, or to go as far as learning or taking up a trade or craft – but just to build on this general appreciation of the differences in approach between traditional and modern.

FOR GENERAL INFORMATION ON THE CARE OF OLD BUILDINGS

Charity organizations
- Society for the Protection of Ancient Buildings (SPAB) – www.spab.org.uk
- The National Trust (England, Wales, Northern Ireland) – www.nationaltrust.org.uk
- The National Trust for Scotland – www.nts.org.uk

The SPAB offers information and runs courses, while the National Trusts show their methods by example through the buildings in their care, and are keen to explain their work; they may also offer some opportunities for hands-on conservation work from time to time.

Statutory heritage agencies
- Cadw (Wales) – www.cadw.wales.gov.uk
- English Heritage – www.english-heritage.org.uk
- Northern Ireland Environment Agency – www.ni-environment.gov.uk
- Historic Scotland – www.historic-scotland.gov.uk

These have a remit to inform their public, and they also keep some buildings in care, which are usually viewable.

Local authority conservation officers

Conservation officers may be contacted through a local authority's planning department, with conservation and local heritage protection information also likely to be available on local authorities' web sites. A conservation officer should be able to offer useful 'first stop' planning advice to enquirers interested in taking on a cottage in their area.

Other sources of training or information

- Some local authorities and organizations run courses in traditional building, such as Essex County Council – www.cressingtemple.org.uk, and the Scottish Lime Centre – scotlime.org, or try your own local authority's web site, or look for information at those of the organizations mentioned above.
- The web site www.oldhouse.info offers general information for owners of old houses, including a home maintenance checklist referred to in this book.
- *Maintaining and Repairing Old Houses: A Guide to Conservation, Sustainability and Economy* by the same author is also published by Crowood (2008), and further examines some of the issues surrounding the traditional constructions mentioned here.
- There are numerous books covering all aspects of the history and development of cottages. Many of these are painstakingly researched and beautifully illustrated and will help the owner understand the local development of materials and styles. There are also many books devoted to the conservative repair of old buildings and to the sustainable adaptation of existing housing.
- Be aware that conservation attitudes, experience and knowledge have changed dramatically in recent decades, and that books are products of their time. Perhaps a book on cottages that dates from the 1970s may not recognize the importance of the 'breathability' issue to the survival of its subject, and a book from the 1950s might not blink at the contemporary destruction of so many original examples, because they were then so abundant.

(Books that cover upgrading insulation to 'ordinary' modern houses, for example, are unlikely to be directly applicable to a cottage for the technical reasons of breathability explained here.)

It is suggested that the sources in the above list are consulted first, in order to get some orientation in the subject. The field of 'home improvements' is a commercially lucrative one and there is a clamour of advertising and 'bandwagon' pressures (some now come in a 'heritage' or 'green' wrapping) that might lead the uninitiated into expensive works and leave them with a building that is a bit of a Frankenstein's monster and no longer really a cottage. Do not forget that many truly traditional repair methods, founded in our much more environmentally sustainable past, still have the potential to bring environmental benefits today, and are technologically simple and possibly even relatively cheap. Help yourself, make the country look better, help the planet.

FOR A BUILDING OR REPAIR PROJECT

Architects

- Architects Accredited in Building Conservation (AABC) – www.aabc-register.co.uk
- Royal Institute of British Architects (RIBA) – www.architecture.com
- Royal Incorporation of Architects in Scotland (RIAS) – www.rias.org.uk
- Royal Society of Architects in Wales (RSAW) – www.architecture.com
- Royal Society of Ulster Architects (RSUA) – www.rsua.org.uk

Structural engineers

- Conservation Accreditation Register for Engineers (CARE) – *see* ICE and IStructE below
- Institution of Civil Engineers (ICE) – www.ice.org.uk
- Institution of Structural Engineers (IStructE) – www.istructe.org

Surveyors

Royal Institution of Chartered Surveyors – RICS – www.rics.org

Planning and building control

- England and Wales – www.planningportal.gov.uk
- Northern Ireland – www.planningni.gov.uk
- Scotland – www.sbsa.gov.uk
- *See also* local authorities' web sites and www.nationalparks.gov.uk

STATUTORY NATURE CONSERVATION AGENCIES

- Cyngor Cefn Gwlad Cymru (The Countryside Council for Wales) – www.ccw.gov.uk
- Environment and Heritage Service (Northern Ireland) – www.ni-environment.gov.uk
- Natural England – www.naturalengland.org.uk
- Scottish Natural Heritage – www.snh.org.uk

Index

Related titles available from Crowood:

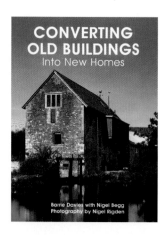

Converting Old Buildings into New Homes

Barrie Davies with Nigel Davies

ISBN 978 1 86126 601 9

192pp, over 150 illustrations

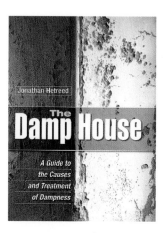

The Damp House
A Guide to the Causes and Treatment of Dampness

Jonathan Hetreed

ISBN 978 1 86126 966 9

160 pages
160pp, 150 illustrations

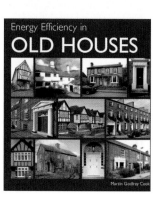

Energy Efficiency in Old Houses

Martin Godfrey Cook

ISBN 978 1 84797 077 0

160pp, 100 illustrations

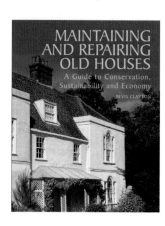

Maintaining and Repairing Old Houses
A Guide to Conservation, Sustainability and Economy

Bevis Claxton

ISBN 978 1 84797 035 0

160pp, over 250 illustrations

Natural Building
A Guide to Materials and Techniques

Tom Woolley

ISBN 978 1 86126 841 9

192pp, over 200 illustrations

Victorian and Edwardian Houses
A Guide to Care and Maintenance

Janet Collings

ISBN 978 1 84797 057 2

160pp, 400 illustrations

In case of difficulty in ordering, contact the Sales Manager:

The Crowood Press Ltd, Ramsbury, Wiltshire SN8 2HR, UK – Tel: 44 (0) 1672 520320

enquiries@crowood.com

www.crowood.com